I0188035

Moaning Low

Also by Van Hawkins

Hampton and Newport News
A look at two historic Virginia towns

Dorothy and the Shipbuilders of Newport News
The story of an iconic American shipyard

The Historic Triangle
How Jamestown, Williamsburg and Yorktown made American history

Plowing New Ground
The Southern Tenant Farmers Union and its place in Delta history

Duty Bound
The Hyatt brothers and Confederates of the Third Arkansas Infantry Regiment

Horizons
A novel

A New Deal in Dyess
The Depression Era Agricultural Resettlement Colony in Arkansas

Smoke Up the River
Steamboats and the Arkansas Delta

Moaning Low

From Slavery to Peonage
Involuntary Servitude in the Arkansas Delta

By Van Hawkins

Moaning Low

From Slavery to Peonage:
Involuntary Servitude in the Arkansas Delta

Printed in the United States of America

First Printing, 2019

ISBN: 978-0-9863992-2-0

Front Cover. Caught! Artist's depiction of fleeing peons, drawn by Frank B. Masters, Cosmopolitan Magazine *42 (March 1907), 485.*

Writers Bloc
Jonesboro, Arkansas

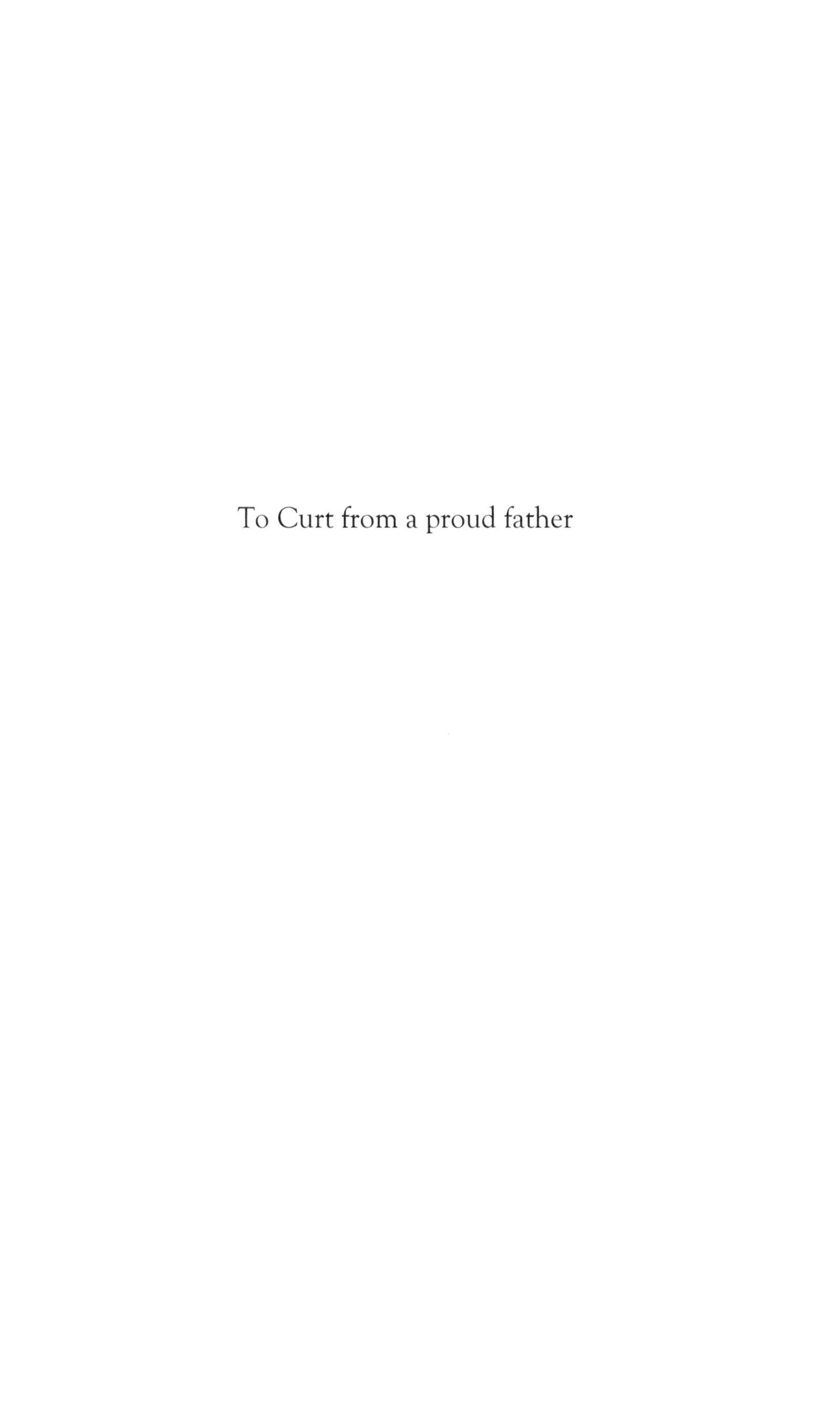

To Curt from a proud father

They took him out to the convict camp . . . .

O children, the tall pines stood and heard him
when he was moaning low.

The other convicts, they stood around him,
When the length of the black strap cracked and found him.

. . .

They nailed his coffin boards together . . .

O Children, the dark night saw where they buried him,
buried him, buried him low.

And the tall pines heard where they went to hide him.
And the wind crept up to moan beside him."[1]

---

[1] Marjory Stoneman Douglas. *Voice of the River* (Sarasota, Fla.: Pineapple Press, 1987), 134.

Table of Contents

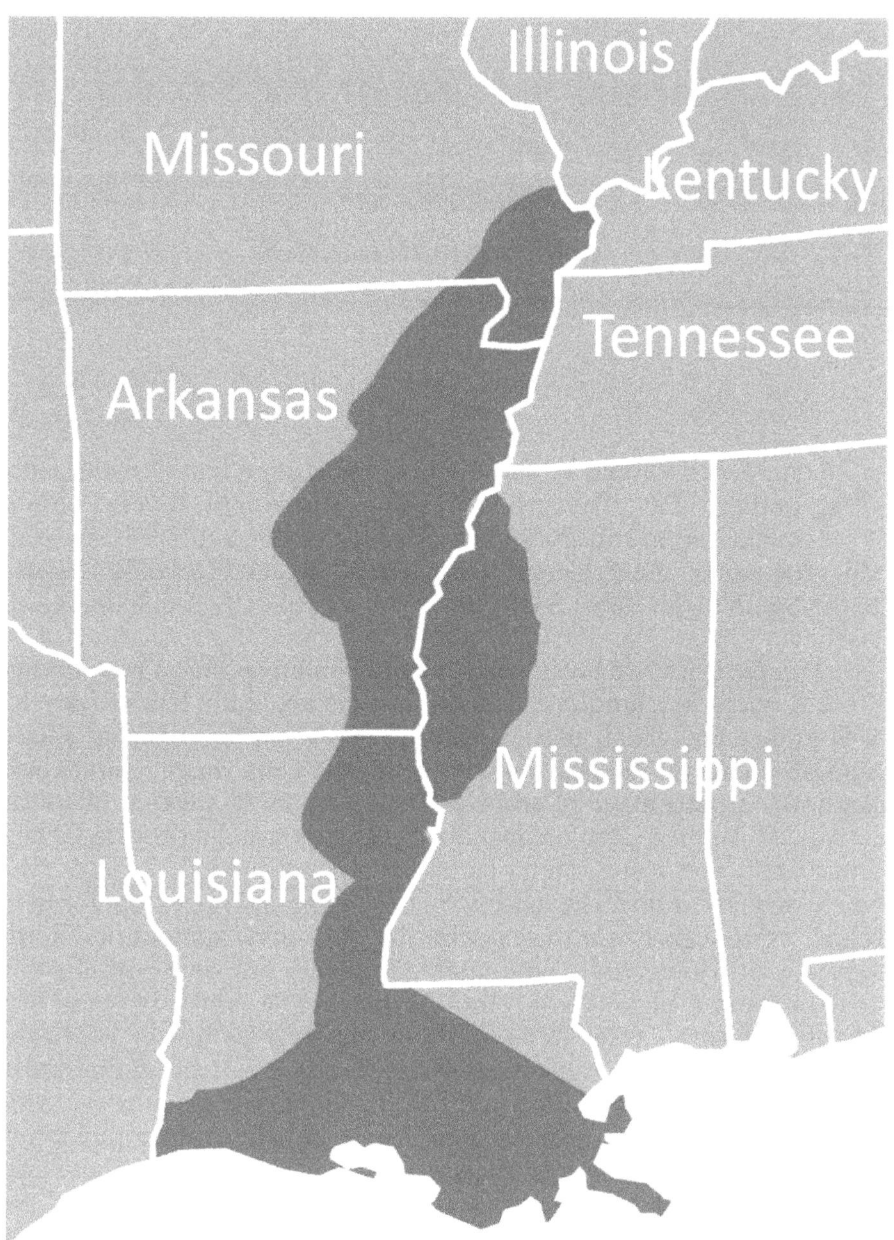

The Mississippi River Alluvial Plain, commonly referred to as the Lower Mississippi River Delta. Illustration by Author.

NOTES AND ACKNOWLEDGMENTS

Some terms should be clarified for readers not familiar with rural southern life. Though the Lower Mississippi River Delta is considered to run from Cairo, Illinois, to the Gulf of Mexico, this story focuses on the Arkansas Delta, hereafter called *Delta*. References to the *South* mean Rebel South, states that formed the Confederacy.

Planter is a word dating back to antebellum southern plantations. Here it refers to a landlord. Tenant farmers generally fell into several well-known and widely used categories. *Cash rent tenants* paid a fixed sum of money for the right to farm property. *Crop share tenants* paid landlords a percentage of crops as rent, such as 25 percent of cotton harvested. In these rent arrangements tenants usually provided labor, equipment, and some inputs necessary for production. Tenants who possessed few or no assets necessary to produce a crop, except for their labor, were called *sharecroppers*. In this arrangement landlords typically provided credit, equipment, and land. For such participation they charged a higher rent, often 50 percent of crops. In some oral histories, farmers refer to working on shares. This can be confusing since sometimes these arrangements do not meet the definition of sharecropping as understood in the Delta. *Furnish* is credit provided to purchase farm inputs and personal items, usually from a plantation store. *Doodlum* was scrip redeemable only at a plantation store. Newspaper reports are identified at point of use and not footnoted. No attempt is made to correct bad grammar or replace offensive language in quotations. They stand as said and written.

This story stops in 1945, though greed and corruption continued. The war didn't change everything, but it substantially reduced the forces that made peonage possible. A vast army of men and women departed the Delta to serve in the armed forces where they learned valuable skills that would earn them a place in a booming manufacturing economy. Some used the GI Bill to complete higher education and gain entry into the professional class. Farming became increasingly mechanized, eliminating the need for numerous laborers. Workers who could operate complicated farm machinery and repair implements that broke down gained bargaining power in the farm labor force. Planters sought them out and had to pay well for their services. Leverage shifted, and to a great extent workers won and planters lost. This would not be true in all cases, but this story recognizes the end of one era at the beginning of another with substantial differences.

Many knowledgeable people helped with this book. Lindsey Tosh, an attorney in Northwest Arkansas, researched court cases and compiled relevant law review articles. Dennis Zolper, a lawyer in Northeast Arkansas, read case summaries and helped with citations. Another attorney, my son Curt Hawkins, reviewed many of the legal cases quoted herein. Jo Ann Steed, an English composition teacher, did copy editing. Much of the material about the Southern Tenant Farmers Union and Dyess Colony is drawn from my books on those subjects. Several knowledgeable readers assisted with this effort. Dr. Michael B. Dougan, Distinguished Professor of History Emeritus at Arkansas State University, shared his encyclopedic knowledge of Arkansas history. Dr Cherisse Jones-Branch, James and Wanda Lee Vaughn Endowed Professor of History at Arkansas State University, provided valuable perspectives. As always, my wife Ruth served as enabler, primary editor, and final arbiter. I can't thank her enough.

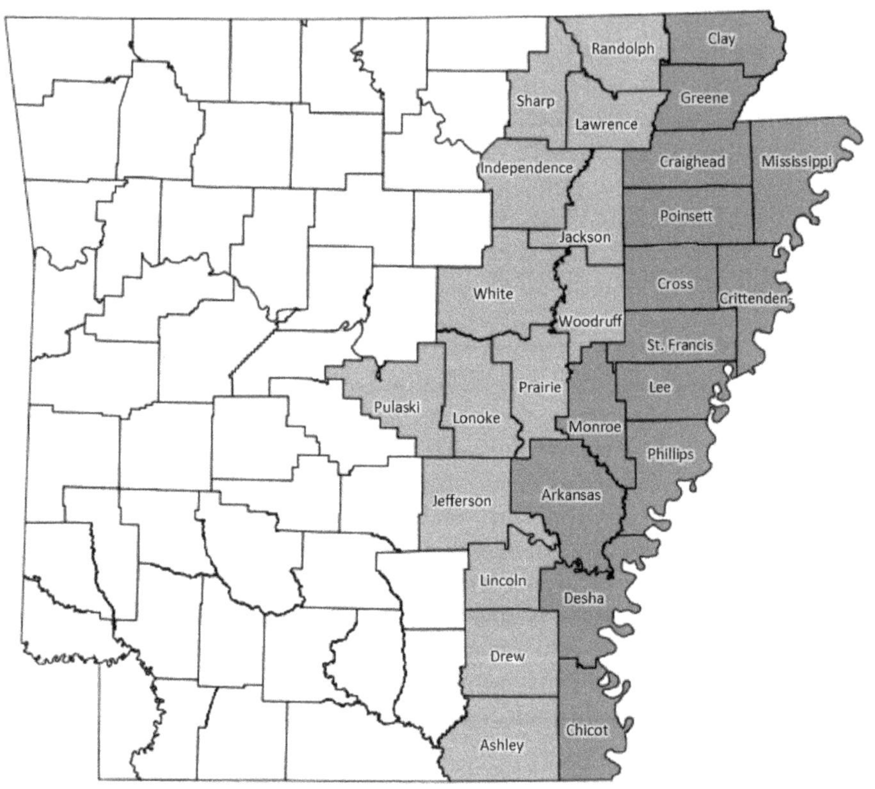

The Arkansas segment of the Mississippi River alluvial plain covers about one-third of the state's 75 counties (shaded areas). It extends westward all the way to Pulaski County. Traditionally, references to the Delta mean those extremely fertile counties closest to the Mississippi River and the drainage basins of its tributaries, including the St. Francis, White, and Arkansas rivers (darker areas). Illustration by Author.

PROLOGUE

This is a story about the ruthless suppression of vulnerable people by unscrupulous Delta planters and powerful business interests. It began when the Civil War ended and freedmen became their target. It continued when black farm workers struggled to protect their families. At the start of the Great Depression, planters suppressed white laborers as well, cheating them out of government assistance. The crime of peonage initially covered labor locked in place by debt, but it became involuntary servitude enforced by many means. These included debt peonage, a term used advisedly since alleged debt often consisted of fiction written by landlords; contract law disregarding Civil Rights; criminal surety frequently accomplished through selectively applied vagrancy laws; work under threat of violence; convict leasing, and kidnapping followed by physical enslavement. Victims found themselves caught in a spider's web, with planters at the center among strands often woven by Jim Crow. Like other American tragedies, this one involved control of land, some of the richest agricultural ground in the United States.

The Mississippi River deposited this soil and formed a so-called delta. Over thousands of years the river created an extraordinarily fertile alluvial flood plain. Though the river made this Delta, devastating earthquakes left their mark as well. Those quakes rank among the worst in American history. Powerful tremors rocked the region in 1811 and 1812. They destroyed towns, created lakes, and caused the Mississippi temporarily to run backward. These quakes helped form gloomy swamps with countless interlaced trees and brush and water covered with a coat resembling green buff velvet.[1]

Valuable soil lay below this inhospitable cover, and a brutal process of recovery at first fell upon the backs of enslaved people. They worked in rancid water amid swarming mosquitoes and endured scalding heat and wilting humidity. Slaves felled trees, cut them into logs, and burned underbrush. In the night sky, flames roared upward amid billowing smoke and ashes like a scene described by Dante. Some who faltered endured unmerciful beatings. Despite formidable obstacles, new ground emerged throughout the Delta. Given the rich soil, temperature ranges, average annual rainfall, and growing season, cotton proved to be an ideal crop. People who questioned whether this inhospitable region could be cleared and farmed efficiently "failed to take into account the determination, rapacity, and cruelty that humans could exhibit if the proper incentives were in place."[2]

Cruelty and rapacity dominated cotton fields throughout the South since production of the fiber required extensive labor. The crop had to be planted, chopped, and picked by hand. Great Britain's mills preferred long-staple American cotton, so demand expanded rapidly. By 1860, southern cotton growers supplied most of the cotton manufactured in Great Britain and in New England's mills. The Union's Civil War blockade ended the boom, causing many British textile factories to go bust. But demand returned after the war, and buyers began to ship approximately one million bales a year through New Orleans. Many white southerners blamed the war's devastation on enslaved persons, so racial hatred and desperation for laborers combined to force workers into peonage conditions some considered akin to slavery. Harnessing a large, subservient labor force to clear unimproved land for cotton continued for many decades in the Delta. It stretched out due to late development of some regions that remained largely untamed until early in the 20th Century.[3] As new ground

---

[1]Timothy Flint, *A Condensed Geography and History of the Western States or the Mississippi Valley*, Vol.1 (Gainesville, Fla.: Scholars' Facsimiles and Reprints, 1970), 189.

[2] James C. Cobb, *The Most Southern Place on Earth. The Mississippi Delta and the Roots of Regional Identity* (New York: Oxford University Press, 1992), 7.

[3] Jeannie M. Whayne, "What is the Mississippi Delta? A Historian's Perspective," *Defining the Delta. Multidisciplinary Perspectives on the Lower Mississippi River Delta,* Janelle Collins, ed. (Fayetteville: University of Arkansas Press, *2015)*, 124.

appeared, so did more cotton. Many planters who victimized black workers convinced themselves, or pretended to believe for economic reasons, that they were doing their victims a favor. Though ridiculous, from their point of view, "Didn't both God and reason . . . declare the Negro inferior to the white Man, and wasn't the black Man thus fulfilling his proper even though lesser station in life by serving a superior class that was at the same time providentially providing him with work and shelter and protection."[4] While searching for additional labor, some landlords looked abroad. They brought in poor immigrants by using spurious promises of financial opportunities. Italians and other Europeans found themselves victims of peonage upon arrival in the Delta. As the 20th Century advanced, so did the arc of abuse. It became a way of life for poor black and white families. During the 1930s and beyond, planters cheated both out of federal assistance provided during the Great Depression.

The same forms of peonage existed throughout the South because planters, legal authorities, business allies, and southern politicians blocked efforts to end them. Some southern dynasties achieved their success this way and refused to admit it. But as Abraham Lincoln made clear in an 1862 message to Congress, we cannot escape history.

---

[4] Jerrold M. Packard, *American Nightmare. The History of Jim Crow* (New York: St. Martin's Press, 2002), 33.

Above, former slaves walking into Union lines to follow the troops for protection. From Harper's Weekly, February 21, 1863. Below, black laborers performing work in a Union camp, such as doing soldiers' laundry and chopping wood. From Frank Leslie's Illustrated Newspaper, July 19, 1862. Library of Congress Prints and Photographs Division.

CHAPTER 1

Spirits Not Subdued

Amanda Worthington, whose wealthy family owned land in the Arkansas Delta's southernmost section, revealed in her diary the intensity of despair throughout the South after the Civil War ended. In 1865 she described her sorrow and humiliation. "Oh! my country, my country, my spirit chafes at the forced submission to our foe & in my soul the fire still smoulders [sic] & waits for a chance to burst forth once more with renewed vigor, and do battle for Vengeance, vengeance for our wrongs!" [1] Unfortunately, many black families became targets when this vengeance burst forth.

Well before the war ended, peonage began. Fugitive slaves watched federal troops march into the South, and black families walked wearily into their camps. Many arrived at night, elderly men "with gray and tufted hair; women with frightened eyes, dragging whimpering hungry children; men and girls, stalwart and gaunt – a horde of starving vagabonds, homeless, helpless, and pitiable, in their dark distress."[2] Since Union troops controlled Helena, Arkansas, by 1863 about 3,600 black persons found refuge there. Families worked on nearby farms

---

[1] Troy Woods, *A Delta Diary. Amanda Worthington's Civil War Diary* (Olivewoods Press, 2008), 105. Worthington began the journal in 1862 when she was 16 and living in Washington County, Mississippi. Her entries describe the comfortable life of a planter family during the antebellum period and the despair and ruin of post-war circumstances.

[2] W. E. B. Du Bois, *The Souls of Black Folk* (New York: Barnes & Noble Classics, 2003),17.

according to rules established by Union General Lorenzo Thomas. They could not negotiate wages or working conditions since landlords typically told federal officials how many workers they needed, and officers filled their orders. Some authorities did not review wage records properly, so many planters cheated black families out of their earnings. Farm workers faced a difficult task putting this war-ravaged land back into cultivation. Union Captain Edward Redington describes a desolate countryside with frightened white people and black families who "swarmed around" federal soldiers for protection.[3] Bitterness of southern whites toward blacks, who they believed caused the war and its physical destruction, was incalculable. Some families lost three generations of their men, and one in five white southern men of military age did not survive. "The war took young, healthy men and rapidly, often instantly, destroyed them with disease or injury."[4]

After the guns became silent, surviving Rebels endured a long walk home. Confederate General Samuel G. French describes what they saw. "A once beautiful country, almost desolate and silent; the busy hum of industry had ceased; the daily smoke of burning buildings, the marching of armies and the dull sound of distant cannon terminated; railroads had been destroyed, bridges were burned, many wagon roads were impassable; agriculture had nearly ceased, draft animals had been taken for war purposes; the flower of the South had fallen in the fight; the noble women were almost paralyzed in mind."[5] The belief that freed slaves could co-exist with southerners who hated them proved to be folly. And returning this ravaged land to productivity became difficult due to a shrunken labor pool. Of an estimated 400,000 black men between the ages of 18 and 45 living in the South before the war, about 200,000 fought for the Union. Of these, approximately 100,000 perished. About 200,000 who did not fight for the Union died performing enslaved labor for the Confederacy. Others left the South once freed, leaving about 75,000 black men in the labor force. Similarly, of approximately 400,000 southern black women, about 100,000

---

[3] Captain Edward Redington, "Transcribed letters, May 14, 1863-October 23, 1863; May 1867," *Account of the Battle of Helena, Arkansas, Wisconsin Goes to War: Our Civil War Experience* (State of Wisconsin Collection, University of Wisconsin System.)

[4] Drew Gilpin Faust, *This Republic of Suffering. Death and the American Civil War* (New York: Alfred A. Knopf, 2008), xi-xii.

[5] Samuel G. French, *Two Wars: An Autobiography* (Nashville, Tenn.: Confederate Veteran,1901), 241.

perished while following northern armies, 125,000 took work in southern cities, and many moved out of the South. Counting youths between 10 and 18, about 285,000 black men, women, and children became potential workers. An additional 200,000 white laborers increased the workforce, but many resented doing jobs previously performed by enslaved persons[6] To dominate available labor, landlords soon developed contracts for black farm workers with provisions similar to slavery. Some versions required employees to remain on farms at night without written permission of an employer to leave, obey all lawful orders, be civil in deportment, and abide by other restrictive rules. These agreements continued a master psychology held over from slavery. As a result of such terms, freedmen suspected these contracts to be devices to keep them enslaved,[7] and they were right. Despite well-founded mistrust, freedmen worked on at least 100 Delta farms by 1865, many operated by pre-war landlords.

To smooth out the South's rocky transition, during May 1865 the U.S. Congress established a Bureau of Refugees, Freedmen, and Abandoned Lands. It came to be called the Freedmen's Bureau. Agency responsibilities included supervising disposition of abandoned and confiscated land and other property; issuing clothes, food, and medicine to needy freedmen, and enforcing labor contracts between workers and planters. Black farm workers needed this help and then some. E. W. Gantt, a bureau agent, predicted a future of peonage for many families if the agency failed to do its job properly. Gantt wrote his supervisor that former slaves faced being "starved, murdered, or forced into a condition more horrible than the worst stage of slavery!" He said that wrath over the lost war would fall on the heads of helpless people, and he was correct.[8] During bureau supervision in 1865 and 1866, agents approved thousands of labor agreements between freedmen and landlords satisfied with a contract labor system largely determined by market forces.[9] Bureau reports made few references to attempts by combinations of planters or freedmen to fix outcomes. However, many freedmen disclosed widespread collusion of planters to control terms of

---

[6] Theodore Saloutos, *Farmer Movements in the South 1865-1933* (Berkeley: University of California Press, 1960), 14-15.
[7] *Farmer Movements*, 16.
[8] Randy Finley, *From Slavery to Uncertain Freedom: The Freedmen's Bureau in Arkansas, 1865-1869* (Fayetteville: University of Arkansas Press, 1996), 152.
[9] Ralph Shlomowitz, "The Origins of Southern Sharecropping," *Agricultural History* 53:3 (July 1979), 560.

employment, a predictable development. Common compensation arrangements included sharing time – freedmen farmed some acreage rent-free in exchange for day labor; standing rent – they paid a percentage of farm production for use of acreage, and wages in kind – workers received farm products as wages. To dominate labor, planters compromised bureau agents when possible. Audacious landlords offered to help with disputes, even when they were the ones being complained about. They offered up the tired canard that white southerners knew their people best.[10]

The superintendent of freedmen filed a report in 1865 about difficulties between planters and black workers in Tennessee and Arkansas. With respect to Helena, the document revealed that the amount of abandoned land led him to secure a large interest to freedmen. Reports attributed about $40,000 as the aggregate income of black lessees. The superintendent claimed that their income would have been much greater had his instructions not been thwarted.[11] He indicated cultivation of about 100 Arkansas plantations consisting of approximately 50,270 acres.

After extensive service in the post-war South, Federal Colonel Samuel Thomas summarized problems between freedmen and white southerners. He said that racists refused to accept that blacks had any rights. They would cheat a "negro without feeling a single twinge of their honor. To kill a negro they do not deem murder; to debauch a negro woman they do not think fornication; to take the property away from a negro they do not consider robbery."[12] Thomas called the reason for such outrages simple. Despite emancipation, white southerners believed that blacks at large belonged to whites at large.

General O. O. Howard, the Freedmen's Bureau director, warned about planter public relations campaigns throughout the South to disguise mistreatment. He expressed his views in a June 21, 1865, letter written to an officer serving in South Carolina. Howard reminded him of planter sophistries and that if they could not have slavery, they

---

[10]Nathan I. Huggins, Martin Kilson, and Daniel M. Fox, eds., *Key Issues in the Afro-American Experience*. Vol. II, Since 1865 (New York: Harcourt Brace Jovanovich, 1971), 11.

[11]Report, Office General Superintendent of Freedmen. Department of the Tennessee and State of Arkansas. (Memphis, Tenn.: December 31, 1864), 36-37.

[12] Samuel Thomas to O. O. Howard, Sept 21, 1865, reel 22, Freedman's Bureau, M752.

wanted conditions as close to it as possible. The general said that if permitted, southerners would use federal officers to accomplish their goals. Unfortunately, the bureau lacked sufficient agents to block their goals.

General John Sprague became assistant commissioner for Arkansas and confirmed that he had too few officers to protect freedmen throughout the state. During summer 1865 he attempted to defend Arkansas freedmen with only nine agents. Though the war department directed military commanders to replace officers being discharged who also were agents, many did not comply. Consequently, totals of mounted troops steadily declined. Captain E. G. Barker, responsible for four counties in southeastern Arkansas, reported that he lacked sufficient troops to deal with numerous complaints about planter abuses of freedmen from three counties in his district.[13] Bureau agents watched helplessly as planter henchmen assaulted and murdered freedmen, and civil authorities did nothing to bring guilty parties to justice. To further complicate matters, planters formed vigilante bands to intimidate workers without landlords being connected to their actions. According to an agent at Camden, disguised thugs accosted freedmen at night, whipping men and women, without being identified and punished. Planters discovered other ways to hide themselves. A landlord near Augusta hired outlaws to invade his property and whip freedmen. When victims attempted to report this to a bureau agent, terrorists beat them again.

Despite planter objections, some agents made them pay freedmen a fair wage. When employers refused to settle-up, these bureau personnel sometimes seized their crops. In most cases this resolved disputes. If landlords still avoided a payday after crop seizure the bureau resorted to more stringent measures. When a Columbia County planter refused after repeated warnings to compensate employees, an agent seized his crop and arrested him. In a few cases, agents sold a planter's crops to satisfy wage claims. But enforcement cut both ways. Agents opposed freedmen using coercion to achieve employment demands considered unreasonable. They also interceded on behalf of planters when poor work or absent employees threatened crop production. A southeastern Arkansas landlord complained to an agent

---

[13] Donald G. Nieman, *To Set the Law in Motion. The Freedmen's Bureau and the Legal Rights of Blacks, 1865-1868* (Millwood, N. Y.: KTO Press, 1979), 14.

that though his employees contracted to work for 26 days every month, they violated their contract by taking off on Saturday afternoons and Sundays. In this case the bureau authorized him to dock their pay. An agent at Washington, Arkansas, arrested and sentenced to hard labor several workers who persisted in fighting after a planter complained. But landlord abuses caused most problems. An agent at Madison discovered a freedman and his wife laboring under a contract "such as no man married or single could have complied with, the compensation being totally inadequate for work performed." The bureau released this couple and made their former employer pay them for time already worked at the county's prevailing wage.[14] Newton Bridges hired Israel Malcom, his wife, and child for food, two suits of clothing, one pair of shoes each, and medical assistance if necessary. They received no wages or crop shares.[15] Some freedmen fared better. In De Valls Bluff, men averaged $17.25 per month as farm hands and women $12 as farm labor or domestic helpers. About 25 percent of freedmen there claimed to be self-employed. Of them, women typically worked as cooks, seamstresses, and laundresses. Men made carpenters and teamsters.[16]

Relationships between farm managers and freedmen often frustrated both. Several entries in Bayner plantation records from 1867 reflected a white overseer's point of view. He complained that during one week nearly half of his black workers on the Jefferson County plantation missed one or more days for a variety of reasons. An entry said, "Damned sorry work week." Other comments displayed the same irritation.

> *I have talked and talked it does no good about getting out of mornings it does no good.*
>
> *There is no use in trying to get them to work on Saturday evening for tis plum folly.*
>
> *Rained on the evening of the 30th of June and none went to work on the 1st.*

---

[14] *Law in Motion*, 214.

[15] Labor Contracts, 1865, Entry 284, Freedmen's Bureau, Field Office Records-Arkansas, National Archives.

[16] Labor Contracts, February-March 1865, Freedmen's Bureau, Field Office Records-Arkansas, National Archives.

My patience worn plum out with Negroes and mules.

This overseer's problems increased when his employees revolted. On May 2, 1867, plantation hands refused to work for him "any longer." The manager resolved this strike at a meeting with laborers, but difficulties continued. On May 18 he recorded "A perfect rebellion amongst the Hands." His workers warned that "if I killed or discharged Alfred that they was not going to work on the place any longer." What Alfred did to put himself at risk is not mentioned, but the overseer fired him anyhow. Worth noting is that these plantation employees had the confidence to strike and make demands, even though they later returned to work. Their disputes with the overseer suggest that freedmen were evolving from a slave mentality into a life governed by their personal needs and priorities.[17]

Black women were carving out places for themselves in this flux, particularly in politics. They attended rallies and participated in efforts to increase black voter registration. William Brian, a Jacksonport bureau agent, observed this development with some incredulity. He said that though it appeared "strange," efforts to increase registration appeared to be "confined to the females."[18] Joseph Thorp, another Arkansas agent, also appeared incredulous at the independence of black women when faced with contracts they did not accept. "Many negro women," he said, failed to work as required in contracts. They claimed that their husbands had no authority over their place in the workforce. Thorp claimed that the lack of "harmony" between freedmen and white employers could be blamed on negro women who refused "to perform their part of contracts."[19]

Though this and other signs of shifting power troubled planters, freedmen carrying firearms became especially difficult to accept by whites attempting to hold onto their historic hegemony. According to J. C. Predmore, a bureau agent in Napoleon, the practice of freedmen

---

[17] Bayner plantation record book, February-December 1867, entry 422, Field Office Records-Arkansas, National Archives.

[18] William Brian Report, August 31, 1867, Field Office Records-Arkansas, National Archives.

[19] Mary-Farmer-Kaiser, *Freedwomen and the Freedmen's Bureau. Race, Gender, and Public Policy in the Age of Emancipation* (New York: Fordham University Press, 2010). 84. Qtd. from Loring and Atkinson, *Cotton Culture of the South*, 13; Assistant Commissioner Records-Arkansas, National Archives.

"carrying pistols is almost universal."[20] To the dismay of planters, the bureau's position held that black men had as much right as white men to arm themselves for self -protection. Freedmen took firearms to the fields and wherever they believed weapons might be necessary. Some created informal militias, which enabled them "to express their determination to care for themselves."[21]

One bureau problem arose because of a section in the statute that established the agency. It gave a commissioner authority to "set apart, for the use of loyal refugees and freedmen, such tracts of land within the insurrectionary States as shall have been abandoned, or to which the United States shall have acquired title by confiscation or sale, or otherwise; and to every male citizen, whether refugee or freedmen as aforesaid, there shall be assigned not more than forty acres of such land, and the person to whom it was so assigned shall be protected in the use and enjoyment of the land for the term of three years at an annual rate."[22] During this period or at the end of it freedmen could purchase the land and receive "such title" as the federal government could convey. Howard devised a plan for them to apply for tracts and expressed hope that the concept would generate additional land distribution. Southern newspapers ran stories about this opportunity and how to apply, but authorities made few grants. The bureau lacked sufficient acreage to provide homesteads for thousands of eligible persons. Additionally, the agency could not transfer guaranteed title to land subject to restoration upon confirmation of an owner's loyalty. President Andrew Johnson created an additional barrier by issuing a general amnesty that restored property rights to most Rebels. This thwarted hopes that the bureau would become an instrument of land redistribution. Former Confederates wanted their land back, and the president let them have it, leaving most freedmen with another broken promise, without 40 acres and a mule.

Stakes were high for landlords during Reconstruction, and they knew it. If freedmen gained financial independence through land ownership, planters would lose an exploitable source of labor, and their plantation model would be threatened. In an article published by

---

[20] Predmore to Smith, January 31, 1868. Assistant Commissioner Records-Arkansas, National Archives.
[21] *Uncertain Freedom*, 65.
[22] Edward Royce, *The Origin of Southern Sharecropping* (Philadelphia, Penn.: Temple University Press, 1993), 90.

DeBow's Review during June 1866, George Fitzhugh expressed views about freedmen shared by planters determined to keep them in peonage. "We should treat them as mere grown-up children, or apprentices, [under] the protection of guardians or masters, and bound to obey those put above them, in place of parents, just as children are so bound." He believed that severe legislation might be required to compel blacks to work on white terms. Demeaning treatment came from a variety of authorities. Sheriff John Thorp in Augusta, Arkansas, established rules for black workers that resembled parental control. They had to go to bed early except on "special occasions" and attend church regularly.[23] Some bureau agents contributed to demeaning restrictions. They would not allow freedmen to congregate in towns or military camps and become idle.

Black families considered land ownership a defense against these forms of subjugation. In some states they formed and financed societies, associations, and companies to settle people on farms. In their search for homesteads, 124 Georgia families petitioned the bureau during 1866 for transportation to Arkansas. They hoped to settle on land made available by a Southern Homestead Act passed by the U. S. Congress. The statute at first restricted sale of large tracts in order to encourage black family farms with small parcels, but many problems plagued this program. Lack of land records hampered transfer of clear titles. Railroad company objections muddied land ownership claims. Poor soil meant that it could not be tilled without substantial investments in time and effort. This prevented freedmen from supporting themselves immediately, a necessity for most. It rendered the Homestead Act of questionable value to them. Only in early months of the bureau's existence did it appear that the agency could help black families live their dream of land ownership.[24] Freedmen soon woke up to the reality that they could only depend on themselves.

In a report to the U. S. House of Representatives written in December 1866, General E. O. C. Ord reported on abusive treatment of Delta freedmen described by agents. Captain Cole at Camden found affairs there deplorable. Several freedmen had been murdered and others denied their share of crop proceeds. Landlords scared off many

---

[23] Sheriff John Thorp Rules, December 5, 1865, Freedmen's Bureau, Assistant Commissioner Records-Arkansas, National Archives.

[24] *Origins of Sharecropping*, 91.

employees to avoid paying them. Cole called feelings against freedmen intense and bitter and said he had affidavits to substantiate abuses. Lt. Eli H. Mix at Osceola released three black persons from slavery. A woman had worked three years without pay. The planter threatened to kill her if she tried to run off, and he whipped her. The other two, a husband and wife, worked for 15 cents per day. The landlord threatened to kill them if they attempted to escape. Major General Sprague projected that Arkansas freedmen would in one year be defrauded out of one-third of their earnings. He also pointed out why injustice continued. "Doubtless there can be found men in every community who would scorn such baseness, but they are too few to make their scorn felt by the community at large." Agents reported assaults and murders throughout the Delta, yet local authorities failed to intervene. Ord reported 52 murders of freedmen in the state during four months without convicted murderers being punished. In southeastern Arkansas white terrorists threatened freedmen if they reported ill treatment to the bureau. Freemen resisted, but many were never heard from again. Ord's report indicated that the number of murders documented fell well below the actual number.[25]

Despite high barriers, some black professional men rose above them and became successful. In the post-war early years, 13 black lawyers practiced in Delta counties, and they were "probably as well educated as their white compatriots."[26] Black attorneys used the law and political activities to attain Civil Rights, and John H. Johnson succeeded on both counts. The first black attorney in post-Civil War Arkansas, he was elected to the state legislature in 1866. The politically astute Johnson presided over a Republican Party state convention. Black men without formal educations continued to seek success through acquisition of land. A spokesman for black southerners, Reverend Garrison Frazier, addressed this issue at a meeting with pastors. "The way we can best take care of ourselves is to have land, and . . . till it by our own labor. We want to be placed on land until we are able to buy it and make it our own."[27] Acquisition of farms by black

---

[25] General E. O. C. Ord, The treatment of freedmen in Arkansas, letter to U. S. House of Representatives, Misc. Doc. No.14, 39th Congress, 2nd Session. From Little Rock, Arkansas, January 4, 1867. University of Arkansas Special Collections.

[26] Judith Kilpatrick, "(Extra) Ordinary Men: African-American Lawyers and Civil Rights in Arkansas Before 1950," *Arkansas Law Review* 53:299 (2000) 307, 309.

[27] Garrison Frazier, "Colloquy with Colored Ministers," *Journal of Negro History*, 16:1 (January 1931), 91.

families faced three major hurdles. They had no capital because of having been enslaved persons, scarcity of available credit, and white hostility toward black ownership. Few white southerners would sell land to black buyers due to pressure from neighbors and local institutions. Black families that sought to purchase land placed themselves in grave danger, but many accepted the risk and pressed ahead. Planters attached possession of land to independence and financial equality, both mortal enemies of peonage. Though land ownership continued to elude them, freedmen still chose to farm under various arrangements. Some planters contracted with laborers in groups, called firms, set of hands, or party of hands. Collective share agreements determined distribution of earnings among members. Working in a share system, working for shares, and contracts for a share of the crop applied to various labor contracts, including sharecropping as generally understood in the Delta.

Call it what you will, freedmen took home too little money for too much work. Women fared the worst. They labored beside men for reduced wages until harvest, when they received a full wage. At crop gathering time, planters recognized the full value of labor to harvest perishable crops. Collective share arrangements for an entire plantation workforce did not prove viable because workers sought terms that matched effort and reward at a family level. Tenant farmers benefited planters in many ways, including an especially important one. They provided opportunities for landlords to cook the books. Price gouging for goods and usurious interest rates on charge accounts continued from one generation to the next. Markups could range from 30 to 100 percent. In egregious cases bureau agents interceded. Agent Glasshoff in Lake Village helped Columbus Paul, a freedman, check a plantation merchant's accounts. Paul criticized outrageous prices and contested a charge for cash loaned by Sunnyside plantation. After reviewing the accounts, Glasshoff discounted the bill and advised this merchant to supply freedmen with weekly transaction balances rather than annual statements.[28]

Divergence between pre-war planter domination and post-war realities in the Delta became clear in an interview with W. B. Mann. His story appeared in a March 12, 1935, Memphis *Commercial Appeal*

---

[28] Glasshoff Report, November 15, 1867, Freedmen's Bureau, Field Office Records-Arkansas, National Archives.

retrospective. The Marianna landlord described a defeated and impoverished region that faced rebuilding what the war tore down. Mann recalled the day his father assembled all the "negroes" to tell them that they were free. The planter said that it was his wish and his advice that they stay and work the growing crop there. However, he followed this offer with what may have been a ruse to hamper worker mobility. Mann's father announced that regional planters planned to meet the following week and develop "fair arrangements" for workers. Such "arrangements" were generally short on "fair" and long on unfair "arrangements." As a result of such collusion, laborers found that nothing could be gained by leaving one onerous relationship in order to enter another just like it. Whether Mann was delusional or disingenuous one cannot say, but he lamented that "customs and habits are gone forever. The confidence and cooperation that existed between the two races has been replaced with distrust and suspicion, until the landlord and cropper now do nothing for each other that the contract does not call for. Such partnership cannot prosper."

Typical contracts between planters and freedmen required workers to provide good and faithful labor. Planters used this code language when accusing hired help of breaking contracts. It allowed landlords to avoid making good on financial commitments to workers. Among Delta planters, good and faithful labor meant an arrangement as close to slavery as possible. Yankee employers who rented plantations and hired freedmen to work for them exhibited less concern about subservience, but also used demeaning contract language to punish freedmen for alleged violations. [29] Some black families remained trapped in incredible situations. John Wesley "belonged" to George Coggrith and lived in Wittsburg during the war. He remained a de facto slave after the conflict. "Four years after freedom we didn't know we was free." While living on Coggrith's farm, his mother would not let the children get far from their house. She had been warned that Indians would steal her children. "They stole children, or I heard they did," said Wesley. "Grown folks and children all kept around home."[30]

---

[29] Ronald L. F. Davis, "Labor Dependency Among Freedmen, 1865-1880," *From the Old South to the New. Essays on the Transitional South,* Walter J. Fraser, Jr. and Winfred B. Moore, Jr., eds. (Westport, Conn.: Greenwood Press, 1981), 157.

[30] Federal Writers' Project: Slave Narrative Project. Vol. 2, Arkansas Part 7, Vaden-Young, 1936. Manuscript Division, Library of Congress, Digital ID: http://hdl.loc.gov/loc.mss/mesn.027.

Freedmen gained some protection from three post-war federal constitutional amendments. Ratified in December 1865, the 13th Amendment established that "neither slavery nor involuntary servitude, except as a punishment for crime whereof the party shall have been duly convicted, shall exist within the United States, or any place subject to their jurisdiction." The 14th Amendment ratified in July 1868 said that "All persons born or naturalized in the United States and subject to the jurisdiction thereof, are citizens of the United States and the State wherein they reside. No State shall make or enforce any law which shall abridge the privileges or immunities of citizens of the United States; nor shall any State deprive any person of life, liberty, or property, without due process of law; or to deny to any person within its jurisdiction the equal protection of the laws." Ratified in February 1870, Amendment 15 stated that the "right of citizens to vote shall not be denied or abridged by the United States or by any state on account of race, color, or previous condition of servitude."[31] Southern racists soon solved problems posed by these three amendments. Kangaroo courts took care of the duly convicted part of the 13th Amendment. Southerners did not concern themselves with 14th Amendment protections since authorities ignored violations. Poll taxes, literacy requirements, and intimidation blocked many black citizens from casting ballots.

Unfortunately, U. S. Supreme Court decisions limited protections these amendments afforded black citizens. The court read narrowly the 13th Amendment's prohibition on involuntary servitude, the 14th Amendment's assurance of due process of law and equal protection for black citizens, and the 15th Amendment's guarantee of voting rights.[32] The amendments mattered little to landlords. White southerners claimed that former slaves would not work unless forced to, so planters used physical compulsion. Employers considered those who asked for reasonable compensation to be uppity. A bargaining process between races would put former slaves on an equal footing with former masters, an intolerable situation for planters. Landlords failed to recognize, or perhaps refused to admit, that freedmen possessed substantial leadership skills and business expertise that they acquired while

---

[31] *Declaration of Independence and Constitution of the United States* (Washington, D. C.: Cato Institute, 1998), 48-50.

[32] Risa Goluboff, *The Lost Promise of Civil Rights* (Cambridge, Mass.: Harvard University Press, 2007), 8.

enslaved. Black overseers ran large plantations for absentee owners. They supervised cotton-ginning, sugar-boiling, and tobacco curing crews in exacting work that demanded great skill and industriousness. Emancipated black managers had wider and deeper experience than their masters realized, and they had practical knowledge about how to farm successfully. [33] Though planters argued otherwise, in the workplace many freedmen were their equals or better.

---

[33] Eugene D. Genovese, *Roll Jordan Roll. The World the Slaves Made* (New York: Vintage Books, 1976), 366-367.

Top, former slaves dressed in old Union uniforms in front of an army barracks. 1864 John C. Taylor Photograph, William A. Gladstone Collection. Bottom, Freedmen's Bureau agent trying to keep the peace. Harper's Weekly, July 25, 1868. Library of Congress Prints and Photographs Division.

Top, white overseers round up field hands. Bottom, the outlook was dim for sharecropper families. Photos by Ben Shahn, Farm Security Administration. Library of Congress Prints and Photographs Division.

CHAPTER 2

Pleading Vainly for Mercy

Black farmers who tried to do something about mistreatment often came to a violent end. Bryant Singfield, a freedman from Texas, attempted to organize former slaves who stayed to work on plantations after the war. Some of them formed an independent colony on abandoned land in Phillips County. They refused to be intimidated by planters, and this became too much for white landowners to tolerate. They blamed Singfield, and planters apparently kidnapped him along with several followers. None were heard from again, but a legend remained.[1]

"There is a broad, sweeping, lonesome bend in Big Creek, only a few miles below Trenton and known as 'The Basin' where the giant alligator gar flounce lazily and the scaly, venomous moccasin lay unmolested on partially submerged logs and tops of fallen trees and where along the shores ancient cypresses standing as silent sentinels rear gaunt and ghost-like against the sky that Negroes contend is haunted and where it is said that in the dark stillness of a moonless summer night the ghost of Bryant Singfield can be seen to emerge from the murky depths and a terrifying voice can be heard pleading vainly for mercy."[2] Though planters took seriously people who challenged

---

[1] M. Langley Biegert, "Legacy of Resistance: Uncovering the History of Collective Action by Black Agricultural Workers in Central East Arkansas from the 1860s to the 1930s," *Journal of Social History* 32:1 (Autumn 1998), 79.
[2] Qtd. in George E. Lankford, ed., *Bearing Witness: Memories of Arkansas Slavery* (Fayetteville: University of Arkansas Press, 2003), 293-294.

their ways of doing things, some observers ridiculed the principles that governed their culture. The *Atlantic Monthly* said that a typical southern landlord possessed a "cast of character which was founded mainly on family, distinction, social culture, exemption from toil, and command over the lives and fortunes of his underlings." Planters considered it the "highest gentility" not to work.[3] Loss of this lifestyle devastated many white landlords. Anne Miller, a former enslaved person, watched her once-upon-a-time "master" go mad after emancipation. He refused to live in a country with free blacks. A year later he committed suicide.[4] Many white southerners agreed with him, but stopped short of suicide. Instead, they turned to political allies and compliant authorities to maintain involuntary servitude. Debt peonage helped keep blacks where whites wanted them.

Booker T. Washington, the prominent black leader and spokesman, said that planters held freedmen in a form of servitude as bad as antebellum slavery. Debt, real or fictional, robbed them of liberty and in some cases their lives. It "winds him deeper and deeper in its meshes each year till he is lost and bewildered."[5] Washington sought to free them from the meshes of debt peonage, especially through educational and business opportunities. He believed that capitalism would neutralize racism in the long run and recommended that blacks seek business opportunities in the New South. Washington said that education would help them become independent farmers, industrial workers, and tradesmen. He marketed this vision to all who would listen, but it was a hard sell in the South. Planters were determined to keep their workforce deep in debt. Sometimes the Ku Klux Klan enforced white priorities. Six former Confederates formed the first klan den during the summer of 1866 in Pulaski, Tennessee. It began as a lark, an opportunity for amusement, but grew into a means of terrorizing freedmen and political enemies. As word spread of klan escapades, so did new dens throughout the South. They became a dark force in white hoods that intimidated blacks and their white allies. Klansmen often attacked prosperous black families because these people had escaped peonage and established a path for others to follow. Though the extent of its involvement in specific acts remains unclear, evidence suggests that in 1868 the klan threatened federal officials,

---

[3] *Atlantic Monthly*, No. 17, February 1866, and No. 39, April 1877.

[4] *Roll Jordan*, 109.

[5] Qtd. in Pete Daniel, *Shadow of Slavery: Peonage in the South, 1901-1969* (Urbana: University of Illinois Press, 1972), IX.

black people, and Republicans. It is estimated that more than 200 Arkansans were murdered on the eve of an 1868 election.[6]

Southern legislators did their part to control black laborers by passing laws that authorities enforced selectively to maintain peonage. One statute charged freedmen with criminal vagrancy if they did not enter into proffered employment contracts. Those who did, but later quit, could be arrested and sent back to their employer. Some states developed ludicrous vagrancy statutes. It could be defined as disorderly conduct, idleness, lewd speech, misspending earnings, and acting disrespectful. Enticement statutes prevented employers from hiring persons working for someone else, which severely hampered employees who sought better conditions and higher paychecks. Criminal surety gave arrested persons a choice between paying fines, which they generally lacked resources to do, or working for planters who paid their fines. Many southerners believed that freedmen lacked the stability to work in a freedom of contract system, so Rebel states passed laws to compel service. Simply put, "forced labor in the South was supported by a web of state laws too complex and varied for the [U. S.] Supreme Court and other courts to disarm."[7] Cynical Mississippi legislators named one of their racist creations "An Act to Confer Civil Rights on Freedmen." It required employees to produce labor contracts when demanded or face arrest by a white person. South Carolina freedmen could not work as craftsmen or store clerks without judicial approval. Northern outrage led to invalidation of some egregious statutes, but southern authorities continued to selectively enforce vagrancy and enticement laws.

"More than any other legislation, the enticement acts embodied the essence of involuntary servitude," according to William Cohen. They established in modified form the proprietary relationship between master and slave. When Rebel states passed enticement laws after the war most made them criminal statutes. Ten states, including Arkansas, passed these statutes starting in 1865 as a common means to control black laborers.[8] Some enticement laws disappeared, but later

---

[6] Thomas DeBlack, "Harnessed Revolution," *Arkansas. A Narrative History,* Jeannie M. Whayne, et. al., eds. (Fayetteville: University of Arkansas Press, 2002), 220.
[7] Benno C. Schmidt, Jr., "Principle and Prejudice: The Supreme Court and Race in the Progressive Era. Part 2: The Peonage Cases," *Columbia Law Review* (May 1982), 3.
[8] William Cohen, "Negro Involuntary Servitude in the South, 1865-1940: A Preliminary Analysis," *Journal of Southern History* 42:1 (February 1976), 31.

reappeared. In 1875, Arkansas enacted a replacement for its 1867 version and increased maximum penalties for convicted persons.

Arkansas statutes required employers to grant discharge certificates to workers "legitimately" leaving their service. Any subsequent employer who hired a worker lacking this certificate could be prosecuted under enticement laws. Many black southerners lacked certificates and opportunities to use them. Black and white women experienced many of the same challenges after the war – the destitute, elderly, widows of soldiers, and wives of unemployed men. Thousands of seamstresses during the war became impoverished after the collapse of military uniform manufacturers. Labor agents contributed to difficulties among black families by recruiting men to distant agricultural employment, leaving women and children behind. Abandoned families wandered the roads and scavenged for food. A widowed washerwoman with six children said, "Sometimes I gits along tolerable. Sometimes right slim; but dat's de way wid everybody – times is powerful hard right now."[9]

Times were powerful hard for poor white women who lost their husbands and property in the war. They begged for bread and foraged for food in desolate regions in a grim struggle for survival. Some families lived in the woods with little or no shelter. Like their black counterparts, poor white mothers exhibited great resourcefulness keeping themselves and their children alive.[10] Black women had to cope with their family's economic and emotional needs while living among white southerners who hated them. Responsibilities of these wives and mothers included their family's daily welfare, wellbeing of kinfolk, and earning modest sums of money doing housework, fieldwork, or both. Most rural black women did "a man's share in the field and a woman's part at home."[11] Housekeeping posed difficulties due to their living space and primitive conditions. A typical shelter consisted of logs or lumber and measured about 15 or 20 square feet. It lacked glass windows, screens to keep out insects, running water, sanitary facilities, and adequate insulation as well as ventilation. Daily living – eating,

[9] Tera W. Hunter, *To 'joy my freedom. Southern Black Women's Lives and Labors after the Civil War* (Cambridge, Mass.: Harvard University Press, 1997), 23.
[10] Jacqueline Jones, *The Dispossessed. America's Underclasses from the Civil War to the Present* (New York: Basic Books, 1992), 65.
[11] Jacqueline Jones, *Labor of Love, Labor of Sorrow. Black Women, Work, and the Family from Slavery to the Present* (New York: Basic Books, 1985), 85.

sleeping, and bathing – took place in one room. Children usually slept on the floor and parents on a small bed in the same room.

Mistreatment of black families continued day after dreary day despite the federal government's good intentions. At first, black people considered the federal government to have a greater potential for tyranny than states, but that view changed. As Senator Charles Sumner observed, the federal government became a "custodian of freedom" for black Americans.[12] When Congress passed a Civil Rights Act, President Johnson vetoed it. He claimed that it placed too much power in Washington and not enough in states, but Congress overrode his veto. Southern legislators agreed with Johnson and maneuvered around federal statutes to control workers. Newspapers assisted by contributing to false narratives. The *Little Rock Daily Conservative* opined on February 2, 1867, that it is "generally conceded that the system of planting on shares is the most successful, as well as the most advantageous to both planter and laborers." This commentary failed to mention planters rigging crop yields, hiding sale proceeds, inflating supply costs, and charging exorbitant interest rates on furnish. Though the state's so-called elite regained influence, Congress slowed their progress, somewhat. The first Reconstruction Act passed in March 1867 dissolved self-reconstructed state governments and put in place five military occupation districts in the South. Still, planters pressed ahead, and Freedmen's Bureau labor contracts often allowed them to achieve significant control over workers.[13] Selective enforcement of laws helped. Vagrancy statutes continued to be a powerful tool in cultivating peonage. Arkansas did not adopt a new vagrancy statute until 1905, but had a serviceable law from the antebellum era. Vagrancy and enticement legislation helped maintain in modified form the relationship between slave and master.[14]

Federal efforts aimed at helping workers included an 1867 Peonage Act. It declared that "holding of any person to service or labor under the system known as peonage is hereby declared to be unlawful, and the same is hereby abolished and forever prohibited" in U. S. territories or states. All acts, laws, resolutions, orders, and regulations "heretofore

---

[12] Eric Foner, *Story of American Freedom* (New York: W. W. Norton, 1998), 106.
[13] Carl H. Moneyhon, *The Impact of the Civil War and Reconstruction on Arkansas* (Fayetteville: University of Arkansas Press, 2002), 214.
[14] William Cohen, *At Freedom's Edge. Black Mobility and the Southern White Quest for Racial Control* (Baton Rouge: Louisiana State University Press, 1991), 31.

established, maintained, or enforced, or by virtue of which any attempt shall hereafter be made to establish, maintain, or enforce, directly or indirectly, the voluntary or involuntary service or labor of any persons as peons, in liquidation of any debt or obligation, or otherwise, be, and the same are hereby, declared null and void." Persons who "hold, arrest, or return, or cause to be held, arrested, or returned, or in any manner aid in the arrest or return of any person or persons to a condition of peonage, shall, upon conviction, be punished by fine not less than one thousand nor more than five thousand dollars, or by imprisonment not less than one nor more than five years, or both, at the discretion of the court."[15]

Planters often evaded accountability by using misinformation. A naïve northern journalist named Benjamin C. Truman obliged them. Landlords convinced him that only poor whites perpetrated outrages. Truman called planters the black man's friend and poor whites his enemy. It was poor white southerners who exposed black people to "contemptible persecutions," he said.[16] Truman failed to understand that though some poor whites applied the lash, planters paid for the whip. An Arkansas Freedmen's Bureau agent described a key challenge in this labor environment. "I am pressing the point vigorously upon our people that bodily coercion fell as an incident of slavery. Many of our best farmers confess that I am right; others growl and wish to be allowed to enforce their contracts, the simple English of which is to whip the nigger." Planter intimidation and thievery may have contributed somewhat to income declines for farm workers, confirmed by U. S. Department of Agriculture (USDA) statistics. The annual value of wages and benefits such as rations for Arkansas farm workers in 1867 came to $158 for men; $94 for women, and $78 for youths. In 1868 they fell to $115; $75, and $67 respectively.[17] But black families had few options since laws providing protection were of little use to people unaware of their provisions or unable to pay legal fees.[18]

---

[15] U. S. Congress, *Congressional Record*, 39th Congress, Session II, 1867, Chapter 187, 546.
[16] Robert Higgs, *Competition and Coercion. Blacks in the American Economy, 1865-1914* (Chicago: University of Chicago Press, 1977), 39.
[17] Report of the Commissioner of Agriculture for the Year 1867 (Department of Agriculture: Washington, D.C., 1868), 416.
[18] Harold D. Woodman, "Post-Civil War Southern Agriculture and the Law," *Agricultural History* 53:1 (January 1979), 321.

Correspondence in bureau files confirmed anecdotal accounts of freedmen abuse during the late 1860s. Agent Eli H. Mix reported the burning of a freedmen church, attributing it to a malignant spirit in the state. White bullies warned freedmen that klansmen would kill their leaders. An account of multiple murders came from Volvey Smith. In one month white terrorists killed eight freedmen, and civil authorities arrested only one person. During the investigation, 25 friends of the prisoner rode into town. They told a magistrate that if the accused man went to jail blood would be shed. A judge released the prisoner, and Smith said that he had been advised to leave the area until things quieted down.[19] Some bureau practices created problems rather than solved them. Bureau director Howard's support of a contract system sometimes led to peonage. To prevent reinstitution of slavery, he decided that the intervening agency between freedmen and planters would be labor contracts. "It was accepted doctrine that the capacity to make a contract was a corollary to freedom." The flaw in this theory was that if authorities forced freedmen to sign contracts without compensation requirements, planters could take advantage of them.[20] And they did.

Freedmen anticipated some improvements in spring 1868 when voters handed Republicans control of the state General Assembly and elected Powell Clayton governor. Unfortunately for black residents and Republicans during that summer, klan activities spread in southern and eastern sections of Arkansas. Clayton mobilized the militia to protect black families from intimidation and violence and declared martial law in ten counties. This led to armed skirmishes between militiamen and klansmen followed by arrests, trials, and some executions. By 1869 klan activities had decreased, but Freedmen's Bureau protection ceased altogether.[21] Withdrawal of its personnel from the South brought violent revenge against bureau agents. Ruffians assaulted Captain John Williams and Anthony Habricht, and killed

---

[19] C. Fred Williams, et al, eds. *Documentary History of Arkansas* (Fayetteville: University of Arkansas Press, 1984), 111-112.

[20] Daniel A. Novak, *The Wheel of Servitude. Black Forced Labor After Slavery* (Lexington: University Press of Kentucky, 1978), 9-10.

[21] Steven Hahn, *A Nation Under Our Feet. Black Political Struggles in the Rural South from Slavery to the Great Migration* (Cambridge, Mass.: Harvard University Press, 2003), 284.

Simpson Mason and Hiram Willis. Racists murdered five freedmen in Osceola within a month of the bureau's departure.[22]

Planters continued to deny freedmen independence by blocking their ownership of land. An 1869 *Southern Cultivator*, No. 27, asked this rhetorical question. "If freedmen become land owners, what will become of white landholders, the upper strata of society?" The writer answered: "It will suffer degradation consistent with the elevation of the lower orders." Black farmers who did not own land worked for landlords in three common categories: day labor, tenants, and sharecroppers. State law distinguished between a landlord-tenant relationship and a landlord-sharecropper one. Statutes classified sharecroppers as laborers agreeing to work for landlords with a portion of crops as wages. They did not acquire dominion or control over premises where they labored. Sharecroppers only had a right to enter and remain on property for required tasks. Tenants acquired possession, dominion, and control over premises for a term covered by their agreement. They paid rent to landlords for use of land, and it did not alter this relationship if rent consisted of a portion of crops produced. Since landlords maintained ownership of a sharecropper's portion of crops until distributed, other creditors lacked security for loans and furnish given to croppers. Thus legal standing became a point of dispute between landlords and creditors. For protection, planters pressured legislators to pass laws extending landlord liens to advances made by them to sharecroppers. In instances where planters became merchants using plantation stores and furnish, collecting debts became simpler and allowed opportunities to manipulate accounts and shares in order to keep renters in debt peonage. If lienholders seized a borrower's property and returned it, those assets became next year's advance. In this manner landlords preserved liens covering old and new debts. Lenders required tenants to give chattel mortgages on personal property in addition to liens on crop shares, which put everything they owned at risk. Damage provisions for breached contracts further weakened tenant protections. They made an employee liable for all money owed to an employer if the worker quit. Landlord terminations were a different matter. If a planter unlawfully fired a tenant, the worker could collect damages only equal to what he might have earned if permitted to continue working under the landlord's contract.

[22] Willis to Bennett, January 31 and July 13, 1868, Freedmen's Bureau, Field Office Records-Arkansas, National Archives.

Furthermore, this amount could be reduced by what the former employee earned in a new job or could reasonably have earned somewhere else during a cancelled contract period.

Born into slavery in Clark County, Anthony Taylor's story brings into sharp focus what happened to black farm workers after the war.

> *Wasn't no law then. I worked all day long for ten cents a day. They would allowance you so many pounds of meat, so much meal, so much molasses. I have worked all day for ten cents and then gone out at night to get a few potatoes. I have pulled potatoes all day for a peck of meal and I was happy at that. I never did know what the price of cotton was.*

Taylor said that freedom came for some at the end of the war, but not all.

> *There was some one going through telling the people that they was free and that they was their own boss. But yet and still, there's lots of them never did leave the man they was with. There was lots of white people that wouldn't let a nigger tell their niggers that they was free, because they wanted to keep them blind to that for years. Kept them for three or four years anyway.*

One of Taylor's memories illustrated the criminality and cruelty of his landlord. The planter seized his family's food set aside to carry them through the winter. He took pigs and hogs that the Taylors fattened with their portion of a corn crop.

> *Took 'em and sold 'em. We didn't even know that we owed him anything. We thought the crops had done settled things. All we children cried. The old man and the old woman didn't say nothing, because they was scared. When our hogs was taken that time, we didn't have nothing to go on that winter. They would allowance us some meat and make us split rails and clear up land for it. It was a cinch if he didn't give it to you you [sic] couldn't get nothing. Wasn't no way to get nothing. Then when crop time rolled 'round again they would take it all out of your crops. Make you split rails and wood to earn your meat and then charge it up to your crop anyhow. But you couldn't do nothin' 'bout it.*[23]

---

[23] Anthony Taylor, Little Rock, Arkansas. Interviewed by Samuel S. Taylor, *Bearing Witness. Memories of Arkansas Slavery. Narratives from the 1930s WPA Collections,* George E. Lankford, ed. (Fayetteville: University of Arkansas Press, 2003), 61-63.

Home of an Arkansas tenant farmer. Photo by Ben Shahn, 1935. Farm Security Administration Collection, Library of Congress Prints and Photographs Division.

CHAPTER 3

A Brief Moment in the Sun

Observing dissolution of a national commitment to assist black citizens, W.E. B. Du Bois, a prominent black educator and spokesman, says that the "slave went free; stood a brief moment in the sun; then moved back again toward slavery."[1] In other writings he added that it is up to "honorable men . . . to see that in the future competition of races the survival of the fittest shall mean the triumph of the good, the beautiful, and the true . . . and not continue to put a premium on greed and impudence and cruelty."[2] Du Bois had a dream, but it would not become a reality in the Delta.

During Reconstruction, greedy and impudent planters tightened the noose around laborers by using suspect contracts. In one example, an 1870 farm lease spelled out common features that gave Delta landlords control over tenants. Blanset, the tenant, had to take harvested cotton to a nearby gin using landlord Barrow's wagon and mules. The tenant would most likely be directed to a gin owned by the landlord or a business associate and thus receive proceeds determined by them. Though Barrow agreed to provide furnish to Blanset, no terms

[1] W.E.B. Du Bois, *Black Reconstruction in America* (New York: Free Press, 1997), 30.
[2] W. E. B. Du Bois, *The Soul of Black Folk* (New York: Barnes & Noble Classics, 2003), 117. Although originally from New England, Du Bois came south to attend Fisk University in Nashville, Tennessee. During summers he taught rural folks and witnessed the many forms of racial injustice they endured. After obtaining a Ph.D. from Harvard, Du Bois taught at Atlanta University, wrote many books and essays, and became a prominent spokesman for black Americans.

were mentioned. Omission of an interest rate might be an oversight or perhaps a means of imposing a rate based on how much the debtor could pay after harvest. Blanset rented 20 acres and agreed to pay one third of the corn, one fourth of the cotton, and one fourth of the sweet potatoes raised during the year. Blanset also agreed to repay Barrow for furnish out of his portion of crops. The landlord could not seize crops unless Blanset attempted to deceive or defraud him. The tenant had to consult Barrow before selling crops. This gave Barrow an opportunity to control marketing and Blanset's share.[3]

Financial desperation and intimidation caused tenants to sign these questionable farm contracts, and the klan sometimes provided the intimidation. Though the organization lacked centralized leadership, its locals shared goals and tactics. Klan membership spanned class lines, but victims blamed the South's so-called upper classes and rightly so. Its leadership included planters, merchants, lawyers, ministers, and deacons. In other words, "the very best citizens."[4] This raised a question about racial violence. How could professed Christians countenance and participate in the beatings and murder of other human beings? Some turned away, not wanting to peer into that hell and share responsibility for it. Others observed, but did nothing, contriving excuses for this inhumanity. A culture grounded in slavery contributed to their behavior. More than malice drove some masters to whip slaves for praying to God. Planters demanded that they address all grievances and wishes to their earthly masters. This attitude continued in the post-war South.

Justice was blind and obedient to planter will. Many southern judges found black men guilty of something when cotton grew ready for harvest. Victims generally had two choices: serve on the chain gang or be leased to a planter who paid their fine. Many died in each situation, but during 1871 a southern court found that they suffered more than one form of death. Virginia's Supreme Court in *Ruffin v. Commonwealth* declared imprisoned persons "civilly dead." The decision declared that during their time in prison, convicts forfeited not only their liberty, but all personal rights. They existed in a state of penal

---

3 Ted Worley, ed., "Tenant and Labor Contracts, Calhoun County, 1869-1871," *Arkansas Historical Quarterly* 13:1 (Spring 1954), 103-104.

4 Eric Foner, *Reconstruction: America's Unfinished Revolution 1863-1877* (New York: Perennial Classics,1988), 433.

servitude, slaves of the state.[5] Some courts became little more than employment agencies for planters. Death rates among leased prisoners ranged from 20 to 50 percent. Those who chose chain gangs to avoid being leased did not better their circumstances. Whipping bosses stood over workers and carried a leather strap about three feet long. A convict said that if the gang did not work "like fighting fire," a whipping boss walked down the line striking indiscriminately.[6]

Despite legal efforts to stop such abuses, opponents carved out loopholes and slipped through them. The Slaughterhouse cases helped make this possible. They developed in 1872 when about 100 persons who made their living butchering livestock in New Orleans sued the state. They claimed that regulations created a monopoly that hampered their ability to practice this trade. The butchers argued that these statutes violated the 13th and 14th amendments. However, the Louisiana Supreme Court found against them, ruling that state police powers allowed actions to protect the safety and health of citizens. After plaintiffs filed a motion to appeal, both sides agreed to a compromise, except for three butchers. The U. S. Supreme Court agreed to hear their case. In December 1872 it ruled against the holdouts, finding that state actions fell within its power to control slaughter of livestock in the city. Justices ruled that constitutional amendments did not apply to acts taken by states if reserved to them under police powers.[7] This point had critical consequences. Throughout the South, states legislated discriminatory statutes under cover of police powers.

Such court rulings prevented peonage victims from getting justice, and lack of political power hampered them as well. As a result, "segregation and disfranchisement strengthened the caste system . . . stripped them of political power, and most significantly, impelled the [black] middle class on a course of self-preservation at the expense of the masses."[8] Planters recognized the danger of black political power and blocked polling booths with intimidation and violence at election time. Consequently, Democrats dominated the 1874 election in

---

[5] *Ruffin v. Commonwealth*, Virginia Supreme Court, 1871. Qtd. in Andrea C. Armstrong, "Slavery Revisited in Penal Plantation Labor," *Seattle University Law Review* (Spring 2012), 4.

[6] Schmidt, Part 2, 5.

[7] *Slaughterhouse Cases*, 83 U. S. 36 (1872).

[8] Fon Louise Gordon, *Caste & Class. The Black Experience in Arkansas, 1880-1920* (Athens: University of Georgia Press, 1995), 71.

Arkansas. Legislators handed county courts and justices of the peace greater authority to settle tenant-landlord disputes. Section 4101 of an 1873 lien law stipulated that landlords who had liens on crops for rent could bring suit before a justice of the peace or in circuit court and obtain a writ of attachment. Section 4080 applied to persons who held liens. If below a threshold amount, they could go before a justice of the peace in the county where their lien existed. They could make a sworn statement of the amount due after all just credits were given.[9] Two problems for tenants stand out in such provisions. One, local justices of the peace often were planters or allies. Two, "all just credits" computed by landlords involved flexible mathematics that invariably added up in their favor.

Other new laws tightened the hold of planters. Theft of property worth more than $2 could be punishable by imprisonment. Landlords who held liens on farm commodities grown on their property had a right to approve or deny tenant sales. Checks for crop sale proceeds had both the tenant's name and the landlord's, so they could not be cashed without endorsement by both parties. Families were prohibited from leaving a landlord before their contract expired. Poor black farm tenants lacked political allies. The state's two dominant parties directed their efforts toward middle-class blacks who considered themselves apart from farm tenants and working-class folks. Those who had climbed into the middle class hesitated to risk their gains by challenging this white power structure. In this sense they "sacrificed the agricultural and laboring classes to white economic exploitation."[10]

Federal legislators sought to enhance minority rights with the Civil Rights Act of 1875, but ran into trouble in the U. S. Supreme Court. That court found the act "beyond Congress's powers under the 13th and 14th amendments." Justice Joseph P. Bradley decided that "it would be running the slavery argument into the ground" to declare private discrimination acts "badges of slavery."[11] Civil Rights efforts declined after an 1877 political compromise. Under that agreement Republicans reduced their support of black citizens struggling to break the chains

---

[9] Edward W. Gantt, *A Digest of the Statutes of Arkansas* (Little Rock, Ark.: Little Rock Printing and Publishing Company, 1874), 741-742.
[10] *Caste and Class*, 14.
[11] Benno C. Schmidt, "Principle and Prejudice: The Supreme Court and Race in the Progressive Era. Part 1: The Heyday of Jim Crow," *Columbia Law Review* (April 1982), 12.

that bound them, and white southerners accepted the Republican presidential candidate in a contested 1876 election. This led to the Rutherford B. Hayes presidency and what many considered to be an end to Reconstruction.

Still, many black citizens continued their resistance despite what some consider a betrayal. Reconstruction was "overthrown, subverted, and betrayed" due to objections about costs, internecine politics, and xenophobia," and was "as good as dead" from 1875 onward.[12] Public opinion had turned against it long before the compromise. A *New York Tribune* in 1870 declared the country "sick and tired" of it. "We cannot forever keep the boy out of the water because he has not learned to swim."[13] The U. S. Supreme Court limited reach of post-Civil War constitutional amendments in order to accommodate political compromise. The court helped purchase peace, and black families paid the bill.

Henry Blake, a former slave and sharecropper, described the results of peonage for his family. "After freedom, we worked on shares a while. When we worked on shares, we couldn't make nothing—just overalls and something to eat. Half went to the other man and you would destroy your half if you weren't careful. A man that didn't know how to count would always lose. He might lose anyhow. They didn't give no itemized statement. No, you just had to take their word. They just say you owe so much. Brother, I'm telling you the truth about this. You had to take the white man's word on notes and everything. Anything you wanted, you could git if you were a good hand. But you better not leave him—you better not try to leave and git caught."[14]

Though planters wanted to retain tenants such as the Blakes, they did not want to maintain indefinitely farmers genuinely in debt to them. Perpetual indebtedness meant giving up real resources, so peonage using fictitious debt made more financial sense. Paying off exorbitant debt, often fabricated, put tremendous pressure on families. A typical black mother had six or seven children, and many mothers worked in

---

[12] Allen C. Guelzo, *Reconstruction. A Concise History* (New York: Oxford University Press, 2018), 114, 129.
[13] Qtd. in Guelzo, 101.
[14] Henry Blake, Little Rock, Arkansas. Interviewed by Samuel S. Taylor, *Bearing Witness. Memories of Arkansas Slavery Narratives from the 1930s WPA Collections*, George E. Lankford, ed. (Fayetteville: University of Arkansas Press, 2003), 320-322.

the fields or homes of white employers. Some held both jobs. They did this in addition to domestic responsibilities and generally received less pay based on gender rather than productivity. A great disparity existed between working wives in Cotton Belt white and black households. In 1870 more than 40 percent of black married women had outside jobs, mostly field work. About 98.4 percent of white wives kept house and had no other occupation. Approximately 24.3 percent of black households, compared with 13.8 percent of white ones, had at least one working child under the age of 16. Despite attempts to climb out of property, most black families occupied the lowest rung on the economic ladder.[15]

[15] *Labor of Love*, 63.

Well-stocked country stores often were owned by planters and extended credit to keep their tenants indebted to them. Photos by Curtis Duncan.

Jim Crow laws, enacted in the late 19th and early 20th centuries, mandated racial segregation of public schools, public places, and public transportation. Blacks had to use separate restrooms, drinking fountains, waiting rooms, and other facilities. Exceptions were made for black domestic workers and caregivers while accompanying their charges. Photo by Jack Delano, 1940. Library of Congress Prints and Photographs Division.

CHAPTER 4

We Wear the Mask

A poem by Paul Laurence Dunbar, *We Wear the Mask*, describes a method used by blacks to hide their secret rejection of whites who sought to dominate them.

We wear the mask that grins and lies,
It hides our cheeks and shades our eyes, –
This debt we pay to human guile;
With torn and bleeding hearts we smile,
And mouth with myriad subtleties.

Why should the world be over-wise,
In counting all our tears and sighs?
Nay, let them only see us, while
We wear the mask.

We smile, but, O great Christ, our cries
To Thee from tortured souls arise.
We sing, but oh, the clay is vile
Beneath our feet, and long the mile;
But let the world dream otherwise,
We wear the mask![1]

[1] Jay David, ed., *Black Defiance. Black Profiles in Courage* (New York: William Morrow & Company, 1972.), 62-63.

In 1881, black South Carolina families removed their masks and formed emigration societies for relocation to Arkansas. A northern reporter saw "just desserts" being served up to their landlords. He said that these planters maintained red-shirted rifle clubs to intimidate black voters during political campaigns, but now found a "Nemesis in human affairs."[2] Though sometimes migrants used agents to assist them, often they did not. Many South Carolina families came to Arkansas on their own. Some left Edgefield County led by John Hammond, a black Baptist minister. His members first sent a three-man scouting party to Arkansas, and they returned claiming government land could be had almost for the asking. After assessing members for trip expenses Hammond's group set out for Augusta by wagon and on foot in search of available land. According to the January 7, 1882, *Gazette* in Huntsville, Alabama, the trip went without a serious hitch.

During the 1870s, more than 36,000 black migrants arrived in Arkansas. Some expected life on easy street, but most found rutted swampland. Planters welcomed this influx since these arrivals enlarged the labor pool and helped hold down wages. But unexpected consequences came with migrants into the state – an increase in black voters. In 1880 they apparently helped elect John Johnson, a black attorney. He suppposedly beat incumbent Poindexter Dunn in the First District Congressional election, so whites devised a scheme to reverse election outcomes by using fraudulent tallies. This became a common weapon used by white authorities to steal elections. According to the July 9, 1878, *New York Times*, a Jefferson County Democratic leader said that the "radicals" may have the numbers and out vote us, but we can "out count" them. By "out counting," Democrats declared Dunn the winner. Despite white chicanery, four black men were elected to the state General Assembly by 1880. In 1890 the Arkansas House had 12 black members, and ten of the 12 had migrated to the state. Southern racists took extreme measures in some cases to maintain political control. Republican John Clayton won the Second Congressional District race, but was murdered during January 1889 while investigating voter fraud in Conway County. Another unwanted development came with migrants. By 1890 more than a dozen all-black towns existed in the state. This progress produced some remarkable results. Liberia City, one such community, created a joint stock

---

[2] *Under Our Feet*, 361.

company that bought 2,000 acres of land and resold it to black farmers. Improvements in education occurred as well, when churches operated private schools for black students.[3]

Two black migrants became spectacularly successful. Born a slave, Pickens Black Sr. came from Alabama to Jackson County, Arkansas, in the 1870s after hearing about good land to be had. He worked on the railroad and saved enough money to buy 40 acres, which started his real estate empire. Pickens Black eventually owned 8,000 acres with a cotton gin, sawmill, and grain elevator. He refused to be defeated by white jealousy. Each time his general store in Blackville burned, he replaced it with a better version.[4] Scott Bond also was born a slave, but in Mississippi. When about 18 he lived with his stepfather in Madison, Arkansas, and began to display his formidable entrepreneurial skills. While in his early twenties, Bond peddled food in a wagon and fish caught on a trotline. Through hard work and frugality he saved $900 and purchased a farm, which he cleared and drained. Bond bought more land and added cotton gins. At the age of 60 he owned 21 farms, several gins, buildings in Madison, and a large and profitable general store there. Memphis businessmen offered him $2 million for his assets, but Bond declined their offer. At one point he owned 12,000 acres, about 50 percent with virgin timber. He cut over the land and milled its timber at his sawmill. Bond added to his fortune through land speculation and other business opportunities. Like Pickens Black, he refused to accept the limitations that Jim Crow sought to impose.[5]

Most migrants to the Delta found fence-row-to-fence-row cotton. The amount of land devoted to that crop rather than others validated its importance. Estimates indicated that in 1879, of more than three million acres of harvested crops, cotton made up about 35 percent. By 1889, the percentage of lands committed to the crop had increased to about 45 percent of all harvested acres in the state.[6] Compensation for

---

[3] Story Matkin-Rawn, "'The Great Negro State of the Country': Arkansas's Reconstruction and the Other Great Migration," *Arkansas Historical Quarterly* 72:1 (Spring 2013), 39-40.
[4] https://encyclopediaofarkansas.net/entries/pickens-w-black-sr-5396/. Accessed Aug. 25, 2019.
[5] Ulysses S. Bond, "Highlights in the Life of Scott Bond," *Arkansas Historical Quarterly*, 21:2 (Summer 1962), 146-152.
[6] Carl H. Moneyhon, *Arkansas and the New South. 1874-1929* (Fayetteville: University of Arkansas Press, 1997), 64.

growing cotton varied, even within the same area. An Arkansas planter said that on 20 plantations around him landlords used about ten different contracts. Despite variations, wage rates and crop shares tended to be higher in Arkansas than in other southern states. Sometimes unscrupulous black recruiters lured migrants with claims of higher incomes. One victim described this betrayal.

> *De white folks would pay niggers to lie to the rest of us niggers to git der farming done for nothing. He'd tell us come on and go with me, a man wants a gang of niggers to do some work and he pay you like money growing on trees. Well we ain't had no money an ain't use to none, so we glad to hear dat good news. We just up and bundle up and go with this lying nigger. Dey carried us by de droves to different parts of Alabama, Arkansas, and Missouri. After we got to des places, dey put us all to work allright on dem great big farms. We all light in and work like old horses, thinking now we making money and going to git some of it, but we never did git a cent. We never did git out of debt. All over was like dat. Dem lying niggers caused all dat. Yes dey did.*[7]

Some recruiter sales pitches reached ludicrous extremes. Henry Green remembered them describing Arkansas as a place "dat de hogs jes layng er round already baked wid de knives an de forks stickin' in 'em ready for to be et."[8] Agents who enticed laborers to leave one Arkansas employer for another risked punishment under state law. It prohibited a person from enticing away a worker contracted with another person without that employer's consent. The enticer could be fined not less than $25 nor more than $500. Additionally, he would be liable for all advances and damages sustained by the employer.

People migrating to Arkansas helped to significantly expand the state's labor force. Its black population increased from 210,666 in 1880 to 309,117 by 1890. One black migrant taken to Arkansas by a labor agent became an NAACP official. William Pickens described how a recruiter told his parents about Arkansas, a "balmy paradise with coconuts, oranges, lemons, and bananas for the picking and with enormous yields of corn and cotton." The father signed a contract to

---

[7] Leon F. Litwack, *Been in the Storm So Long. The Aftermath of Slavery* (New York: Vintage Books, 1979), 309.
[8] *Uncertain Freedom*, 99-100.

work until repayment of transportation debt and furnish charges. Penniless upon arrival in the balmy paradise, they labored for a year and found themselves deeper in debt. The next year they ended up with more debt. As a result, the elder Pickens went to Little Rock on a pretext to find a better situation. There he met a reputable landlord who advanced transportation money to relocate. Within a year the family had paid off its new transportation debt. Reflecting on exaggerated claims of labor recruiters, John Van Hook said that "Some of those labor agents were powerful smart about stretching the truth."[9] Other migrants had better luck with agents. Recruiters representing planters in higher-wage states – Mississippi, Arkansas, Louisiana, and Texas – recruited thousands of black families from the lower-wage states of Alabama, Georgia, North Carolina, and South Carolina.[10] Honest recruiters provided accurate information about wages and opportunities. In some cases they helped pay moving costs, guaranteed employment, and saw to it that transitioning workers were not charged with vagrancy or prosecuted for leaving an employer.

Unfortunately, many migrants moved to the Delta during exceptionally tough times. Economic difficulties in the 1880s contributed to formation of several farm organizations in Arkansas, but racial animus and fractured solidarity hampered them. Their formation developed due to increased tenancy, low crop prices, the crop-lien system, discriminatory railroad shipping costs, and statutes favoring mortgage holders. In response to these and other issues, black Prairie County farmers organized a local alliance in 1882. Other black farm workers formed an organization named Sons of the Agricultural Star headquartered in Monroe County. The Agricultural Wheel, founded in Arkansas in 1882, eliminated "whites only" eligibility at its 1886 state convention and allowed separate black Wheel chapters.[11] Still, membership rules and common causes did not eliminate racial antipathy. The state organization required black Wheels to pay dues, but during a July 1887 convention the white Wheelers attempted to deny recognition of black delegates from St. Francis County. In reaction

---

[9] *Storm So Long,* 309.

[10] David E. Bernstein, *Only One Place of Redress. African Americans, Labor Regulations, and the Courts from Reconstruction to the New Deal* (Durham, N. C.: Duke University Press, 2001), 10.

[11] Fon Louise Gordon, "From Slavery to Uncertain Freedom: Blacks in the Delta," *The Arkansas Delta. Land of Paradox,* Jeannie M. Whayne and, Willard B. Gatewood, eds. (Fayetteville: University of Arkansas Press, 1993), 107-108.

to this color line, black Wheels organized a Colored State Agricultural Wheel.

No matter how hard they tried, black residents could not change the hearts and minds of many white southerners. Black southerners faced a catch-22. Whites denied them a proper education, then declared them too illiterate to vote, serve on juries, and enjoy other citizenship privileges. When hard work led to financial success, black families had to remain in the shadows for protection. Several witnesses described their dilemma. A black woman recalled that a white playmate told her, "You think you are white because your folks own their own home; but you ain't, you're a nigger just the same, and my paw says if he had his rights he would own niggers like you, and your home, too."[12] Viral racism spread from parent to child, family to family, neighbor to neighbor, and often grew worse along the way. This contagion may have been exacerbated by what an Italian researcher calls group polarization. Quoted in the January 9, 2016, *Arkansas Democrat Gazette*, Michela Del Vicario said that like-minded people speaking to each other end up believing a more extreme version of what they originally thought. They accept opinions they agree with and reject those they do not. What results is a "proliferation of biased narratives fomented by unsubstantiated rumors, mistrust, and paranoia."

Biased narratives supported many forms of mistreatment. Benjamin Mays says that his mother always kept him clean and well-dressed. Yet one day while he waited for mail at the post office a white doctor struck him and said, "Get out of my way you black rascal. You're trying to look too good anyway." Mays says that his only mistake was trying to look too good.[13] When white thugs went to Eunice Rivers's home and beat up her father, the only reason the family could come up with was that they were living too well. The girl's father worked two jobs, owned his small home, and had achieved financial independence. After nightriders shot up the family's house, the Rivers moved into a rent cabin, and harassment ended.[14]

---

[12] A Southern Colored Woman, "The Race Problem: An Autobiography," *The Independent* 56 (March 17, 1904), 589.

[13] Benjamin E. Mays, *Born to Rebel. An Autobiography* (Athens: University of Georgia Press, 1986), 45-46.

[14] Ruth Hill, ed. *Black Women Oral History Project* 7 (Westport, Conn.: 1991), 221-222.

The major American writer Richard Wright spent part of his boyhood in the Delta. In his book *Black Boy*, Wright shares his reaction to the death of an uncle at the hands of white murderers. He was eight when thugs killed his uncle because of the man's prosperity derived from a saloon in Elaine. Wright says that "Uncle Hoskins had simply been plucked from our midst and we, figuratively, had fallen on our faces to avoid looking into the white-hot face of terror that we knew loomed somewhere above us. This was as close as white terror had ever come to me and my mind reeled." Bewildered by his family's passivity, Wright asked his mother why. But "the fear that was in her made her slap me into silence."[15]

Jim Crow made some exceptions to second-class status of black female domestic workers and caregivers. They could take children or dependent adults onto public transportation and into spaces reserved for whites while accompanying their charges. Otherwise, rules barred them from these places. Some public parks featured signs such as "No Negroes Allowed on the Grounds Except as Servants." White employers depended on them and in some instances claimed black helpers to be part of their family, but still insisted on a dividing line between races. It went like this cradle to grave. Little Rock citizens sought to convert a cemetery used for black burials into an exclusively white cemetery. But with no money available to remove black corpses and bury them elsewhere, grave diggers placed white bodies on top of them. An Alabama resident objected to any racial integration in cemeteries. "If a colored person was to be buried among the whites, the latter would all rise from their graves in indignation. How they tolerate the niggers in heaven is a mystery, unless the mansions there are provided with kitchens and stables."[16] Apparently, white southerners demanded that blacks know their place at all times, even in Heaven or Hell.

Many merchants welcomed black and white customers in their country stores, and some storeowners took advantage of both. A critic

---

[15] Richard R. Wright, *Black Boy: A Record of Childhood and Youth* (New York: Perennial Library, 1945), 47-48. Born during 1908 in Mississippi, Wright wrote six novels, novellas, short stories, seven non-fiction books, and many articles, essays, and poems. First published in 1945, *Black Boy* received great critical acclaim and made him the first bestselling black author. In 1947 he became a French citizen and lived in Paris until his death in 1960.

[16] Leon F. Litwack, *Trouble in Mind. Black southerners in the Age of Jim Crow* (New York: Vintage Books, 1998), 236.

of their financial practices claimed that store owners sometimes ignored the maxim that "honesty is the best policy." Another observer said that a merchant's decision about right and wrong depended largely on the alertness of customers.[17] Many forced farmers they furnished to plant only cotton by denying advances for other crops. Since merchants sold foodstuffs, the idea of financing competition from gardens did not appeal to them. Customers usually restricted purchases to the three M's – meat, molasses, and meal. A poor family's diet included staples such as salt pork, cornbread, and molasses. Those permitted to have gardens also had beans, tomatoes, potatoes, okra, peas, onions, turnips, and collard greens. High merchandise prices and carrying charges depended on monopolies. A typical distance between country stores was about nine miles, and this established barriers to competition. A farmer who wanted to compare prices at two stores located that far apart had to travel 18 miles by wagon and team, according to the January 1870 *Rural Carolinian*. This would exhaust the better part of a day. So country stores had small but secure monopolies.

Devices to protect a merchant's territory became consistent throughout the South. A crop lien system exploited farmers who were charged exorbitant prices and had to settle up at harvest time. Merchants financing tenants required cotton since that cash crop provided income when harvested to pay their bills. These businessmen wore many hats. Bill Nixon served as a railroad ticket agent, freight agent, and postmaster. Others issued marriage licenses and performed weddings. Records indicated that some lacked accounting skills. In one set of books a merchant penciled this note at the top of a page: "Suit of clothes for who!" [18] In another: "Rec' for something." [19] However, sketchy accounting could produce useful results for stores. Bookkeeping frequently showed a debt at the close of each year for an industrious laborer. Records could be made to balance exactly for a cropper ordered to move on. This achievement perplexed customers not good enough at ciphering to keep pace with a shady bookkeeper. A person who demanded too close a look could be branded a troublemaker and run out of the county by an obliging sheriff. It made a great deal of difference whether merchants became landlords or

---

[17] Jacqueline P. Bull, "The General Merchant in the Economic History of the New South," *Journal of Southern History* 18 (February 1952), 40.

[18] W. H. Henderson ledger, 1891:92, W. H. Henderson papers. University of Kentucky Library.

[19] J. H. Johnson's cashbook, May-December, 1871, Johnson papers. Qtd. in Bull, 43.

landlords became merchants. In the former, merchants threatened planter elites. In the latter, planters retained control and reduced country stores to a secondary role as in the antebellum era. So when possible, planters opened their own stores.[20] To help achieve this transition, landlords launched ideological attacks backed up with laws depriving merchants of first liens on crops.

Need for credit from one source or the other resulted in part from scarcity of bank financing in southern states. In 1865, Rebel states had approximately one-fourth of the nation's population and less than two percent of the banks. This ranked substantially below its 15 percent share prior to the war. Though the number of banks increased, by 1890 the South's portion remained less than its prewar percentage. Additionally, southern banks had limited capital and deposits. A National Banking Act stifled recovery of southern banks by requiring a minimum of $50,000 of paid-in capital to establish a national bank. Regulations prohibited national banks from possessing mortgaged real estate with loan amortizations of more than five years. Small bank woes dated back to 1865, when Congress passed a ten percent tax on note issues of all non-national banks. This measure virtually eliminated state bank note issues throughout the country, which harmed small southern banks that relied on them.[21] Illiteracy put many borrowers at a disadvantage when sitting in front of a loan officer. Monitoring bank accounts and loan disbursements required financial skills, and farmers had few. Many tenants could not read, much less understand notes payable and associated paperwork. Lack of liquidity also hindered credit worthiness. Loan drawdowns began early in the year with no repayment until end of the year. Tenants had little security to pledge in addition to crops, which made farm loans risky. It took a gutsy banker to make such loans, and they were rare.

---

[20] Harold D. Woodman, "Sequel to Slavery: The New History Views the Postbellum South," *Journal of Southern History* 43:4 (November 1977), 546-547.
[21] Roger L. Ransom and Richard Sutch, "Debt Peonage in the Cotton South After the Civil War," *Journal of Economic History* 32:3 (September 1972), 646.

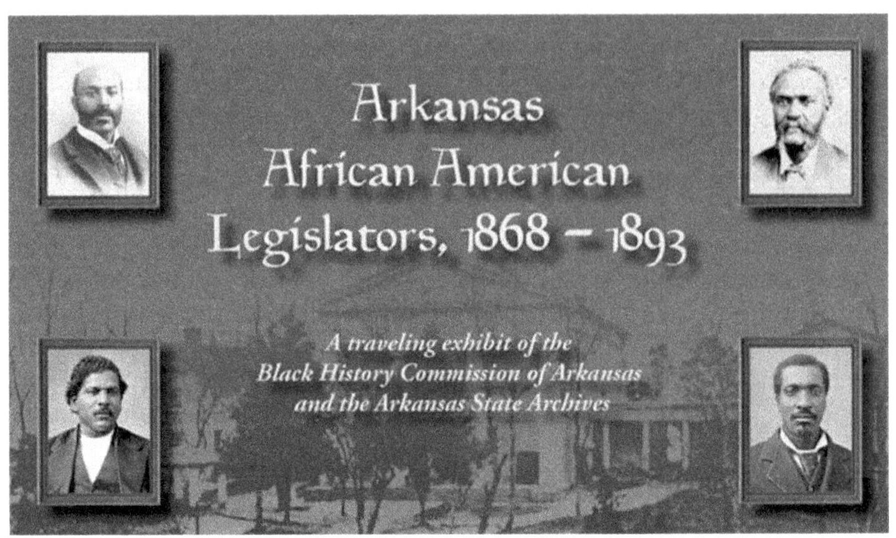

No. ________ **Poll Tax Receipt, 189**__

Office of Collector of ________________ *Co., Ark.* ________ *189*__

RECEIVED OF ________________________________

*One Dollar in payment of Poll Tax charged against him for year 189*__

____

Collector ________________ *County, Ark.*

________________________________ *D. C.*

Brown Printing Co., Little Rock—1894.

A traveling exhibit celebrates the 85 African Americans known to have served in the Arkansas General Assembly between 1868 and 1893. Despite the many obstacles in their paths, these legislators included successful lawyers, merchants, ministers, educators, farmers, and other professionals. Gains were short-lived, however, when more restrictive election laws were passed in 1891, along with an 1892 poll tax amendment. All black legislators were voted out of office by 1894. Exhibit created by the Black History Commission of Arkansas and the Arkansas State Archives.

CHAPTER 5

Downtrodden Sons of Toil

Ida Wells-Barnett, a famous black crusader against racial injustice, said in 1892 that during previous decades racists murdered hundreds of black people for allegedly participating in insurrections. No insurrections materialized, however, so white people needed another excuse. Disputed voting rights became a flashpoint. Black people had the right to vote, but not protection to exercise it. They believed that in a ballot there was a "subtle something which stood for manhood as well as citizenship, and thousands of brave black men went to their graves, exemplifying the one by dying for the other." Barred from voting, that could no longer be an excuse for murder. Lynching next became a response to avenge alleged assaults upon white women. Racists declared black men to be "virile monsters," and violence continued under that ruse.[1]

---

[1] Jacqueline Jones Royster, ed. *Southern Horrors and Other Writings: The Anti-Lynching Campaign of Ida B. Wells, 1892-1900* (Boston, Mass.: St Martin's Press, 1996), 76-77. Born a slave in Mississippi, Wells became a militant anti-lynching crusader. After attending Rust College in Mississippi, she taught in public schools. Wells bravely sued a railroad company for discrimination and won, but lost on appeal. She later took up journalism and campaigned against racial injustice, particularly lynching.

In one assessment, during the 1890s black resistance "had long ceased to be an important deterrent to white aggression."[2] But not in Arkansas. Black leaders continued to spar with Jim Crow and retained some political power before restrictive acts curtailed their participation. Approximately 70 percent of black adult males voted in the 1890 gubernatorial election, mostly for Republicans, and they held 11 of 95 state representative seats in 1891. This probably ranked as the second highest percentage of black representatives in any state legislature at that time.[3] At mass meetings black participants passed resolutions denouncing bills in state legislatures that forced separation of races into different train cars.

Despite resolutions and reasonable counter-proposals, black travelers remained segregated and humiliated. Planters protected and preserved their class, and disfranchisement remained a valuable tool for ratcheting down black political influence. Cumulative poll taxes punished poor folks, black and white, though black citizens remained the primary targets. If necessary to achieve desired election outcomes, authorities issued poll-tax receipts to fictitious persons, dead persons, and nonresidents. Men convicted of crimes that politicians associated with black violators could not vote. And passing a literacy test in some states became mandatory, though not in Arkansas. Test questions often pertained to matters in a state's constitution, and white voters invariably gave correct answers and black voters the wrong ones. An editorial writer declared that "if every Negro in Mississippi was a graduate of Harvard . . . he would not be as fitted to exercise the rights of suffrage as the Anglo-Saxon farm laborer."[4] Given the agenda of people scoring these tests, black Harvard graduates probably would have a mysteriously high failure rate.

When black workers protested suppression, and many did, they often faced overwhelming violence. A September 12, 1891, Memphis *Commercial Appeal* reported a possible Delta cotton picker strike during that fall harvest. R. M. Humphrey led the Colored Farmers Alliance, a group primarily made up of field hands and sharecroppers. He demanded a one dollar wage for every hundred pounds of cotton

---

[2] C. Vann Woodward, *The Strange Career of Jim Crow* (New York: Oxford University Press, 1957), 64.
[3] Morgan Kousser, "A Black Protest in the 'Era of Accommodation': Documents," *Arkansas Historical Quarterly* 34:2 (Summer 1975), 151.
[4] *American Nightmare,* 68.

picked. At that time Delta planters paid 50 cents. Humphrey expected wide-spread support throughout Texas and Arkansas, but in the Delta only Lee County pickers staged a significant rebellion. Intimidation by white thugs and small raises for pickers discouraged participation. Fear of violent reprisals caused most field hands to avoid confrontations. Ben Patterson, a union organizer from Memphis, focused on Lee County, and at least 25 local pickers agreed to strike.[5] The incident that set off a violent series of events developed from conversations between a landlord, J. F. Frank, and his plantation manager, Tom Miller. After Miller complained about a slow harvest, Frank authorized him to increase wages if necessary. When pickers heard this and struck they received 60 cents per hundred. Other planters sent Frank a letter printed in the Lee County *Courier* warning that 50 cents was the price, "and we are not going to pay any more, neither are we going to permit [more] to be paid in this neighborhood." The strike began on September 20 when employees of H. P. Rodgers demanded 75 cents per hundred. After Rodgers fired them they encouraged others to join a walkout, and some did. According to a September 29, 1891, Memphis *Commercial Appeal*, an observer reported that "all the fields, covering several thousand acres, were white with cotton." But in a 30-mile stretch he saw only two men picking. Planters convinced Lee County's sheriff to form a posse of strike breakers. When strikers clashed with men still working, two laborers died. Three days later someone killed Tom Miller on his way to join the sheriff, and the white posse sought revenge.

After setting fire to a plantation cotton gin, Patterson and his allies worked their way through cane breaks to Cat Island in the Mississippi River. They hoped to catch a steamboat and escape, but the posse caught up with them, killed some, and arrested others. Patterson managed to board a riverboat, but vigilantes murdered him. An October 1, 1889, Chicago *Daily Tribune* reported what happened to the captured strikers. "Sheriff Riddick and posse left Cat Island . . . with nine of the thirteen rioters conveying them to Marianna's jail. They were overtaken by an armed band of white regulators and after a desperate struggle [a dubious claim] nine black prisoners were taken from the Sheriff and his men. Without any ceremony the negroes were dragged to the nearest tree and inside of fifteen minutes nine bodies were swaying with the breezes. The mob directed the Sheriff to go home with his men, and he did so without delay." Press coverage did not mention casualties among

---

[5] *Legacy of Resistance*, 82.

the sheriff's men after the alleged "desperate struggle." Planters murdered other black workers as well, according to *Commercial Appeal* coverage.

Black pastors preached against lynching and other acts of violence, and racists marginalized them when possible. In a letter written on March 24, 1892, Reverend Malcolm Argyle despaired about the murder of numerous black men throughout the state. They strung up victims on telephone poles, burned them at the stake, and shot them. "In the last 30 days there have been not less than eight colored persons lynched in this state."[6] A June 12, 1895, Helena *Weekly World* questioned the motives of two black preachers and ridiculed their congregations. "Jim Harvey and Sim Gibson are just a couple of common negro broilers, neither of them know anything about Christianity, nor are they governed by any consideration except the desire to work the gullible fools in the congregation for all the money they can get." Efforts to upset the status quo sometimes see-sawed from pulpits to politics and contributed to a populist political movement in the early 1890s. An Arkansas convention attracted 170 delegates, among them 82 Confederate veterans, 32 ex-Union soldiers, and 11 black men. Their platform included opposition to poll taxes and convict leasing. Of particular interest to black participants, the plank denounced lynching and vowed that the party would support "downtrodden sons of toil," regardless of race. After introduction by a black delegate, an anti-lynching resolution passed unanimously.[7] Their egalitarianism made Arkansas populists unpopular. A June 30, 1892, *Arkansas Gazette* insisted that "This is white man's country, and white men are going to rule it, and when the third party opened its arms to the Negro at its state convention, it invited its certain death at the polls next fall," an accurate prediction.

Democrats swept the 1892 election and ended a fusion system that had allowed white Democrats to maintain some influence in areas with black Republican majorities. In that system black Republicans and white Democrats had shared responsibilities for such functions as tax collection and road maintenance. Prior to elections, leaders from both

---

[6] Grif Stockley, *Ruled By Race. Black/White Relations in Arkansas from Slavery to the Present* (Fayetteville: University of Arkansas Press, 2009), 127.

[7] John William Graves, "Negro Disfranchisement in Arkansas," *Arkansas Historical Quarterly* 26:3 (Autumn 1967), 203-204.

parties allotted each other places on the ballot. This compromise gained Democrats black votes, and Republicans gained representation in county governments. After fusion ended, Delta voters elected Democrats in both state and county races, according to the September 9, 1892, *Arkansas Gazette.* During the next two years voters eliminated black candidates from nearly all public offices. Election fraud took care of some challenges to the state's ruling elite. During one investigation, the speaker of the Arkansas House of Representatives addressed the floor. He asked if any member would deny that someone stole nine ballot boxes from the Pulaski County clerk's office. The January 3, 1889, *Arkansas Gazette* announced that a Pulaski County member denied the charge, claiming that only six were stolen. A new election law passed with a poison pill. It placed election machinery in Democratic Party hands. In 1891, about 93,000 white Arkansans and 116,665 black persons could neither read nor write. They made up approximately 26.6 percent of the state's population. Instead of allowing friends or party members to assist these voters the new law required that precinct judges mark their ballots. This allowed partisan Democrats to ensure election tallies favoring their candidates. One newspaper called this change a positive development. A Pine Bluff *Commercial* on September 4, 1894, declared that "The ignorant and uneducated whites and blacks cannot vote the ticket, which ought to be, and is a blessing to the state, for ignorance should never rule a great commonwealth like Arkansas." The General Assembly proposed in 1892 a poll tax amendment to the state constitution. It required potential voters to display receipts of timely paid poll taxes prior to voting. The amendment was ratified by voters under dubious circumstances, but a replacement amendment became law in 1908.

A famous court decision in the late 1800s added to the burdens carried by black Americans. A Louisiana law required railroads to provide equal but separate accommodations for races. In *Plessy v. Ferguson* the U. S. Supreme Court in 1896 found this law constitutional. With that decision Jim Crow maintained a separate, unequal, and unconscionable existence for black citizens. Many absurd practices evolved from this case. White and black laborers could not work in the same rooms, use the same entrances, draw their pay from the same windows, drink from the same bucket, or use the same toilets. Asked why blacks could not borrow books from the public library, a librarian answered forthrightly, "Southern people do not believe in social equality.[8]

The mid-1890s became especially hard times for cotton producers. A year's labor brought little more than $100, and sharecroppers received about $50. They failed to obtain any proceeds if lien holders took it all.[9] Some landlords admitted the degraded conditions they forced on black workers. One said that "No other laborer of whom I have any knowledge, would be as cheerful, or so contented on four pounds of meat and a peck of meal a week, in a little log cabin . . . with cracks in it large enough to afford free passage to a large sized cat."[10] Many black women in such cabins endured enormous hardships, but prevailed. Though financial resources and social status affected the difficulty and extent of their work, virtually all of them performed a staggering amount of it. They did this while bearing babies, nursing the sick, and tending to the dying.[11] When asked about what work she did, Laura Abramson replied, "What is I been doing? What ain't I been doing be more like it. I raised fifteen of my own children . . . I worked on the farm purty nigh all my life."[12]

Black tenants, women and men, had difficulties getting their earnings "purty nigh" all their lives. Even reasonable efforts led to violent confrontations. One occurred in October 1898. The *Helena World* reported that a Phillips County sharecropper, Charles Munn, asked his landlord, Frank Barry, for settlement information. His request infuriated the planter, who threatened Munn. The tenant then burned down Barry's house, and his landlord died in the fire. Munn received a speedy trial, conviction, and hanging, all started by a dispute concerning a reasonable request. Another incident merited an 1898 *Helena World* report. A planter named Ferrell ordered his tenant to gin where he directed, but the sharecropper refused. Ferrell killed him, but authorities filed no charges. Despite intimidation and violence, some

---

[8] *American Nightmare,* 91.
[9] C. Vann Woodward, *Origins of the New South 1877-1913* (Baton Rouge: Louisiana State University Press, 1951), 207.
[10] A. W. S. Anderson, *Proceedings of the Third Semi-Annual Session of the Alabama State Agricultural Society* (Montgomery, Alabama, 1888), 93-95.
[11] *The American Slave,* 8, 22.
[12] Elizabeth Anne Payne, "What Ain't I been Doing?: Historical Reflections on Women and the Arkansas Delta," *The Arkansas Delta. Land of Paradox,* Jeannie Whayne and Willard Gatewood, eds. (Fayetteville: University of Arkansas Press, 1993), 139.

black Arkansans worked their way into the middle class, which included railroad workers, teachers, physicians, dentists, postal employees, and land-owning farmers. Between 1890 and 1920, this group made up nearly one-fourth of the state's black population. Still, many black families existed in hopeless conditions.[13] A Hampton Institute graduate wrote from Arkansas in 1899 that racism's impact on southern blacks made it "impossible for them to know of a better way of living, and having known no other they are content to exist in this miserable way with no effort at improvement."[14]

[13] *Caste & Class*, 70.
[14] *Trouble in Mind*, 163-164.

Rolling cages transported convicts to work sites such as sawmills and road paving jobs in Arkansas and throughout the South. A heavy chain from one end of the cage to the other shackled prisoners at night. National Archives.

A southern chain gang, early 1900s. Library of Congress Prints and Photographs Division

CHAPTER 6

Where it Tries Men's Souls

A black Delta resident expressed his frustration with life in the region in a letter to the NAACP, calling it a place where it "tries mens' [sic] souls to live." W. E. B. Du Bois put the problem of racial inequality in a wider perspective. "Herein lie buried many things which if read with patience may show the strange meaning of being black here in the dawning of the Twentieth Century. This meaning is not without interest to you, Gentle Reader; for the problem of the Twentieth Century is the problem of the color-line."[1]

After a relatively restricted beginning on public transportation, Jim Crow pushed segregation into almost every corner of life. Fanaticism dominated due to a general weakening and discrediting of forces that previously had held it in check. White people often prevailed by playing one race against the other. Tom Watson, a populist politician from Georgia, told both races that "You are made to hate each other because upon that hatred is rested the keystone of the arch of financial despotism which enslaves you both. You are deceived and blinded that you may not see how this race antagonism . . . beggars you both."[2] In 1905, the U. S. Department of Justice advised Ulysses S. Bratton, an

[1] *Souls of Black Folks,* 3.

[2] Thomas E. Watson, "The Negro Question in the South," *Arena* 6 (October 1892), 548.

Assistant U. S. Attorney in Arkansas, of a department goal to end peonage wherever it existed. He and his boss, William Whipple, accused nine men from Portland, Arkansas, of peonage. Seven of them pled guilty, telling a federal judge that they did not know they were breaking the law. Two men went to trial, and the court convicted one. According to an *Arkansas Gazette*, these were the first cases of this kind ever known in Arkansas."[3]

Despite some peonage convictions in the South, difficulties achieving justice for victims remained the rule, not the exception. Though accused men escaped punishment in a Florida case, it led to an important U. S. Supreme Court decision validating the peonage act. Fred Cubberly, an attorney and U. S. Commissioner, learned about seizure of escapees from a Georgia turpentine camp. This became the *Clyatt* case. It caught Cubberly's attention when James R. Dean told him about a raid on his Florida work camp by men from Georgia along with a local deputy sheriff. Samuel M. Clyatt led this raid and handcuffed at gunpoint Will Gordon and Mose Ridley, two black workers who escaped from Clyatt's turpentine camp allegedly owing him money. Clyatt took the two men back to Georgia where they promptly disappeared. Cubberly informed U. S. Attorney John Eagan of his intent to use this case to test constitutionality of the 1867 peonage law. While Cubberly and Eagan prepared their case a Pensacola attorney told Eagan how peonage worked at turpentine camps throughout the South. A law officer assisted camp operators with holding workers in a "worse state than when they were slaves," said W. O. Butler. Employees would never get out of debt, regardless of their earnings. Workers who rebelled suffered severe beatings.[4] They were defenseless because a black man would be murdered if he brought charges in local courts about a white man beating him. But in November 1901, a grand jury indicted Clyatt, and he stood trial. H. S. Sutton, a Florida county sheriff who assisted Clyatt, testified that he was unaware that law officers could not legally serve warrants issued in a different state. The deputy sheriff said that he did not question the warrants because he left his spectacles at home and could not read the documents. A court found Clyatt guilty and sentenced him to four years in prison. For southern employers who depended on peonage for their

[3] Robert Whitaker, *On the Laps of Gods. The Red Summer of 1919 and the Struggle for Justice that Remade a Nation* (New York: Crown Publishers, 2008), 74-75.
[4] *Clyatt v. United States*, 197 U. S. 207 (1905).

workforce, this was an ominous development. So businessmen paid two Georgia politicians to handle the appeal, and they got their money's worth. Senator Augustus Octavius Bacon and Congressman William G. Brantley argued in the U. S. Supreme Court that only unlawful arrest could be proven in *Clyatt*. Since the two men disappeared after returning to Georgia, it could not be proven that they were held in peonage. In March 1905, Justice David J. Brewer delivered the court's opinion. It stated that the peonage act prohibited holding, arresting, and returning a laborer in peonage. But without victim testimony, the court ruled in favor of Clyatt and ordered a new trial. Prosecutors dropped the charges, lacking victim testimony, but they validated constitutionality of this peonage statute.[5]

Despite some legal successes, peonage still spread throughout the South like kudzu and proved as difficult to eradicate. News of such cases and anecdotal evidence of other abuses became fodder for northern reporters. When they dished out criticism of worker mistreatment it proved hard for the South to swallow. A July 24, 1903, *New York Post* charged that peonage cases "illustrate very clearly the need of outside criticism if the South is to be held up to its duty towards the negro race." According to that edition, southerners insisted that they be "left alone" to deal with problems their way. But their way would not eliminate peonage and would help perpetuate such practices. As prosecutors learned to their dismay, peonage prosecutions mostly failed to win guilty verdicts, particularly those involving black laborers. Southern white jurors accepted any method used by Delta planters to force workers into a cotton patch. Complaints from federal prosecutors to the attorney general expressed frustration and incredulity that clear-cut cases could not be won. The *Savannah Press* on March 20, 1905, recorded the frustration of a federal judge in Georgia. Emory Speer shared with a jury his thoughts on peonage. "No crime is so subtle in its operation, more destructive in its results than that which degrades the public conscience, until it can tamely and without protest witness the unlawful slavery of the citizen."

Prosecutors found plenty of "unlawful slavery" in lumber camps. Firms acquired millions of timber land acres in southern states, including Arkansas. Cutovers produced a proliferation of sawmills, which typically required from 50 to 70 men. Upper management

---

[5] *Wheel of Servitude*, 50.

consisted of a superintendent, foreman, and bookkeeper. Specialists included sawyers, blade filers, and log jackers to position logs on a moving carriage. At the low end of the employee totem pole stood plank carriers, stackers, and "dust monkeys," usually young boys huddled beneath whirling blades to keep them free of sawdust. Whites invariably held the good jobs and blacks the bad ones. Their work tended to be exceptionally dangerous. Flying chips put out eyes; taut cables came loose, separating human limbs from bodies, and rolling logs crushed legs and arms.[6] Saginaw Lumber Company operated a Hot Springs County facility aptly named Dead Man Camp. Though legal status of all workers there is unknown, what is known are its horrible conditions. Shacks and lean-tos of rough pine lacked floors and adequate sanitation. Prisoners contracted typhoid, malaria, and other diseases. The death rate from illness and abuse gave this camp its name.[7] Unfortunately, this Arkansas site typified those throughout the South. A sociologist used official reports, inmate testimony, and personal observations to develop a vivid description of such facilities. They consisted of bunkhouses, cages, and tents with vermin-infested bedding. Lack of sanitation led to tuberculosis, pneumonia, and other diseases. In this brutal world, ill health did not excuse poor work or provide relief from punishment. Bosses pushed sick men to their limits and beyond. For those who could not stand or walk, leather straps lacerated their flesh and left raw wounds discharging blood and pus.[8] Convict camps sometimes consisted of rolling cages that followed work sites deep in a forest or swamp.

Another form of labor intimidation that prevailed throughout the South was called whitecapping. It consisted of intimidation used by whites against blacks to force them into abandoning their jobs, homes, or both. Whitecappers attempted to run off black plantation employees, industrial workers, farmers, and land owners. Farming could be the first step toward land ownership for poor white families, so competition

---

[6] Edward L. Ayers, *The Promise of the New South. Life After Reconstruction* (New York: Oxford University Press, 1992), 127.
[7] Dennis Holt, "The Legend of Dead Man Camp," *Arkansas Historical Quarterly* 9:2 (Summer 1950), 118.
[8] Vivien M. L. Miller, "Murder, 'Convict Flogging Affairs,' and Debt Peonage. The Roaring Twenties in the American South," *Reading Southern Poverty Between the Wars, 1918-1939* (Athens: University of Georgia Press, 2006), 81.

from black farmers threatened them.[9] Whitecappers made clear their aims and targets in newspaper notices. A March 15, 1915, *Arkansas Gazette* ran this headline. "Negroes Warned to Leave Pine Bluff." Another account in that edition spelled out the white agenda. "Negroes Beware. We want your jobs. You are given two weeks to leave the city or suffer the penalty of death."

In May 1906, Judge Jacob Trieber found five Arkansas County men guilty of violence against black railroad workers. He fined each man $500 and sentenced them to one year in federal prison. The *Russellville Courier Democrat* on May 3, 1906, quoted from his decision. It read in part, "Here were men who were willing to work and anxious to work, and there were others who were willing to give them employment, and yet there seems to be on the part of a few men in the state a disposition to prevent these men from working because, in this instance, they happen to be negroes." Trieber called the crime "almost as serious an offense as can be committed." He said that "Every man has a right to employ whomsoever he pleases; every man has a right to accept employment to do honest work."[10]

Two additional Arkansas incidents helped convince the state's attorney general to take a public stand against whitecapping, and the U. S. Attorney General agreed. After a justice department investigation, authorities produced two indictments. The first, *United States v. Morris,* charged 11 white men with intimidating sharecroppers. The second, *United States v. Hodges,* charged 15 men with intimidating black workers at a sawmill in White Hall, forcing them to quit their jobs.[11] Trieber heard the case and interpreted the 13th Amendment to be a substantial extension of federal power allowing prosecution of persons preventing others from contracting for their labor. He ruled that labor contracts were a freedom granted by this amendment.

---

[9] Jeannie Whayne, *Delta Empire. Lee Wilson and the Transformation of Agriculture in the New South* (Baton Rouge: Louisiana State University Press, 2011), 120-121.

[10] Jewish immigrants, Trieber and his family settled in Helena, Arkansas, during 1868. Trieber became a prominent lawyer, and President William McKinley appointed him to the federal bench. He was the first Jewish attorney to become a federal judge in the United States.

[11] The only published district court decisions in *Morris* and *Hodges* are reported together as *United States v. Morris,* 125 F. 322 (E. D. Ark. 1903).

The government failed to secure convictions in *Morris* because prosecutors could not produce direct testimony of alleged intimidation. The court convicted three *Hodges* defendants, and they appealed to the U. S. Supreme Court. What then became *Hodges v. United States* addressed whether the amendment protected a right to contract for labor. If so, was protection a federal or state responsibility? Did reach of the 13th Amendment stretch that far? Did an amendment prohibiting slavery extend to all enslaved persons, regardless of race? After deliberating this amendment's intent and whether the federal government had authority to protect any rights granted, justices overturned the district court's conviction of the three Arkansas men. The court ruled that what is prohibited in the 13th Amendment are slavery and involuntary servitude. Given this interpretation the court refused a 13th Amendment basis for prosecution of whitecappers.[12] This substantial limitation on the amendment and federal powers of enforcement eliminated from the amendment's scope protection against many "labor- and race-related harms beyond slavery and involuntary servitude."[13]

---

[12] *Hodges v. United States*, 203 U. S. 1 (1906)
[13] *Lost Promise*, 136.

Illustration links slavery and peonage in the United States as one and the same. New York Public Library.

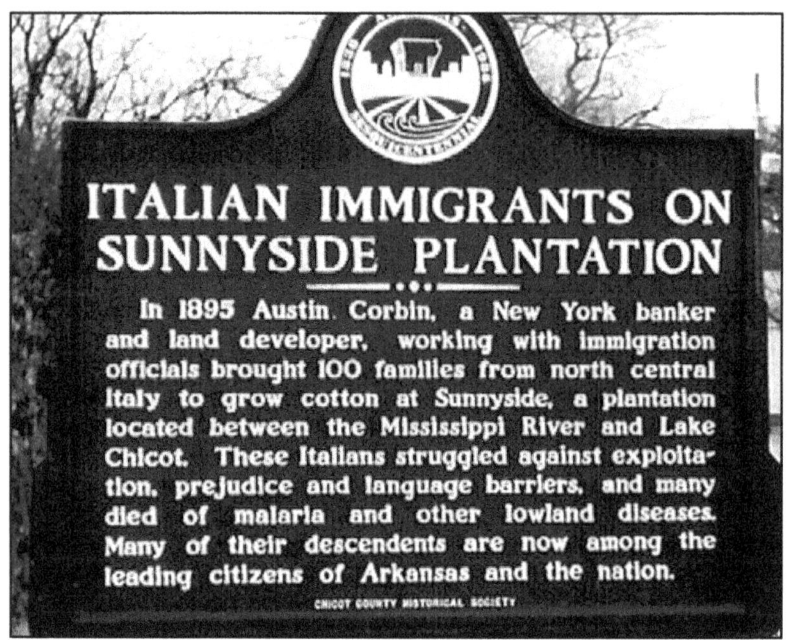

Above, historic marker in Lake Village, Arkansas. Below, Mary Grace Quackenbos. U. S. Department of Justice.

CHAPTER 7

Organ Grinders and Banana Vendors

Many planters seeking to enlarge their labor pool recruited foreign workers. Italians immigrating to the Delta may have suited landlords, but not newspaper critics. An April 17, 1891, *Fort Smith Elevator* called them "organ grinders and banana vendors, . . . so filthy that the inspecting physicians will not allow them to land." A *Fayetteville Republican* edition complained that the country was becoming too strongly tainted with foreign odors. On November 29, 1895, the *Monticellonian* groused about "a lot of Dagoes from Italy. We are not anxious for them out here."

Delta newspaper reviews may have been offensive, but Italian immigrants had a stalwart defender in New York City. In an effort to help Italians with New York connections trapped in southern peonage, attorney Mary Grace Quackenbos went south to see for herself. She had an important ally in Assistant Attorney General Charles W. Russell. His peonage investigations, which would culminate in a 1907 report, led him to call the crime involuntary servitude rooted in laws controlling black laborers. A narrow reading of the 1867 peonage act limited federal prosecution to cases with forced labor to satisfy debts. However, Russell pointed out that throughout the South, forced labor existed without a claim of debt, and the peonage act provided no protection in cases lacking a connection to debt.[1] Quackenbos agreed.

She took on a case that exposed major abuses of Italian immigrants in the Delta. Edmondo Mayor des Planches, Italian Ambassador to the United States, wrote a letter to the U. S. Secretary of State on June 4, 1907, asking for an investigation into treatment of Italian immigrants at Sunnyside plantation in Arkansas. The ambassador mentioned "numberless complaints" about management's business dealings, and he wanted Quackenbos in charge.[2] Unfortunately for owners of several southern plantations, she accepted the challenge. How Italians ended up in the Delta is a sordid tale. It began with a planter on the lookout for laborers he could control, and he found them in Italy. The first group began their odyssey when Austin Corbin searched for families to populate Sunnyside at the Arkansas Delta's southern end. Corbin, a New York financier, bought this Chicot County property and soon learned that vast acreage required a large, pliable labor force. After employing black workers and convicts unsuccessfully he decided to take a different route, one that led to Italy. Planters needed these immigrants because of stiff competition from other southern employers. Cotton mills, phosphate mines, double tracking railroad crews, cotton oil mills, saw mills, and builders of roads and levees competed for available labor.

Immigration advocates emphasized several points, among them scarcity of labor and dissatisfaction with the quantity and quality of black workers. As might be expected, throughout the South a need for agricultural labor dominated.[3] Corbin's plan to recruit Italians began at a meeting in New York attended by Alessandro Oldrini, chief agent of

---

[1] Charles W. Russell, Report Relative to Peonage Matters, U. S. Attorney General Annual Report (Washington, D. C.: 1907), 208.

[2] Edmondo Mayor des Planches to Secretary of State, June 4, 1907, Department of State General Records, Rg. 59, 866.55 6923/8-9, National Archives. The first female Special Assistant United States Attorney, Quackenbos concentrated on exposing peonage throughout the South. After graduating from law school, the wealthy New Yorker founded the People's Law Firm to assist poor migrants. Following an investigation in the South with Assistant Attorney General Charles Russell she became a special U. S. District Attorney for the Southern District of New York. However, her appointment would be expanded to cover peonage throughout the country.

[3] Shannon Klug Craig, "Arkansas and Foreign Immigration: 1890-1915." M. A. Thesis. University of Arkansas, May 1979, 29-30.

the Italian Bureau of Information and Protection. To meet his needs, Corbin claimed that he would sell small parcels of land to immigrant farmers and provide financing. Despite this apparent generosity, Sunnyside owners may never have intended for immigrants to independently own plantation land, according to Robert L. Brandfon's theory. He calls the plantation an agricultural business model integrating all of its parts – land, cotton gin, houses, a store, barns, tools, equipment, and warehouses. Sale of any part, especially land, would fracture the system.[4] Nevertheless, Corbin convinced Francesco Fava, a previous Italian Ambassador to the United States, of his plan's merits. Though Fava reacted positively to the idea he encouraged Corbin to develop it as a business arrangement, not an official one. This led Emanuele Ruspoli, mayor of Rome, to Sunnyside, where he formed a partnership with Corbin. Since a federal statute prohibited importation of farm contract laborers to this country, Corbin subdivided acreage into plots, each with 12 and one-half-acres and a house.

In November 1895, the first families arrived in New Orleans bound for the Delta. At Sunnyside they found that a house and farm package cost $2,000 and came with a 21-year amortization at five percent interest. Contracts spelled out financial arrangement between Italian settlers and the company.[5] Management would purchase their ginned cotton at the current market price less associated expenses, not to exceed $1 per bale. Contracts established an arbitration commission to resolve disputes between immigrants and the company - - - one arbitrator selected by the Italians, one by Sunnyside managers, and a third by the two arbitrators. Buyer's remorse soon set in, and settlers claimed to be victims of false advertising. Complaints ranged from irritating problems to existential challenges, including swarming mosquitoes, unsanitary water, uneven land quality, prohibitive credit from a plantation store rather than cash advances, and potentially deadly diseases. Father Pietro Bandini, whose ministry included aiding Italians relocating from New York to the Delta, verified deficiencies to Fava. Despite negative assessments, Ruspoli assigned agents to recruit prospects for Sunnyside. Leopoldo Belvederesi described his family's

---

[4] Robert L. Brandfon, "The End of Immigration to the Cotton Fields," *Mississippi Valley Historical Review* 50:4 (March 1964), 605-606.

[5]Willard B. Gatewood, Jr. "Sunnyside: The Evolution of an Arkansas Plantation, 1848-1945," *Arkansas Historical Quarterly* 50:1 (Spring 1991), 24.

recruitment. "I live[d] in Montignano, which is governed by the priest and Prince Ruspoli. When I was born my father went to the priest to register my birth . . . and found out that Prince Ruspoli was sending families to America. We were five in the family, my parents and three boys. If we had not been boys, the prince would not have sent our family to America to work on the cotton plantations. We stayed in America eight years."[6] Typical arrangements called for landlords to provide boat tickets and immigrants to have at least 55 lira. Transportation costs and cash advances went on plantation accounts at ten percent interest. So Italians arrived at Sunnyside in a financial hole without any digging.

In June 1896, Corbin died in an accident, and the project became a problem for his heirs. Ruspoli issued a favorable report after inspecting Sunnyside, and a second group of colonists with 72 families arrived. They also learned that Ruspoli's agents misled them. Among immigrants who made their first cotton crop, more than one third did not pay out and faced a second crop with debt remaining from the first. A tenant committee in May 1897 presented complaints to Sunnyside managers. The list included unhealthy drinking water, few independent labor opportunities, inadequate housing, unreasonable prices at a plantation store, and exorbitant interest charged on accounts, common features of peonage. These complaints caused Italian officials to investigate Sunnyside. Guido Rossati, an agronomist and director of an Italian bureau in New York, visited in February 1898, and his report painted an ugly picture of conditions. He demanded improvements and advised that without them he could not recommend that Italians remain in such a "life-threatening environment." Still, Ruspoli's influence with Italian officials prevented significant corrective actions.[7] A management change did not help. Three prominent businessmen took over Sunnyside in 1898 – Leroy Percy, O. B. Crittenden, and Morris Rosenstock. At that time only 30 Italian families lived there. From Greenville, Mississippi, Percy ruled one of the South's most powerful empires and began pulling strings to tie up more Italians. He arranged a tour for Ambassador des Planches, who departed unimpressed. After Ruspoli died in 1899, Percy enlisted other recruiters

[6] Paul V. Canonici, *The Delta Italians* (Madison, Miss.: Creative Designs, 2003), 5-6.
[7] Ernesto R. Milani, "Peonage at Sunnyside and the Reaction of the Italian Government," *Arkansas Historical Quarterly* 50:1 (Spring 1991), 34.

who enabled O. B. Crittenden and Company, a leasing entity formed by the three investors, to increase their plantation roster.

When des Planches requested in his June 4 letter that Quackenbos head up an investigation, she was serving as a justice department special assistant concentrating on immigrant abuses. Quackenbos identified 40 regional plantations that held from one to 180 Italian families, but turned her immediate attention to Sunnyside. When Quackenbos arrived, about 170 Italian families lived there. Sunnyside gained their entry into America by violating the alien contract labor law. That statute made it a crime to import immigrants using labor contracts made in their native countries. In order to disguise their true status upon arrival in the United States, immigrants received primers giving safe answers to questions that would be asked by inspectors.[8] Quackenbos's plan to undertake a confidential investigation of Sunnyside fell apart when the identities of two federal agents became known during their conversations with Italian farmers. Local authorities arrested one investigator, Charles Pettek, and held him overnight in the company store. The following day a justice of the peace found Pettek guilty of trespass and fined him $100 or three months on a chain gang. Quackenbos paid the fine. This confrontation put Percy and Quackenbos in a power struggle. After he blocked her attempts to enter the plantation, Quackenbos asked Acting Arkansas Governor Xenophon O. Pindall to intervene, and he did. In a July 20, 1907, letter to Crittenden, Pindall said that Quackenbos intended to conduct a fair and complete investigation. He added that she had the right to make this inquiry and would receive his support.[9] Quackenbos reported that in a private conversation Pindall verified widespread violations of peonage and alien contract labor laws in the Delta. But he admitted that "politics are such that no District Attorney will care to antagonize the powerful interests of the state for the sake of these poor Italians."[10] Quackenbos gained access to the plantation, but owners littered her path with obstacles. Managers restricted investigation hours and monitored interviews. Notes and interview transcripts disappeared

---

[8] Mary Grace Quackenbos, Sunnyside Report, September 28, 1907, 7. Department of Justice File No. 100937. Accessed at William Alexander Percy Library, Greenville, Miss.

[9] Pindall to Crittenden, July 20, 1907. Department of Justice. Accessed at William Alexander Percy Library, Greenville, Miss. Items 142-143.

[10] Quackenbos to the U. S. Attorney General, July 20, 1907, Department of Justice, Rg. 60, 74682, National Archives.

from her hotel room in Greenville. Thomas Catchings, a Percy ally and retired congressman, returned them. However, Quackenbos would not be intimidated. After interviewing 70 families and inspecting the plantation store's accounting records she found violations of alien contract labor laws, state usury laws, price gouging, substandard living conditions, profiteering on medical care charges, intimidation, and other deficiencies.

Quackenbos sent a report to Percy dated August 17, 1907, that included these recommendations:

- *Install screens on houses to protect against insects.*
- *Install artesian wells.*
- *Lower plantation store prices.*
- *Provide commissary expense records to tenants.*
- *Allow more freedom in cotton marketing and lower fees.*
- *Charge 6% interest on accounts, not 10%.*
- *Eliminate flat interest charges.*
- *Allow a cooperative store with prices controlled by tenants.*
- *Make advances one-half in store credit and one-half in cash.*
- *Increase advances.*

She justified this last recommendation by using Florini Giovanni's family. The husband, wife, five children, and their mule received no more than $18 per month. Though inadequate allowances were bad enough, Quackenbos revealed management's venality in their charges for medical care. The physician billed from $2.50 to $5.50 for individual visits and $12 to $25 for special cases. A plantation manager admitted that the company took 20 percent of the doctor's fee and charged tenants an additional 10 percent interest. Quackenbos recommended that the current doctor be replaced by an Italian physician selected by the Italian consul at New Orleans. She proposed that medical fees be reduced and management take no percentage of charges. At the end of her report, Quackenbos said that "These suggestions are respectfully submitted and I earnestly hope that they will be approved and accepted."[11] She could not have been more wrong.

---

[11] Quackenbos to Percy, August 17, 1907, Department of Justice. Accessed at William Alexander Percy Library, Greenville, Miss. Items 106-117.

After reading her letter, Percy must have been livid, having his business practices attacked and his honor impugned by a woman lawyer, a Yankee no less. He shot back a reply that quashed her hopes for substantive cooperation. The planter dealt with her recommendations one by one.

- *They refused to screen houses because of costs.*
- *He did not agree to provide tenants with artesian water, calling it impractical.*
- *He claimed plantation store prices were competitive with prices at other stores. This may have been true since other stores also gouged their customers.*
- *Store managers would note purchases on customer books.*
- *He refused to charge less than 10 per cent interest per annum on accounts.*
- *He did not agree that advances should be half in cash and half in supplies. He declared one dollar per acre sufficient to supply a tenant family and their stock.*

As to cotton marketing and associated fees, Percy claimed that "This is the only real complaint that the tenants, so far as I am advised, have ever made about their business at Sunny Side." Percy offered farmers several marketing options.

After being caught profiting from sick people, Percy offered some improvements. He agreed to have the Italian consul locate a doctor for Sunnyside who would charge tenants one dollar per visit. If unable to pay, tenants would receive advances at six percent interest. Sunnyside would expect no rebate from the doctor. In conclusion, Percy said that "We have given your criticisms and suggestions full, careful and patient consideration, and to the extent that we have considered it practical, in fact, I may say even beyond this, that we have tried to adopt them. I sincerely trust that with the information you have gained from a personal investigation of the property, the knowledge that you have acquired as to the practical operation of it, and the explanations given you, that you will concur with us, that we have conceded everything which can reasonably be expected."[12] Percy could not have been more wrong.

In a September 28, 1907, report to the attorney general, Quackenbos criticized labor practices at Sunnyside. She charged that "Sometimes it is spoken of as a model of foreign settlements; but whatever has been said of the prosperity of Sunny Side [sic], it is a complete failure as an Italian colony." She called it a cotton plantation where Italians worked for American bosses. Using extensive testimony from colonists and an analysis of financial materials, Quackenbos pointed out numerous inconsistencies and concluded that "Something is radically wrong." Her report indicated that O. B. Crittenden & Company made no pretense of running a colony or promoting immigration. It was an investment for cotton production.[13] This report quoted from a letter Percy wrote to Quackenbos. "We are not operating the property as an eleemosynary institution. I appreciate the Italian peasant as a farm laborer and I am desirous of keeping those who are capable of making crops on Sunny Side."[14]

Investigators found a questionable, if not blatantly illegal, recruitment process in which corrupt Italian agents induced poor Italians to leave their homes. According to the report, in order to hide immigration violations recruiters instructed Italians not to mention work status or prepaid passage.[15] Quackenbos said that nearly every plantation in the region had a resident agent earning as much as $25 per family. Upon arriving in Greenville, colonists expected a warm welcome, rather than guards herding them into boats to cross the river. After a two-hour boat ride managers took them to empty cabins. Quackenbos called these immigrants tenants in name only. "They have no rights as men who lease land and in Mr. Percy's own words are regarded merely as farm laborers." The Italians could not read their contracts written in English, but a plantation interpreter encouraged them to sign anyhow. Quackenbos said that management forced men, women, and children to "labor in the merciless sun to pay back the last farthing. I saw a little girl of ten years thus working and her yellow green face, pale lips and dying eyes, the visible extremities of her bones,

---

[12] Percy to Quackenbos, August 17, 1907, Department of Justice. Accessed at William Alexander Percy Library, Greenville, Miss. Items 118-129.
[13] Sunnyside Report, 1.
[14] Sunnyside Report, 3.
[15] Sunnyside Report, 7-8.

covered with the sun-dried skin, will never be cancelled from my mind."[16]

Quackenbos excoriated planters for bringing people into a country where state laws protected involuntary servitude and allowed arrest for debts rarely proven. Laws relating to trespass, enticement, vagrancy, and contract-jumping applied to their relatives and even government inspectors. "The definition of peonage is to my mind too technical and too narrow, and so long as such singular interpretation is given it – slavery will flourish and our country will be disgraced."[17] Percy made clear his intention to eliminate freedom of movement among Sunnyside Italians in a letter to Umberto Pierini, a recruiter operating in Mississippi. Percy said that "It is perfectly evident that you can remain on friendly terms with those interested in the Sunnyside property, including myself, only by pursuing one course, and that is by declining to have anything to do with the [re]locations of Italians who leave Sunnyside, simply stating to them that your relationship with the owners of the property is such that you don't care to have anything to do with locating on other places tenants desiring to leave there.

"In other words, I feel that my friendly attitude towards you has been of service to you. I know that an unfriendly attitude on my part would be an injury to you, and I don't want to assume it without cause, but I will do so unless you are willing to say that you will have nothing further to do with endeavoring to [re]locate Italians leaving Sunnyside."[18]

Apparently this woman lawyer was really getting on Percy's nerves. He retaliated after Quackenbos's severe criticism by using a sympathetic press to attack her motives and methodology. A September 8, 1907, *Vicksburg Herald* called her a socialist agitator. A September 29 *Greenville Times* criticized her for stirring up Italians, suggesting that such a thing might be expected of a professional woman. In a letter to the U. S. Attorney General dated October 8, 1907, Quackenbos became more adversarial, advocating an expansion of peonage prosecutions. She said, "I beg to assure Your Honor that only prosecutions for peonage and prosecutions under the Alien Contract

---

[16] Sunnyside Report, 35.
[17] Sunnyside Report, 64.
[18] *Delta Italians*, 13.

Labor Law, and the restriction of immigration" would improve matters. Quackenbos recommended that charges be filed against Crittenden for two peonage violations, and she provided the following details. Two Italian men left Sunnyside and boarded a train in Greenville after purchasing tickets for Birmingham, Alabama, to seek temporary work. Crittenden, a policeman, and two other men entered the train and ordered the Italians to get off. After they refused, Crittenden and his henchmen dragged them from the train with threats of arrest and the chain gang if they did not return to Sunnyside. Upon landing in Arkansas, a manager met them and warned, "I'd like to give you as many kicks as you never heard of in your life and throw you into the Mississippi River." He marched them home between riding bosses.[19] The Jackson, Mississippi, *Daily News* on October 26, 1907, announced arraignment of Crittenden before United States Commissioner L. B. Mosely at the federal building on the charge of peonage. The newspaper called arrest of Crittenden the "most sensational peonage story that has been brought to light since the Federal authorities commenced investigations." A *Vicksburg Herald* on October 26, 1907, gave Percy's side of the story. He said that "There is no peonage in Sunnyside and no merit whatever in the charge. It was made at the instance of Mrs. Mary Grace Quackenbos, a woman lawyer sent to investigate labor conditions in the South by the attorney general's office and is doubtless due to her displeasure at my forbidding her and her employees going upon the Sunnyside plantation, although this was only done after every courtesy had been extended to her and every facility for making a thorough investigation of the condition of the colony afforded her." Powerful interests blocked the Crittenden case from going forward.

The politically powerful Percy asked President Theodore Roosevelt to rid him of this troublesome woman. On November 13, 1907, Percy wrote Roosevelt urging that Quackenbos's claims not be made public, casting this request as his civic duty. He wanted details verified by "competent, reliable, practical men, appointed for that purpose." Percy expressed concern about bad publicity, that it might harm immigration to the Delta and hinder economic development. He warned that publication of an unfavorable report would be "absolutely fatal" to securing immigration. In this self-serving diatribe, Percy also criticized an unwarranted peonage prosecution, apparently the Crittenden case.

---

[19] Quackenbos to U. S. Attorney General, October 8, 1907, Department of Justice. Accessed at William Alexander Percy Library, Greenville, Miss., Items 150-153.

Though the planter did not admit it, he wanted the Quackenbos report gutted by reliable men chosen by him. Percy made a surprising admission that he had not seen the report, but knew from the "very nature of things" that it could not be unbiased. The planter's main line of attack centered on Quackenbos's lack of familiarity with agricultural matters. After more than a dozen pages of criticism directed at Quackenbos and arguments about why he considered her report seriously flawed, Percy made this ridiculous claim. "I have no desire whatever to have her report suppressed. I only ask that no publication be made of it and no action taken under it until it has been verified . . . through men of character and practical sense."[20] Quackenbos sent a rebuttal letter to the attorney general on November 18, 1907. She said that "It is obvious that Mr. Percy is endeavoring to embarrass and delay the pending peonage case against his partner Mr. Crittenden . . . and take advantage of the Administration's friendly feeling toward the South." She called Delta peonage conditions localized, confined to about six out of 40 plantations. Quackenbos made a forceful defense, but lost to Percy's offense.[21]

In February 1908, the U. S. State Department acknowledged receipt of a Quackenbos report dated January 10, 1908, on conditions at Mississippi Delta cotton plantations. At the outset she said that on about 40 plantations in Mississippi and Arkansas, Italian immigrants worked growing cotton. [22] Quackenbos described conditions at Sunnyside and exposed other Arkansas operations, including Premier Cotton Mill at Barton. The mill had a high wood fence surrounding it. At an entrance gate a sign warned, VISITORS NOT WANTED OR ALLOWED ON THESE PREMISES. The mill employed Italian women and children, and Quackenbos described a dreadful scene from her inspection. She saw "a few ragged Italian babies . . . crawling on the steps and in the road, their hands tied up with cloth and on their wrists and arms large ugly sores, the result of a mosquito plague, fever, and cotton lint." Women and children worked in the mill from 5:45 a.m. to 6:30 p.m. with a half hour off for lunch and half a day on Saturdays.

---

[20] Percy to Roosevelt, White House, November 13, 1907. Accessed at William Alexander Percy Library, Greenville, Miss. Items 155-167; 4,10.
[21] Quackenbos to U. S. Attorney General, Department of Justice, November 18, 1907. Accessed at William Alexander Percy Library, Greenville, Miss. Items 168-172, 1-3.
[22] Report of Mary Grace Quackenbos, General Conditions on Delta Region Cotton Plantations, January 10, 1908, 4. Accessed at William Alexander Percy Library, Greenville, Miss.

The superintendent explained that the company needed child labor because this work required "little fingers." [23] Maria Tomassini Grattafiore provided a statement to Quackenbos that exposed the company's duplicity. A recruiter lured her into peonage by lying about most everything. He promised the widow with seven children that her youngsters would earn from 50 cents to $1.50 per day. Provided tickets and a small advance, she sailed to New York with them. Grattafiore told immigration inspectors what she had been coached to say and made her way to Arkansas. "At Barton my children Mariano sixteen years, Amerio fifteen years, Letizia fourteen, and Marianna twelve years, went to work in the mill. The boys made 25 cents and Letizia 14 cents a day." Eugenio, nine years old, earned 10 cents. "The first three weeks I received from the combined efforts of my four children not more than $3 because they took off half the weekly earnings to pay for our transportation debt. I have been paying my debts off every week and now owe $185." Quackenbos described children standing uneasily before enormous machines, "tiny mites with sickly stunted bare limbs and pale faces, lips pressed firmly together, little fingers winding in and out among large skeins, little heads covered with cotton, intent upon the work, strained eager eyes nervously watching, while the extended arms guided the thread patiently lest some mistake occur for which they would be docked."[24]

Quackenbos also reported on conditions at Red Leaf plantation near Sunnyside. John T. Hardie's Sons & Co. owned this enterprise, and R. D. Owens managed it. The report described the plantation's location as an intensely hot and feverish place. At the first house inspected she found Urengarelli Antonio with a high fever lying on a stoop. He arrived in Arkansas with his wife and child and had a $300 debt when Quackenbos investigated. The family rented 20 acres for $7 per acre. Her report called a majority of farmers there helpless.[25] Quackenbos said that ill treatment at Red Leaf existed because Owens occupied a "double position" of plantation manager and justice of the peace. Evidence of his power became clear when Owens officiated in the trial of a justice department employee who entered the plantation for an official inspection. Authorities arrested and fined him $100. In another example of abuse, Owens had Luigi Piersimoni arrested. The court

---

[23] General Conditions, 20.

[24] General Conditions, 21-22.

[25] General Conditions, 92.

sentenced him to eight days in jail and a fine of $80 for trespassing by peddling goods on area plantations. After authorities eliminated this source of supplies, tenants returned to plantation stores for purchases at higher prices and steep carrying charges. Peppe Rocconi and his brother Paolo also came from Italy to Red Leaf. They became "rich only in toil, illness, and pain. The word happiness was hardly a part of our vocabulary. It was a word we seldom used during our early years in America."[26]

About 16 miles from Pine Bluff, a New Gascony plantation broke the familiar patterns of peonage, at least in part. The Quackenbos report described its owner, John P. Gracie, as a "large-hearted Southerner, very enthusiastic about Italians." Gracie studied Italian grammar and encouraged his Italian tenants to learn English. According to the report, he charged high rent, but provided mules free of charge. Two tenants worked with share arrangements; others paid one-third of their cotton crop. Quackenbos heard complaints about sickness and that the doctor charged $3 per visit, which she considered exorbitant. The plantation had a school and a Catholic church. Despite many positives at New Gascony, it shared an important negative found throughout the Delta. Quackenbos said that Gracie broke alien contract laws in the way he imported Italians, and she had paperwork to prove it. [27] While investigating this and other southern plantations, Quackenbos traveled many country roads. She saw the callous abuse of vulnerable families, but in the end, she could do very little about it.

---

[26] *Delta Italians*, 35.
[27]General Conditions, 105.

Top, Italian immigrants arriving by train at Sunnyside Landing. Bottom, mill workers at Sunnyside Plantation. Photo by J. C. Coovert. Jccoovert.com, D. Gorton and Jane Adams.

CHAPTER 8

Babylonian Wine Drinkers

A blurred view of what made a person white or black caused some problems for immigrants held in peonage. Southerners considered northern Europeans white, but southern Europeans not always so. Political power, wealth, and social status grew in proportion to the whiteness of one's skin. Many Delta residents considered Europeans from Mediterranean areas racially questionable. Lack of assimilation also caused problems. The unwillingness or inability of Italians to embrace southern culture marked them as un-American. Conservative rural southerners disliked their Catholicism, their incomprehensible language, and their "Babylonian wine drinking, music, and dancing."[1] Quackenbos criticized recruiters who lied to immigrants about the discrimination they faced. She accused agents of misrepresenting work, magnifying wages, and ignoring state peonage laws. Canvassers with bright stories sought out unsophisticated people in small villages and represented America as a place where fortunes could be made and immigrants would be welcomed.[2]

A federal official who investigated Sunnyside and other peonage complaints became the justice department's point man for fighting the crime. Assistant Attorney General Charles Russell prepared reports in 1907 and 1908 that exposed legal issues concerning peonage. In a section entitled "What Peonage is, Legally Speaking," he pointed out that under criminal law, peonage caused compulsory service to be

[1] *End of Immigration*, 608.
[2] General Conditions, 9-10.

rendered to an employer to work out debt, real or claimed. But even where there was no indebtedness, real or claimed, a conspiracy to cause compulsory service of citizens was punishable. Russell called compulsory service the equivalent of involuntary servitude. He said that a man may be in peonage if held by threats of force, threats of prosecution, or by threats of bodily harm. Federal Judge Henry Clay Niles of Mississippi charged that holding by threat of prosecution under even a valid law constituted peonage. A law did not justify causing compulsory service by intimidation. Russell complained that state laws in the South intended to compel service of working men.[3]

Russell also targeted licensed agents in New York who reaped a rich harvest from the price per head for laborers supplied to planters. He denounced their disregard for truth and honest dealings with immigrants and employers. Russell said that the justice department succeeded in procuring some revocations of licenses, and this achieved a good effect. New York's widely ignored license law stipulated that "Whenever such licensed person or any other acting for him agrees to send one or more persons to work as contract laborers in any one place outside the city in which such agency is located the said licensed person shall file with the mayor or the commissioner who granted licenses, within five days after the contract is made, a statement containing the following items: Name and address of employer, name and address of employee, nature of work to be performed, hours of labor, wages offered, destination of person employed, and transportation terms."[4]

However, recruiters generally ignored the law and sent immigrants south where peonage entrapped them. As justice department criticism increased and eyewitness accounts piled up, peonage became an increasing problem for the South's image. Southern congressmen went on offense, and three led the charge – Frank Clark from Florida and two Mississippians, John Sharp Williams and Benjamin G. Humphrey. They first attacked the messenger. Clark claimed that the justice department, "instead of looking after the . . . business of the United States government, began a crusade in certain States to regulate

---

[3] Charles W. Russell, Jr., Supplement to February 14, 1907, Report on Peonage (Washington, D. C.: Government Printing Office), Appendix B, 216-217. In addition to his many years of experience in the justice department, Russell served as the U. S. Ambassador to Persia.

[4] Russell, supplement, Appendix B, 219-220.

sociological conditions."[5] Humphrey raged against Quackenbos, claiming that she perpetrated an outrage on Mississippi. He protested her investigation of Sunnyside, calling the plantation a model farm community. Clark attacked Attorney General Charles J. Bonaparte for focusing on peonage prosecutions in the South. Several Florida newspapers supported Clark's public relations efforts. A January 27, 1907, *Tampa Morning Tribune* praised him for exposing Bonaparte's "absurd rant about the exercise of the peonage abomination by southern men." A *Jacksonville Times-Union* on January 22, 1907, lauded Florida Congressman Stephen M. Sparkman for sponsorship of a bill to prevent recognition of peonage charges by federal courts.

The national press viewed Florida's peonage record differently. Richard Barry published a story in the March 1907 edition of *Cosmopolitan* magazine about peonage in the South. He interviewed Quackenbos for his article and criticized prominent businessmen and authorities. Florida's legislature passed a resolution condemning Barry and William Randolph Hearst, whose New York *Evening Journal* reprinted the article.[6] Barry described the status of several Florida prosecutions. In December 1906 a judge in Pensacola sentenced five Jackson Lumber Company officers to seven years in prison. Florida authorities also requested 17 indictments against prominent businessmen. According to Barry, "charges were all the same – slavery! The law calls it peonage, which means the holding of a man to unwilling labor to work out a debt. But on this peonage these crafty and cruel employers had ingrafted the ante-bellum implements of bondage – the lash and the bloodhound. It is difficult to find a man of prominence in Florida who does not condone the system." Though the wheels of justice were grinding slowly in the South, at least they were moving. This may be attributed to the fact that victims of peonage included white men. According to Barry, "The monumental error made by the employers in Florida was in going beyond the black man with their slavery. Had they stuck to the racial division they might have escaped castigation, as they have for a decade. But, insatiate, and not finding enough blacks to satisfy their ambitious wants, they reached out and took in white men."

---

[5] U. S. Congress, House Congressional Record, 60th Congress, 1st session, 1908, 42, pt. 3: 2750.

[6] Jerrell H. Shofner, "Mary Grace Quackenbos, a Visitor Florida Did Not Want," *Florida Historical Quarterly* 58:3 (January 1980), 279-280.

Barry declared that peonage corroded politics, blackened industry, retarded immigration, and clogged the wheels of justice.

On March 2, 1908, the U. S. House of Representatives passed a resolution requesting the Immigration Commission to investigate the treatment of immigrants on Mississippi Delta cotton plantations, including those in Arkansas. The commission was a bipartisan group formed in February 1907 by Congress to study various facets of immigration to America. After passage of this special resolution the subject of peonage was set apart and made a separate investigation. A subcommittee was established – the peonage committee of the Immigration Commission – to investigate peonage abuses. [7]

The subcommittee's investigation came to the absurd conclusion that instances of peonage had occurred in 1906 and 1907 in some southern states, but they were "sporadic instances." The commission found no general system of peonage anywhere. One of the so-called sporadic instances included in their report, a flagrant one, took place in Arkansas:

> *In the Arkansas case, an immigrant was arrested as a vagrant, convicted before a justice of the peace, and sentenced to pay a fine of $10 and costs. There was added to his sentence, without authority of law, the expenses and mileage of the constable who came to the town where he was arrested, and the expenses and mileage of the constable and prisoner going from the place of arrest to the convict farm, the lessee of which paid to the county where the arrest took place 25 percent of the fine only and the justice's costs, but held the prisoner to work out both the legal and illegal expenses at the rate of 75 cents a day. In this case the prisoners were kept in a barn, 80 men being kept in a moderate-sized building with no special arrangements for ventilation or sanitation. On Saturday nights the men were locked in the building and kept there until Monday morning. There was a good deal of sickness among the men, despite the fact that during the week days they were healthfully employed out of doors. While at work the men were guarded by 'trusties' [sic] armed with shotguns. There were both white and colored men*

---

[7] Report on Peonage, Abstracts of Reports of the Immigration Commission, 61st Congress, 3rd session 1910-1911, no. 747, II:443.

> *among the trusties [sic]. Members of the subcommittee were present in the United States circuit court in Little Rock when the proprietor of this particular farm was the unsuccessful defendant in the suit for damages brought by a prisoner who had been so illegally detained and in whose favor the jury gave a substantial verdict. These prisoners, held to work at illegal sums and some of whom were whipped and otherwise illtreated, illustrate what is commonly accepted as peonage.*[8]

Russell's 1908 report about peonage focused on selective use of vagrancy laws, such as Arkansas's 1905 version. It defined vagrants as able-bodied persons more than 14 years old without a home or means of support and not seeking a job. If law officers wanted someone to be a vagrant they hauled him into court for a conviction. Fines ranged from $10 to $100. He could be imprisoned, put to work on a chain gang, or leased to an independent contractor.[9] The police used such dodgy statutes to declare criminal whatever they chose to call a crime.

Intervention by a foreign embassy on behalf of its citizens held in peonage increased federal attention. An October 1, 1909, letter from the U. S. Secretary of State to the attorney general illustrated this. It concerned George Scharmer, a German subject. In 1908, authorities arrested Scharmer in Malvern and fined him $20 for trespassing on a train. He could not pay the fine and court costs, so Frank Tillar did. He had a contract with the county to pay fines and put convicts to work on his property. The state department heard from the German Embassy that Tillar held Scharmer longer than necessary to pay his fine. The attorney general called facts in the case unclear due to "unsatisfactory information" received from the Arkansas governor. A letter from the justice department to the U. S. Attorney in Little Rock encouraged more support for the German national than what American citizens normally received. "It is desirable and important that the facts be ascertained, and that if any [peonage] offense has been committed, punishment be secured." The letter stressed that the attorney be "zealous." Arkansas Governor G. W. Donaghey asked the state attorney general to examine facts surrounding Scharmer's arrest and punishment and issue an opinion as to their legality. The state department forwarded to the

---

[8] Peonage sub-committee report, 444.

[9] William Fosgate Kirby, *Supplement to Kirby's Digest of the Statutes of Arkansas* (Indianapolis, Ind.: Bobbs-Merrill Co., 1911), 2059.

embassy a state attorney general's opinion which said that "The fine and subsequent imprisonment of Scharmer are proper under the laws of the State."[10]

Another Arkansas peonage case involving justice department intervention drew considerable press attention. A July 24, 1909, *Colliers* magazine article said that authorities arrested Joseph Callas when his train stopped in Little Rock. Callas said that a man put a gun to his head and asked where he was from and if he had a job and any money. Callas admitted having only ten cents and was charged with vagrancy. Originally fined $10, by the time Callas reached southeast Arkansas his fines and fees had reached $90. He described treatment received along with other convicts, totaling 85 prisoners, black and white. According to him, guards herded them to cotton fields with picking sacks tied to their backs. A whipping boss and guard with bloodhounds stood by. The boss whipped men who could not pick fast enough and beat one man to death. An overseer flogged two or three men each day and sometimes up to ten. Callas somehow sent letters to the justice department about the situation, and agents obtained his release. At a national prison association meeting held in New Orleans a speaker who studied convict leasing said that prisoners in the South, mostly black men, were in many cases "worse off than they were in the days of slavery."[11]

After 1900, the justice department focused on southern peonage for several reasons – progressive impulses, political gain, and judicial concern for freedom of contract and freedom to labor. But reformist impulses often dissolved after declarations of principle, and landmark cases failed to be followed up with necessary law enforcement.[12] An exception occurred in Alabama. The *Birmingham News* on November 29, 1910, reported southern Alabama to be "swarming with secret service agents, yellow magazine writers and reformers from the North." They responded to reports about hundreds of white men held in bondage. White men in bondage generated outrage not present with black men in bondage. Bonaparte assigned Russell to coordinate federal investigations, seek indictments, and manage prosecutions.

---

[10] Department of Justice, Mail and Files Division, Reel 13, 50-144.
[11] Mary Church Terrell, "Peonage in the United States: The Convict Lease System and the Chain Gangs," *Nineteenth Century* 68 (August 1907), 309.
[12] Schmidt, part 2, 7.

Warden and trusty hold bloodhounds at bay at Tucker Unit, Arkansas Department of Corrections. UALR Center for Arkansas History and Culture.

RKANSAS G

LITTLE ROCK SATURDAY, MARCH 24, 1888.

A HELL IN ARKANSAS.

The Light Thrown On the Coal Hill Convict Camp Through an Official Investigation---No Hearsav, But Blood-Curdling Facts.

Men Beaten to Death, Half Starved, Half Clothed, But Worked All the Same.

Facts Kept From Everybody, Lessees and Warden Included—Three Wardens Who Killed Seven Men By Brutality Alone.

In order to obtain more definite knowledge of the way things are conducted at the Coal Hill convict camp the board of penitentiary commissioners left this city Thursday morning for the purpose of making as thorough as possible an investigation of affairs. The board is composed of Gov. S. P. Hughes, Secretary of State E. B. Moore and Attorney-General Dan W. Jones. They were accompanied by Dr. G. M. D. Cantrell, penitentiary physician at Little Rock, and a GAZETTE representative.

The party arrived at Coal Hill at 3 o'clock p.m. and went immediately to the stockade, a little over two miles from the station, and remained there until dark. Investigations were resumed again yesterday morning by 8 o'clock and continued until 11 o'clock when the party boarded the train

all night, hit him ninety-six licks in the morning and within an hour the negro was dead. Mark Elder is the white man whose body was exhumed by Coroner Blythe, and thirty-four fearful gashes were found on the back and he was kicked and bruised otherwise. It was developed that Scott whipped him last fall, leaving the flesh bleeding and sore, the flies blew it and it became poisoned. After Gafford succeeded Scott he added some more lashes and Elder died.

SHOT IN THE MINES.

Frank Tolbert ran off and hid in the mines about Christmas because he was whipped for failure to do his task. They looked for him almost a week. One morning Tom Gaddis, an ex-convict, who was pit boss, came up and told Scott about it, and said he could not get the negro to come out. Scott handed Gaddis a pistol and

Daily Arkansas Gazette *article exposed Coal Hill mine atrocities.*

CHAPTER 9

Our Word is Nothing

A May 8, 1911, edition of *The Crisis* published this letter written to W. E. B. Du Bois.

I am not an educated man. I will give you the peonage system as it is practiced here in the name of the law.

If a colored man is arrested here and hasn't any money, whether he is guilty or not, he has to pay just the same. A man of color is never tried in this country. It is simply a farce. Everything is fixed before he enters the courtroom. I will try to give you an illustration of how it is done:

I am brought in a prisoner, go through the farce of being tried. The whole of my fine may amount to fifty dollars. A kindly appearing man will come up and pay my fine and take me to his farm to allow me to work it out. At the end of a month I find that I owe him more than I did when I went there. The debt is increased year in and year out.

You would ask, "How is that?" It is simply that he is charging you more for your board, lodging and washing than they allow you for your work, and you can't help yourself either, nor can anyone else help you, because you are still a prisoner and never get your fine worked out.

> *This is in the United States, where it is supposed that every man has equal rights before the law, and we are held in bondage by this same outfit.*
>
> *Of course we can't prove anything. Our word is nothing. If we state things as they are, the powers that be make a different statement, and that sets ours aside at Washington and I suppose, in Heaven, too.*
>
> *What I have told you is strictly confidential. If you publish it, don't put my name to it. I would be dead in a short time after the news reached here.*

In an egregious Arkansas case, six black persons filed suit against a family in Ashley County that held them in a state of peonage. They described inhumane treatment, imprisonment, and being bound like beasts and paraded through public streets. The white family compelled them to do hard labor without receiving any compensation. In another Arkansas case with unusual circumstances – two white female victims – a state court convicted a wealthy family for illegally holding the girls from St. Louis. The judge forced their employer to pay one of them $1,000 in damages and the other $625.[1] When some victims escaped Arkansas injustice they risked being hauled back into jeopardy. A black newspaper in Chicago, *The Defender*, reported one attempt in 1910. A black man named Steven Green killed his Arkansas landlord in a shootout that injured Green. He fled to Chicago to avoid being lynched, but police there held him for extradition. While waiting for an Arkansas sheriff to arrive, Civil Rights activists Wells-Barnett and Ed Wright began legal efforts to block extradition. Despite their intervention, police turned Green over to an Arkansas sheriff, and they boarded a southbound train. According to a newspaper report, the sheriff told Green about a reception committee waiting with a fire. [2] Wright telegraphed cities along the train's route seeking help. In Cairo, Illinois, Sheriff Fred Nellis had received Wells-Barnett's support for his appointment to office and now returned the favor. When the Arkansas lawman and his prisoner exited the train to cross the Mississippi River by ferry, Nellis seized Green and returned him to Chicago. A judge

---

[1] "Convict Lease System," 310.

[2] Ethan Michaeli, *The Defender. How the Legendary Newspaper Changed America* (New York: Houghton Mifflin Harcourt, 2016), 35-36.

invalidated the extradition order after hearing testimony by Wright and Green that the shooting was in self-defense and he would be lynched if returned to Arkansas.

Despite threats of lynching and other violence, black families continued to acquire land. According to the June 23, 2019, *New York Times*, black people owned nearly 16 million acres in America by 1910. Attempts to evict them came in different guises. "White tax assessors routinely overvalued their land," forcing these property owners to bear heavier tax burdens than whites. If their property became valuable and desired by whites, "local officials could simply declare the property tax-delinquent and sell it at a tax sale." Because white authorities controlled the courts, blacks who acquired land became vulnerable to several forms of land seizure. Motivated by greed and determined to divest black citizens of independence, thieves stole their land when possible.

Courts throughout the South provided little assistance. Justice for black people depended on unbiased southern juries, a rare commodity in the Delta and elsewhere. The *Anderson Daily Mail* on April 29, 1910, reported an example in South Carolina. Though Joshua W. Ashley engaged in peonage, according to the newspaper, a not guilty verdict failed to surprise residents. "For while everybody knows that he is guilty it is equally well known that he is not anymore guilty than scores or perhaps hundreds of other men." As a result, it would "hardly be justice" for him to be convicted and punished for doing what many others are doing. Despite racist efforts to impede progress in and out of the courtroom, black families forged ahead. In 1900 about five of ten black adults could not read. By 1913 only three of ten could not. But whites invariably accommodated black advancement only when it converged with white interests.[3]

During the early 1900s, timber companies sold cut-over Delta acres to white farmers at low prices. Enormous enterprises such as the Chicago Mill and Lumber Company cleared acres, milled lumber, and shipped it to manufacturers. That company ran an operation at Helena. J. F. McEntyre located Memphis Veneer and Lumber Company at Pine Bluff. These businesses and others like them acquired thousands of

---

3 Derrick A. Bell, Jr., "Brown v. Board of Education and the Interest Convergence Dilemma," *Critical Race Theory* 22. Qtd. in Aziz Z. Huq, "Peonage and Contractual Liberty," *Columbia Law Review* (March 2001), 1.

acres and turned new ground into farmable plots. An instance of labor unrest in a regional lumber operation contradicted claims of inferior black labor. White workers protesting at Hinds Lumber Company in Craighead County caused the firm to terminate its black employees at an Anderson Spur mill. But after assessing production of an all-white workforce, Hinds rehired its black employees. In such cases Delta employers exposed contradictions in attitudes about black workers. They called them shiftless and unreliable, but attempted to retain them using every method available, including peonage. A. C. Hervey of Hickory Ridge reported violations in a letter to the U. S. Attorney General in 1911. He complained about convict abuse by a planter named Ranks. After hearing from eyewitnesses, Hervey called this one of the worst cases of peonage in the country. Ranks supposedly paid convict fines and court costs to trap them into working for 75 cents per day, and additional charges helped keep them in debt. According to Hervey, Ranks had a whipping boss and guards overseeing convict labor. Hervey provided two specific examples of abuse. A crippled man, Tom Grady from Wynne, served 29 days for getting drunk. Authorities arrested R. MacComber from Hickory Ridge for disorderly conduct and gave him 60 days. According to Hervey, MacComber told them that he would "make it hot for them" so authorities turned him loose. An assistant attorney general wrote Hervey that the matter would receive careful attention.[4]

Southern legislators continued to help planters make peonage possible. They developed contract-enforcement language to prohibit employee mobility. A typical version warned that "Any person, who, with intent to injure or defraud his employer, enters into a contract in writing for the performance of any act or service, and thereby obtains money or other personal property from such employer, and with like intent, and without just cause, and without refunding such money, or paying for such property, refuses to perform such act or service, must, on conviction, be punished as if he had stolen it."[5] Most white southerners supported such restrictive laws. In 1911, a U. S. Attorney concluded that "The public sentiment in regard to the peonage laws is in a most deplorable condition, many people not hesitating to say the negroes will be compelled to work out labor contracts even if a few of them have to be lynched in order to terrorize the remaining ones into

[4] Department of Justice, Reel 13, 50-146.
[5] Alabama code, 3812, 1886.

complying with these iniquitous contracts.[6] Sometimes public officials did the terrorizing. Orley Lilly, a Helena alderman, and two other men ran a plantation near Marked Tree where they worked 36 black families recruited from Mississippi. A witness advised Judge Jacob Trieber about conditions there. The planters confined people on the farm, guarding them with guns. These captives worked in mud, rain, and snow, in the severest weather and on Sundays. Some men ran away at night and later sent for their families, but managers refused to release family members.[7] A Craighead County court tried Lilly, Daniel H. Robertson, and Robert E. Bailey. After one hour of deliberation the jury delivered a not guilty verdict. A U. S. Attorney from eastern Arkansas said that "an impartial jury would have convicted them, but the atmosphere was unfriendly, not to say hostile, with sympathy clearly resting with the planters."[8]

By the time of *Bailey v. Alabama* in 1911, the federal anti-peonage statute had been further defined in district court prosecutions. It applied in the following cases:

1. *Whenever a debtor is held by coercion, whether that coercion consists of the threat of violence or of prosecution under an apparent, but void, provision of a law.*
2. *Whenever an employer falsely pretends that another is guilty of a crime and bribes a prosecutor or judge in order to induce a laborer to enter into a contract to reimburse the sum paid.*
3. *Whenever an employer causes a person to be arrested on a warrant procured directly or indirectly by him and procures his release after the worker agrees to work out debt.*
4. *Whenever an employer falsely accuses a laborer of a crime in order that he may be convicted and either sentenced to hard labor in the accuser's service or forced to work out his fine in the accuser's service.*
5. *Whenever a magistrate or police official is knowingly involved in an arrest or conviction for the purpose of placing a person*

[6] Alexander Akerman to the Attorney General, August 24, 1911. Department of Justice, Rg. 60, 50-211.
[7] Black witness to Judge Jacob Trieber, March 18, 1912, pf, Reel 3.
[8] William G. Whipple to U. S. Attorney General, May 23, 1912, Department of Justice, file 161148, Reel 13.

in peonage. The act applies even if officials in question are operating under state or municipal law.[9]

To tighten the noose around peonage victims, Alabama legislators in 1903 amended the state's contract labor law concerning workers who took money from an employer and failed to pay it back. Breach of contract became prima facie evidence of intent to defraud an employer. Prosecutors did not have the burden of proving motive, since lack of repayment served as evidence of fraudulent intent. In a 1905 case, Montgomery City Court Judge William H. Thomas declared the statute unconstitutional, but the state supreme court disagreed. It ruled that legislators could establish what was prima facie evidence so long as it did not make such evidence conclusive proof of fraud and did not bar a defendant's right to present evidence in rebuttal. However, a state rule of evidence prevented testimony with respect to uncommunicated motives, purposes, and intentions.[10] Booker T. Washington and allies, many of them white and participating in secret, decided to use Alonzo Bailey for a test case. This black farm hand contracted to work for a year and received a $15 advance. Bailey quit his job after about a month without repaying the advance, and authorities arrested him. His attorney petitioned for habeas corpus before Judge Thomas, but he denied this writ on authority of the state supreme court. The U. S. Supreme Court settled the matter. Justice Charles Evans Hughes delivered its opinion during January 1911 and made several critical points. A jury may not indulge in unsupported conjectures and speculations as to intentions. By not being able to testify, Bailey lacked the presumption of innocence. The state may not compel a man to labor in payment of debt by punishing him as a criminal. The law served as an "instrument of compulsion peculiarly effective as against the poor and the ignorant, its most likely victims." This decision declared that the law violated the peonage statute under 13th Amendment provisions.[11]

The national press greeted *Bailey v. Alabama* with enthusiasm and false assumptions. On January 21, 1911, *Outlook* called it "one of the most important decisions of the Supreme Court in recent years" and

---

[9] *Wheel of Servitude*, 52. Cases cited: *Clyatt v. United States* 197 U. S. 207 (1905); *In re Peonage Charge* 138 Fed. 686 (Fla. 1905); *Peonage Cases* 123 Fed. 671 (Ala. 1903); *United States v. Clement* 171 Fed. 974 (S. C. 1909)

[10] Schmidt, part 2, 19.

[11] *Bailey v. Alabama*, U. S. 219 (1911).

ranked the case with *Dred Scott* as a symbol of "that sense of human brotherhood that was inevitably to render slavery unbearable." The *Nation* on January 1, 1911, claimed that the decision "will cause rejoicing North and South," a mistaken conclusion about southern reactions. The writer assumed that "The Supreme Court's decision will be heartily welcomed by broad-minded southerners everywhere; for they understand that vexing as the labor problem is, the solution lies in other directions than involuntary servitude." Despite *Bailey,* illegal employment contracts continued to exist among supposedly "broad-minded" southerners. Many employees did not know their rights, and sometimes employers "reclaimed" laborers and forced them to work off debts. Journalist Ray Stannard Baker issued a warning to commentators heaping praise on the *Bailey* decision. In an *American Magazine* article he admitted that Bailey became a symbol in this struggle for freedom. But slavery would prevail so long as many white men were shortsighted enough to take advantage of another man's "ignorance and poverty." [12]

Baker also shared several observations about criminal-surety:

> *One of the things that I couldn't understand in some of the courts I visited was the presence of so many white men to stand sponsor for Negroes who had committed various offenses. In one case in particular, I saw a Negro brought into court charged with stealing cotton.*
>
> *"Does anybody know this Negro?" asked the judge.*
>
> *Two white men stepped up and both said they did.*
>
> *The judge fined the Negro $20 and costs, and there was a real contest between the two white men as to who should pay it – and get the Negro. They argued for some minutes, but finally the judge said to the prisoner:*
>
> *"Who do want to work for, George?"*

[12] Qtd. in Schmidt, part 2, 27.

> *The Negro chose his employer, and agreed to work four months to pay off his $20 fine and costs. Behind the system lay the terror of the chain gang.*

An October 1, 1910, *Arkansas Gazette* exposed the transparent corruption that allowed this form of peonage to flourish. A Memphis judge indicated how southern justice worked when cotton matured. He announced in the newspaper that black persons charged with vagrancy would be freed if they accepted job offers, and policemen intended to "renew their efforts to clear the city of all vagrants and loiterers." In addition to contracting through surety these so-called vagrants and loiterers, Delta planters continued to lease convicts. The state first completed a penitentiary in 1849 and leased prisoners to private individuals who either employed the men or sub-leased them to contractors. The state legislature passed Act 46 in 1873, which allowed leasing of convicts inside the penitentiary. Lessees agreed to provide guards, food, clothing, and appropriate medical care in return for all profits from enterprises. Investigators in 1881 found a high mortality rate there, and the Journal of the Arkansas House of Representatives published these humiliating conclusions. It said that although the penitentiary committee is "satisfied the contract system is cruel, barbarous and [an] inhumane one, and is totally at variance with the civilization of this age, yet taking into consideration the present embarrassed condition of the State, they forbear to make any recommendation."[13] A minor political party and labor unions took a stand against the practice. During 1888 the Union Labor Party of Arkansas pledged to "do its utmost" to abolish the contract system and require that all convicts work inside penitentiary facilities. Agricultural Wheel, Farmers' Alliance, and Knights of Labor endorsed this proposal.[14]

With leased prisoners spread throughout the state, proper supervision became impractical. Due to incompetence, corruption, and lack of funds, convict treatment remained deplorable. A mining camp near Coal Hill exhibited typical deficiencies. The *Arkansas Gazette* called the camp "Hell in Arkansas," and state legislators decided to investigate. Though brutality of treatment varied with wardens, a

---

[13] Calvin R. Ledbetter Jr., "The Long Struggle to End Convict Leasing in Arkansas," *Arkansas Historical Quarterly* 52:1 (Spring 1993), 6.

[14] Jane Zimmerman, "The Convict Lease System in Arkansas and the Fight for Abolition," *Arkansas Historical Quarterly* 8:3 (Autumn 1949), 175.

March 24, 1888, *Arkansas Gazette* revealed ghastly treatment there. An investigation uncovered the following: A camp with about 140 men who slept in a building about 90 feet long, 80 feet wide, and 12 feet high. It contained bunks in three tiers. The ill and injured slept beside other prisoners, which caused contagions. Investigators had trouble obtaining testimony from convicts there. Men they questioned would say, "Gentlemen, if I talk, when you go away, I will be beat to death; we can't tell anything about how we are treated." But one convict risked punishment and admitted that guards whipped them with ten to 150 licks at one time on their naked backs for failure to perform tasks. A drunk warden during one night whipped about 75 men with about 50 licks using a leather strap with a piece of shoe leather on the end. The convict said that "blood ran out on the floor." They slept in filthy, blood-soaked clothes, with raw backs covered by sores the size of a man's finger nail to the size of his hand. Guards forced men to work, though severely beaten, sick, or injured. Some men smelled so bad that other convicts could not stand to be around them. Prisoners worked in pairs, and if they did not make their quota of coal, guards lashed them. Workers complained about lack of props to keep the mine roof from caving in, and many accidents resulted from falling slate. Air in the shafts sometimes grew so foul that lamps would not burn. After returning to Little Rock, investigators said they were sickened by what they saw.

In his first message to the Arkansas General Assembly during January 1903, Governor Jeff Davis pledged to clean up the penitentiary system. He said that "there is a crowd of leeches and bloodsuckers that are trying to build up a penitentiary dynasty and political penitentiary ring, the object and purpose of which is to control the politics of Arkansas, and incidentally loot the state treasury while doing it."[15] At that time more than 91 percent of convicts worked outside prison walls for planters, railroad companies, mine operators, and other businessmen. Living conditions varied depending on who ran the site. Legislative committee members inspected facilities and made recommendations, including the following: abolish the lease system; have all convicts work on state accounts; put black convicts on farms and whites inside the walls; do not allow black persons to guard white convicts, and require ten-hour work days. An ex-convict named William N. Hill wrote a book about his experiences while imprisoned in

[15] Arkansas House Journal (1903), 35-39, 40-55.

Arkansas. He describes men "worked, starved, and whipped until they lost their health and died." Hill says that guards exposed prisoners to terrible weather and worked them barefooted in snow. Dishonest guards accepted bribes for better rations from convicts who had something to offer.[16]

A. C. Miller, a Methodist minister, investigated Cummins Prison Farm and found atrocious conditions. He blamed penitentiary board members too busy to properly supervise activities. Miller's report recommended several improvements, including more inspections by board members and that solitary confinement replace whippings. When the state superintendent of prisons released a 1906-1908 report, a December 6, 1908, *Arkansas Democrat* recorded its findings: an average of 850 prisoners each month; a black-white ratio of approximately 70-30; 21 female prisoners; 214 escapes; 276 pardons, and 95 deaths. Loopholes and lethargy saved convict leasing until Governor George Donaghey attended a conference of governors in December 1912. During a meeting he learned that Governor Cole Blease of South Carolina pardoned convicts to reduce leasing. After returning to Arkansas, Donaghey pardoned 360 prisoners, which hampered leasing arrangements. Governor Joe Robinson ended the practice during February 1913.[17]

Though reformers appeared altruistic, some objected to convict leasing for financial reasons. Businesses that worked convicts had a competitive economic advantage over those who did not. Jennifer Roback evaluates convict leasing using the cold calculus of economics. Those who leased prisoners had "no interest in keeping the convicts alive past the end of their sentence" since they had no "scrap" or "resale" value. In this sense leasing was worse than slavery. Since slave "owners" received the "full capitalized value" of an enslaved person's output throughout his life, planters had an incentive to keep him healthy."[18] The 8th Constitutional Amendment proscribed excessive bail, excessive fines, and cruel and unusual punishment. But prisoners working on state farms often endured cruel punishment and a hidden penalty as well. They experienced social death. This form of slavery stripped

---

[16] William N. Hill, *Story of the Arkansas Penitentiary* (Little Rock, Ark.: Democrat Printing & Lithographing Co., 1912), 141.

[17] Whayne, "Reasonable Progress," *Narrative History*, 279.

[18] Jennifer Roback, "Southern Labor Law in the Jim Crow Era: Exploitive or Competitive?" *University of Chicago Law Review* 51 (Autumn 1984), 1170.

inmates of their human dignity by compelling them to work using physical force and coercion. Convicts believed that they had no choice.[19] For the most part courts took a hands-off approach to prison administration and inmate rights. Though forced penal labor could be ruled unconstitutional if beyond an inmate's strength, plaintiffs had to show that officials knew about it and were indifferent. So it hardly mattered to southern administrators.

Concern about peonage diminished early in the 20th Century. From 1907 to 1912 the U. S. Attorney General's annual reports referred to about 80 peonage investigations each year, but only a handful of indictments and few convictions. A 1913 report listed an average of seven peonage investigations per month producing only 21 prosecutions. The 1914 report indicated an average of nine per month. Investigations and indictments ran about the same in 1915. Future reports recorded declines. During 1916, indictments fell to five, and in 1917-1919 the reports did not refer to any peonage charges, though violations abounded.[20] A U. S. Attorney in Little Rock referred to a report of convict farm peonage in a March 6, 1914, letter to the attorney general. He enclosed an article from the *Newport Daily Independent* that contained grand jury testimony about conditions at a Jackson County convict farm. The attorney said that if substantiated this grand jury report indicated existence of peonage there. He proposed an investigation and prosecution if warranted. The justice department asked if the state took any action against persons involved, but resolution of the matter was unclear.[21]

Two Alabama peonage cases in 1914, *United States v. Reynolds* and *United States v. Broughton*, reached the U. S. Supreme Court and affected cases throughout the South. A state court convicted Ed Rivers of petty larceny, and Reynolds paid his fine. In consideration, Rivers contracted with Reynolds to work off his debt. Reynolds threatened Rivers with arrest if he violated their contract. Following several months of abuse, Rivers ran off, and authorities rearrested him. In the second case, a court convicted E. W. Fields of selling mortgaged property, and Broughton paid his fine. Fields claimed that during his

---

[19] Andrea C. Armstrong, "Slavery Revisited in Penal Plantation Labor," *Seattle University Law Review* (Spring 2012), 7, 9.
[20] Reports of the Attorney General of the United States, 1916-1920.
[21] Department of Justice, Mail and Files Division, Reel 13, 50-155.

employment Broughton threatened him with arrest and imprisonment. Fields refused to work for Broughton after a few months, and authorities rearrested him. Since both cases had similar facts, the U. S. Supreme Court decided to hear them together. Alabama statutes allowed third parties to act as sureties for criminals fined by the state and enter into contracts with guilty persons to pay their fines. Failure to fulfill contracts could result in rearrest and additional fines. However, the Supreme Court ruled that when Reynolds and Broughton paid fines owed to the state, the convicted parties had completed their punishment. The state was no longer a party to the transaction, so a subsequent arrest could not be based on failure to pay a fine. It had to be for failure to complete a contractual obligation between two private parties. Therefore Alabama's statute was ruled unconstitutional.[22]

United States v. Reynolds, United States v. Broughton, 235 U. S 133 (1914).

CHAPTER 10

Blood Red in the Delta

After World War I ended, race riots broke out in about 25 American cities, and in many of them white mobs faced black men who survived combat in Europe and refused to be victimized at home. Those days of homicidal white rage came to be called Red Summer, and they were blood red in the Delta. Starting in 1919, white terrorists tortured and murdered hundreds of black Delta citizens, and it came to be called the Elaine Massacre.

When World War I began in Europe during August 1914 it depressed commodity markets. Several U. S. exchanges failed to open, and cotton prices fell by about $10 per bale. Buyers watched and waited like vultures on a telephone line. Finally forced to sell, many farmers unloaded their crops at ruinous prices. Some hauled their crops to town, failed to find a buyer, and returned home with them. [1] Fortunately, prices rose dramatically when America entered the war in April 1917. Southern textile mills achieved growth in excess of 100 percent. Prosperity tasted sweet for the subjects of King Cotton. [2] Soldiers needed uniforms, and cotton growers helped provide them. Improved prices held throughout the war and generated higher incomes for farm workers. Though the war brought prosperity to the Delta, it created difficulties for planters competing with manufacturers and the military for employees. Competition meant fewer opportunities

[1] George Brown Tindall, *The Emergence of the New South 1913-1945* (Baton Rouge: Louisiana State University Press, 1967), 33-34.
[2] "Cotton's Magical Rise Enriching the Nation," *Literary Digest* 53 (1916), 1577.

to control workers and hold down wages. Poor people who now had a little money in their pockets wanted to spend some of it. A *St. Louis Star* article about this new affluence claimed that workers living around Pine Bluff splurged in reckless abandon. Observing farmers and field hands committing "extravagant buying," planters feared that employee expectations had become too high with respect to incomes and independence. Labor agents caused additional problems since they recruited workers to better jobs in other parts of the country. Delta tenant farmers shared in the bounty, and some had the audacity to buy a $45 suit. (That suit would have cost $1,059 in 2019.) A newspaper reporter called them little children to whom some good fairy has paid a visit. Another observer said that Arkansans could not stand prosperity.[3] Both Delta planters and draft boards had trouble finding help. During summer 1918, Phillips County board members blamed low recruitment numbers on labor agents luring workers to other regions. Planters often won competitions with military recruiters after calling upon political allies to gain exemptions for their help. A Craighead County board objected to drafting black men, calling them quite necessary as laborers. Board members said military training of black men would intensify race problems, which turned out to be an accurate conclusion. "The South will do the negro's fighting, if he is left in the fields,"[4] according to the board. Black soldiers posed two problems for planters. They remained unavailable for work and sent money home to relatives. Planters found dependents receiving government checks difficult to starve into submission.

During the war, lumber mills around Elaine found the worker pool so shallow that they hired women. Unfortunately for planter wives depending on domestic help, mills paid higher wages. Rather than increase pay checks, employers pulled political strings to hold them down. A U. S. Commissioner of Labor terminated thousands of black workers employed on military projects, and about 500 returned to Phillips County. However, some landlords found it advantageous to run off tenants and take their crops. Planters used them to put in and maintain crops, but drove them away at harvest time to avoid sharing sale proceeds. Other questionable business practices flourished, and F. B. Crews described one experienced by many Delta tenants. Near the

---

[3] "Cotton's Rise,"1521.

[4] Nan Elizabeth Woodruff, *American Congo* (Cambridge, Mass.: Harvard University Press, 2003), 50.

war's end his father expected to get one dollar per pound for his cotton and shipped the bales to a Memphis cotton merchant. Many months later the company paid Crews two cents a pound and billed him $1,400 for storage.[5] *Johns v. Patterson* improved tenant rights in one respect when it reached the Arkansas Supreme Court in 1919. The previous year Nathaniel Meyers signed a contract with H. C. Patterson to work for crop shares. But Meyers left Patterson to work for F. Johns, allegedly owing Patterson $51. Patterson advised Johns of the contract, but the latter refused to dismiss Meyers. Patterson sued him citing an enticement statute making it a crime for persons to lure away an employee under contract with another party. The court ruled that enticement laws provided a remedy for employers who lost money or labor as the result of another person enticing an employee under contract to others. But it applied only when a third party knew about an existing contract. The court found in favor of Johns since Meyers left Patterson before Johns hired him. Meyers could not be lured away from a job he no longer held.[6]

Though they sought to hinder labor mobility, planters refused to increase wages, which would have been one solution to their problems. E. C. Morris, a black minister from Helena, said that black families continued heading north not for a better climate, but for a better life. This exodus continued despite landlords putting up barriers to block the exits. Authorities in Helena arrested two recruiters for a northern railroad company, fined the men $500 and sentenced them to one year in jail for labor agitation. Black soldiers returning home after the war may have been considered a positive development by planters looking to replace departing laborers, but it turned out to be a negative. These soldiers earned money and self-esteem during military service. William Brown from Phillips County walked away from a cotton farm to fight in France. He wrote his grandmother that "I am awful proud that I came over to France to fight for my country for now that we have gone over the top we can go back home with our chest's [sic] stuck out like a peacock's about it."[7] Delta prosperity ended when a huge cotton crop harvested at the end of 1919 caused plunging prices. The U. S. Secretary

---

[5] Deanna Snowden, ed., *Mississippi County, Arkansas: Appreciating the Past and Anticipating the Future* (Little Rock, Ark.: August House, 1986), 68, 71.
[6] *Johns v. Patterson*, 138 Ark. 420 (Ark., 1919).
[7] Randy Finley, "Black Arkansans and World War One," *Arkansas Historical Quarterly* 49:3 (Autumn 1990), 264.

of Agriculture released a report indicating that the country harvested the second largest crop in its history. Combined yields of ten principal crops increased by 13 percent above a five-year average preceding the war. Along with cratering farm prices, another development concerned white southerners. They faced proud black soldiers in uniform. Fred Sullens, a captain in military intelligence during the war, described meetings with southern whites and his message to them. He pointed out that black soldiers returning from Europe would not be the same as before they donned their uniforms.[8] White southerners recognized that fact and did not like it.

Tension between races led to a massacre of black Arkansans in the Delta. It began when farm workers organized to achieve fair pay and honest crop settlements. Robert Hill, an Arkansas sharecropper, recruited members for the Progressive Farmers and Household Union of America and went to Phillips County to organize laborers. The union located several branches in the area, and Hill assisted members at Elaine, Hoop Spur, and nearby communities with contracts to govern arrangements with planters. Union members planned to deliver a proposal to landlords and strike if planters refused to negotiate. Violence erupted on several fronts. During fall 1919 some black workers decided to sue landlords and hired a Little Rock attorney, Ulysses S. Bratton. In September a union member asked Bratton to represent 68 of them who worked on Theodore Fauthauer's plantation. The planter refused to provide itemized statements of accounts and sold cotton without compensating tenants. When Bratton's son, also an attorney, arrived at Ratio by train approximately 25 black farm laborers met him to discuss strategy. Unfortunately, armed white thugs rode up on horses and kidnapped the attorney. He remained in Helena's jail for 30 days. Ulysses Bratton and his three sons, all lawyers, had to move to Detroit, Michigan, to avoid reprisals for their union representation.

The *Nation* ran a Walter F. White article explaining this union's goals and requirements. Membership material stated that the organization existed to advance the intellectual, material, moral, spiritual, and financial interests of the "Negro race." Those seeking membership had to answer these questions under oath: "Do you believe

---

[8] Captain Fred Sullens, Memo to Major Brown, November 30, 1918, Department of Justice, Bureau of Investigation, Record Group 65. Qtd. in Kornweibel, *Federal Surveillance of Afro-Americans*, Reel 22.

in God? Do you attend church? Do you believe in courts? Will you defend this Government and her Constitution at all times?" Despite commendable union goals, Delta planters and business allies recognized that the organization threatened their business practices. A local merchant hired a black detective from Chicago to gather information, and he warned planters of a potential strike. Employers threatened black laborers with dire consequences should they join the union. An October 2, 1919, *Arkansas Gazette* quoted a planter saying, "I told my negroes about two weeks ago that if they joined that . . . union I would kill every one of them." Animosity soon turned into violence. Precise information about how and why the massacre began and continued for many days remains elusive. Jeannie M. Whayne refers to a "mass of rich but contradictory and even tainted evidence."[9] In one account, carnage began when Hoop Spur union members met at a local church. Phillips County Deputy Sheriff Charles W. Pratt, W. A. Adkins, a railroad agent, and Kidd Collins, a black trustee at the county jail, observed this meeting from a car parked near the church. In an exchange of gunfire Pratt was hit and Adkins mortally wounded. Collins called authorities in Helena to report the shootings, claiming that their car broke down by the church and that someone fired at them first. Those in the church said that men in the car fired at them to break up the meeting, and they defended themselves, a more believable scenario.

A false narrative spread throughout the region about black rioters assaulting white residents and seizing their property. Armed thugs rushed to the area, robbed the homes of black families, and hauled away men to detention locations, at least those they didn't murder. An October 2, 1919, *Arkansas Gazette* reported that union opponents sent the Helena sheriff a message claiming that 1,000 to 1,500 black residents had begun a race war. White women and children departed for Helena. Black families departed for canebrakes to hide from marauding terrorists, estimated to be from 600 to 1,000 men. Sheriff Frank Kitchens called what happened next a "nigger hunt."[10] During this turmoil white kidnappers murdered four prominent black citizens.

---

[9] Jeanne M. Whayne, "Low Villains and Wickedness in High Places: Race and Class in the Elaine Riots," *Arkansas Review. Journal of Delta Studies* 32:2 (August 2001), 102.

[10] Grif Stockley, "The Legal Proceedings of the Arkansas Race Massacres of 1919 and the Evidence of the Plot to Kill Planters," *Arkansas Review: Journal of Delta Studies* 32:2 (August 2001), 142.

Dr. D. A. E. Johnston, a dentist from Helena; Dr. L. H. Johnston; Leroy Johnston, a disabled army veteran, and another brother were headed to Helena after a hunting trip. Learning of violence there they switched to the train. Near Elaine several white men removed the four and forced them into a car. Kidnappers consisted of O. A. Lilly; Amos Jarman, county treasurer; Deputy U. S. Marshall W. H. Molitor, and another man. They chained the four victims together and held them in the rear seat, according to Jarman. The Johnstons never made it to Helena. They were shot to death and their bodies dumped beside a road, according to an October 3, 1919, *Helena World*. Though heinous, these murders became only one act in a horror show.

Due to widespread violence, Arkansas Governor Charles J. Brough declared martial law and sent about 580 soldiers to the area. They brought small arms and 12 machine guns to restore order. Upon arrival, many troopers reportedly aided vigilantes. Determined to place blame for violence on farm workers, white Phillips County businessmen formed a seven-man committee to issue a report that contradicted eyewitness and press accounts. An article in the *Nation* revealed interrogation techniques. According to two sources, suspects brought before this committee were seated in a chair charged with electricity. If prisoners did not say what questioners wanted to hear, the tormentors turned on the electricity until they did. The committee declared that it secured many confessions from "Negro suspects." An October 7, 1919, *Helena World* published the committee's conclusions. "The present trouble with the negroes in Phillips County is not a race riot. It is a deliberately planned insurrection of the negroes against the whites directed by an organization known as the Progressive Farmers and Household Union of America, established for the purpose of banding negroes together for the killing of white people." Governor Brough called the affair a "damnable conspiracy to murder white citizens and take possession of their property." [11] At the time of this so-called damnable conspiracy the county's population consisted of 7,176 white and 26,354 black persons. One would expect that alleged insurrectionists could have killed more than five white persons, but that was the body count.

---

[11] Richard C. Cortner, *A Mob Intent on Death: the NAACP and the Arkansas Riot Cases* (Middletown, Conn.: Wesleyan University Press, 1988), 73.

Wells-Barnett reported a different version of events. She interviewed John Martin, a union member at the Hoop Spur gathering, and he offered this account. "I was at Hoop Spur Church that night. I do know that four or five automobiles full of white men came about fifty yards from the church and put the lights out, then started shooting in the church with about 200 head of men, women, and children. I was on the outside of the church and saw this for myself." When Martin learned of prowling white ruffians he surrendered to soldiers for protection, which proved to be a mistake. "I was carried to Elaine and put in the schoolhouse, and I was there eight days. Then I was brought to Helena and put in jail and whipped near to death and was put in an electric chair to make me lie on other negroes." After his release, Martin learned that white thieves stole everything he owned, including livestock and crops. "These white people know that they started this trouble. This union was only for a blind. We were threatened before this union was there to make us leave our crops."[12] According to victims, torturers used a variety of methods to elicit desired testimony: beatings, electric shock, whipping, and insertion of formaldehyde up the nostrils of prisoners. Witnesses reported barbaric acts such as cutting off ears and toes of murdered black people for souvenirs.[13]

H. F. Smiddy participated in the torture and murder of numerous black people. He admitted whipping prisoners to make them say what interrogators wanted to hear, which was that black residents planned to murder whites and steal their property. In one instance of barbarity, "We began firing into the thicket from both sides thinking possibly there were negroes in the thicket and we could run them out and kill them. As we marched down the thicket to the southwest I saw about five or six negroes come out unarmed, holding up their hands, and some of them running and trying to get away. They were shot down and killed by posse members."[14]

Black women, some union members, faced the same threats and violence experienced by men, but whites underestimated their

[12] Ida Wells-Barnett, *The Arkansas Race Riot* (Chicago, Ill.: Home Job, 1920), 17-18.
[13] Grif Stockley, *Blood in Their Eyes. The Elaine Race Massacres of 1919* (Fayetteville: University of Arkansas Press, 2001), 48.
[14] "Legacy of Resistance," 87.

"strength and tenacity."[15] In one instance a white mob searching for Ed Ware demanded that he come out of his house. Instead, his wife Lulu Ware appeared and boldly asked, "What are you going to do with us women?" This confrontation allowed her husband and another man to escape. Authorities jailed her for four weeks, and when released she returned home and found it stripped of their belongings. Many women endured beatings while held by white authorities and also found their possessions missing when they returned home. Thugs drove Mary Moore from their farm following her husband's arrest and jailed her in Helena where she was "whipped nearly to death to make me tell stories on the others." While the Moores suffered in jail, looters stole their family's property.[16] Louis Sharpe Dunaway, an eyewitness, observed 28 dead black persons thrown into a pit and burned. Additionally, he saw 16 victims hanging from a bridge. Dunaway calls a "fair count" to be 856 murdered blacks with a wounded list probably five times greater.[17] Other estimates reported fewer people killed, but regardless, many were women who resisted.

A major problem with hiding these and other atrocities was what southern whites called the "radical negro press." U.S. Attorney General A. Mitchell Palmer joined critics declaring these newspapers antagonistic to the white race and assertive of their own equality. By 1919 approximately 450 periodicals were being published by or for blacks, including 220 newspapers and at least seven general-interest magazines. Their readership tripled in the previous five years and helped give black citizens a stronger sense of unity. Newspapers written for black audiences challenged slanted white journalism and publicized abuses. The June 18, 1919, *Veteran* reported that "Men, Women and Children Writhe under Cruel Peonage System" on southern cotton plantations. The paper concluded that "slavery in so many respects could certainly have been no worse." To suppress negative publicity, planters prevented postal carriers from delivering these periodicals to tenants. White-controlled newspapers sometimes defended outrageous criminal behavior. Helena residents threatened to lynch black men accused of crimes if "Elaine rioters" were not executed and in

---

[15] Cherisse Jones-Branch, "Women and the 1919 Elaine Massacre," *The Elaine Massacre and Arkansas. A Century of Atrocity and Resistance, 1819-1919*, Guy Lancaster, ed. (Little Rock, Ark.: Butler Center Books, 2018), 183.
[16] *Race Riot*, 17.
[17] Louis Sharpe Dunaway, *What a Preacher Saw Through a Keyhole in Arkansas* (Little Rock, Ark.: Parke-Harper Publishing Company, 1925), 36-37.

November 1921 made good on their threat. After police arrested Will Turner for allegedly assaulting a white girl a mob murdered him and burned his corpse across from the county courthouse. A disgusting editorial in the November 20, 1921, *Helena World* expressed regret, but added an appalling justification. It stressed that since 12 black men convicted of murder had not yet been executed, "Who can say truthfully that . . . provocation was not great, or that . . . forbearance had not been taxed beyond that of any community in the American Union?"

This story moved from canebrakes to courtrooms where justice initially would be denied. Control of the Arkansas criminal justice system began with election of white circuit court judges. They appointed jury commissioners for each court term who selected reliable men, primarily white, to serve on juries. Phillips County planters and businessmen made certain that juries in these cases excluded black citizens. After the massacre a grand jury charged 122 black men with crimes. More than half of them faced murder charges, a questionable proposition given a white death toll of four county residents and one soldier. During their trials all-white juries found 11 guilty of first degree murder and 38 of second degree murder. They convicted some of assault and other crimes, and 67 received long prison sentences. Twelve considered to be leaders of the "insurrection" received death sentences. Hill, the union organizer, escaped to Kansas, and that state's governor refused to extradite him. The Arkansas trials disgraced all involved except the accused. Defense attorneys called no witnesses and conducted minimal cross-examinations. Courts sentenced the 12 to be executed that following December and January. After three Little Rock attorneys and the NAACP came to their defense, this legal contest moved back and forth between federal and Arkansas courts. One of the three defenders, Scipio Africanus Jones, became a nationally prominent attorney due to the case and led what some called a new generation of black lawyers. He served as secretary-treasurer of the National Negro Bar Association, which supported "members of our race who have rights, liberties, and properties to protect."[18] Jones attacked the convict labor system in Arkansas that exploited black and white prisoners and had sued a planter for $75,000 in federal court for mistreatment of leased convicts.

---

[18] "(Extra) Ordinary Men," 352.

Jones's efforts helped save these Elaine defendants when the U.S. Supreme Court delivered an opinion revolutionary in its Civil Rights implications. It said that the 12 sharecroppers had been denied a fair trial and reversed the federal appeals court's decision. It remanded the case for reconsideration of the facts.[19] Writing a majority opinion in *Moore v. Dempsey*, Justice Oliver Wendell Holmes said that their convictions came at the hands of an all-white jury when Phillips County was two-thirds black. He called these trials a charade and that "if the case is that the whole proceeding is a mask – that counsel, jury, and judge were swept away to the fatal end by an irresistible wave of public passion, and that the state courts failed to correct the wrong – neither perfection in the machinery for correction nor the possibility that the trial court and counsel saw no other way of avoiding an immediate outbreak of the mob can prevent this court from securing to the petitioners their constitutional rights."[20] In 1925, authorities released the twelve men sentenced to die and 75 others. No white killers were charged.

---

[19] David Levering Lewis, *W.E.B. Du Bois. The Fight for Equality and the American Century 1919-1963* (New York: Henry Holt and Company, 2000), 9-10.
[20] *Moore v. Dempsey*, 261 U. S. 86 (1923)

Top, a mob gathered at Elaine to observe what appears to be the body of a victim in the ditch. Bottom, body of a woman with her throat cut during the massacre. Arkansas State Archives

Ku Klux Klan rally at unknown location. John S. Beebe Photographs. University of Arkansas Special Collections.

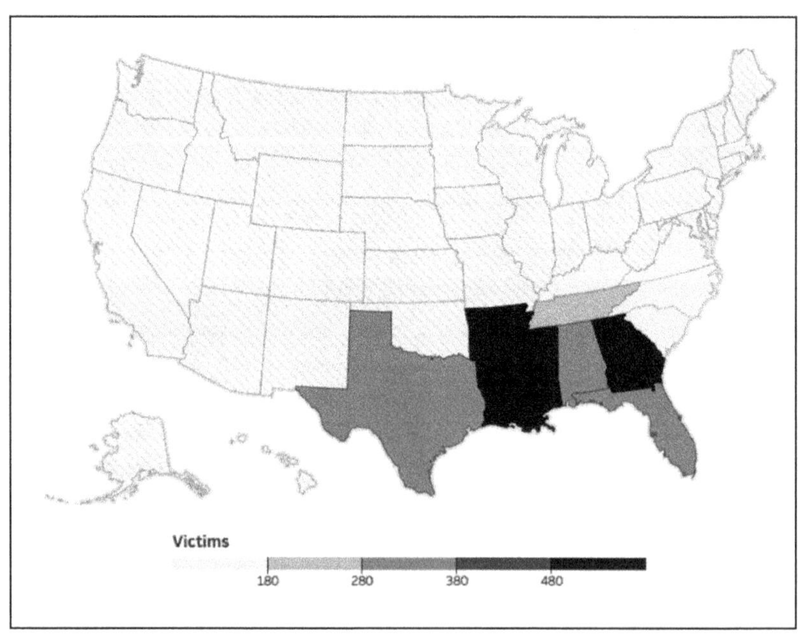

A gauge of lynchings in the South, 1877-1950. Equal Justice Initiative.

CHAPTER 11

We Ain't Got Nothin'

Complaints about Delta planters abusing farm workers poured into the NAACP. H. L. Henderson, a Crittenden County NAACP member, described several cruel Delta landlords and their abuses.

> *Crosby "beat a colored man half to death and run him off."*
>
> *Johnson beat a man "and taken his mule and hogs and chickens and household goods."*
>
> *E. Williams "got all of his people starving and in debt . . . and won't pay them."*[1]

Walter Rowland, a tenant farmer from Holly Grove, summed up his opinion of the sharecropper's dilemma. "De landlord is landlord, de politicians is landlord, de judge is landlord, de shurf is landlord, ever'body is landlord, an we ain't got nothin!" [2]

Some black residents successfully rebelled against white authorities during January 1920. A sheriff and two deputies arrested Dock Hays about ten miles from Dumas. They charged him with

[1] H. L. Henderson to Mary White Ovington, November 28, 1921, NAACP Papers, Group1, Box G11.
[2] Tom E. Terrell and Jerrold Hirsch, eds., *Such As Us: Southern Voices of the Thirties* (Chapel Hill: University of North Carolina Press, 1978), 56.

stealing hogs from a nearby plantation, but armed black men freed Hays. Fearing a violent confrontation, the sheriff and Dumas city marshal called for support. The governor dispatched about 130 soldiers who arrived on January 22 and departed the next day after discovering a peaceful town. Some white residents blamed this trouble on pro-union literature circulating in the area and union organizers, but *Arkansas Gazette* interviews discredited this theory. They pointed out that racial tension had long been present in the vicinity. As was the case throughout the South, when black residents armed themselves for defense, authorities often played the insurrection card. Black families needed weapons in part for protection from nightriders using intimidation and violence against them, and sometimes authorities intervened against these terrorists. A Marion court fined three klansmen $500 and sentenced them to 12 months in prison for threatening black families in Crittenden County. Planters opposed nightriding when it did not further their interests. A Craighead County court convicted 31 men for barn burning and other property destruction. In some instances landlords hired klan members to protect their workers from nightriders, an irony indeed. Though klansmen probably took part in or approved of 28 lynchings in Arkansas during the 1920s, humiliation and beatings were more common. Some courageous black men retaliated against planter-inflicted humiliation and violence. D. M. Peak on the Fletcher plantation in Lonoke County sued Tom and Burel Fletcher for $10,000 after they forced Peak to his knees and pistol-whipped him. As a result of this elderly man's lawsuit the Fletchers made his family gather their possessions and leave the plantation.[3]

Some black protesters paid the highest price possible. Perhaps the most infamous lynching in Delta history developed from a crop share dispute. By the early 1900s, planters avoided Christmas settlements because the money gave renters too much independence. Landlords claimed that if tenants received Christmas settlements they would not work until the money was gone and then ask for advances. This position ignored the fact that crop settlement money belonged to tenants, and planters had no right to withhold it. Henry Lowery confronted his landlord, O. T. Craig, about the tenant's share of money earned from Mississippi County crop sales, but the planter refused to settle-up. Lowery returned to Craig's house on Christmas Day and demanded his

---

[3] *American Congo*, 136.

money. The planter reportedly threatened him, and Lowery shot to death Craig and his daughter and wounded two sons. Lowery's escape took him to El Paso, Texas. Unfortunately, he wrote a friend in Mississippi County about plans to relocate his family, and the postmaster gave Lowery's letter to authorities. When Arkansas deputies brought him back, vigilantes blocked the train at Sardis, Mississippi, and seized Lowery. After this kidnapping a *Memphis News Scimitar* in January 1921 publicized plans to lynch him. One headline read, "Lowery Lynchers Announce Program. Negro to Pay Mob's Penalty for Crime." The newspaper printed a map with the location of this well-publicized lynching, and another story provided details. "Lowery Nears Tree On Which It is Planned to Hang Him." Instead, the mob chained him to a log, surrounded it with leaves soaked in gasoline, and slowly roasted Lowery. The *Hayti Herald* in Missouri reported on February 5, 1921, that it took 40 minutes until his last "death agony." Members of the mob remained until the victim's body became a "charred mass and life was extinct."

The definition of lynching and number of Arkansas victims are problematical. What separated those who lynched from those who murdered? How many black men disappeared in swamps without a trace and remain uncounted? An accurate count seems unlikely. The NAACP in 1940 proposed the following requirements for lynching: "there is evidence that a person was killed; the killing was illegal; at least three people were involved in killing the victim; and the killing was justified with reference to tradition, justice, or honor."[4] Many lynchings in the Delta possessed these requirements and often resulted from disputes about debts, earnings, and working conditions. In 1918 a mob murdered Elton Mitchell in Crittenden County for allegedly wounding W. M. Langston's wife. A June 22, 1918, *Chicago Defender* reported that the dispute developed when Mitchell refused to work for the planter without compensation. Members of the mob carved him up and hanged his remains in a tree. In another incident, a mob lynched Clyde Ellison during June 1919. He supposedly assaulted the daughter of a Lincoln County farmer, David Bennett. One account indicated that the lynch mob put a noose around Ellison's neck and forced him to jump off a bridge. However, a July 5, 1919, *Colorado Statesman*

---

[4] Guy Lancaster, ed. *Bullets and Fire. Lynching and Authority in Arkansas, 1840-1950*. (Fayetteville: University of Arkansas Press, 2018), 5.

attributed the murder to Ellison's refusal to labor in Bennett's cotton patch for a paltry 85 cents per day. The planter invented an assault charge to scare Ellison into working for him, but the ruse failed. A mob tortured Ellison with a hot iron and left his body hanging from a bridge. They posted a sign saying that "This is how we treat lazy niggers." Sometimes law officers encouraged a lynching. In 1927 a mob seized Owen Flemming after he allegedly killed an overseer named J. H. Woods in Phillips County. Some members of the lynch mob asked Sheriff J. D. Mays to take Flemming into custody, but he refused. "I'm busy. Just go ahead and lynch him," the sheriff supposedly said. The mob shot Flemming to death. According to a June 18, 1927, *Pittsburgh Courier*, "Along with other phrases, this will go down in history as one of the most notable ever delivered, for it conveyed into the hands of a white mob of five hundred people the living form of Owen Flemming ... and made of him one more sacrifice upon the bloody altar of the reign of this country's uncrowned sovereign – 'King Lynch Em.'"

Lynch mobs contained people from all classes of southern society, and remarkably, law officers could never identify their members. Methods used in these killings included beating, cutting, hanging, burning, shooting, and sometimes several of them. Participants and onlookers generally numbered in the teens, but sometimes in the thousands. Many onlookers considered lynchings a form of entertainment, and newspapers announced these sadistic coming attractions. Journalist H. L. Mencken, no fan of southern culture, or lack of it, said that "lynching often takes the place of the merry-go-round, the theatre, the symphony orchestra, and other diversions common to larger communities.[5] Unfortunately, newspaper headlines that facilitated attendance at lynchings made Mencken's dreadful observation uncomfortably close to the truth. Many black people died after objecting to denial of their voting rights, attempting to sue an employer, and involvement in union activities. Accusations of rape made up a large category, but sassing a white person or giving a fresh look could lead to violence. This last infraction came to be called reckless eyeballing. Actions deemed disrespectful to whites brought outrageous reactions. In July 1922, murderers shot to death John West in woods near Guernsey for insubordination. Mobs killed women as well. A Georgia mob murdered the pregnant Mary Turner because she

---

[5] Walter White, "The Mind of the Lyncher." Qtd. in *Bullets and Fire*, 116.

threatened to give authorities the names of those who lynched her husband. After hanging her they burned Mrs. Turner's body.[6]

Such atrocities had a chilling effect. As a result, though letters to the NAACP during the early 1920s reported numerous cases of peonage, few witnesses agreed to testify. White juries acquitted peonage defendants regardless of guilt, and judges imposed light sentences in rare convictions. Victims hesitated risking their lives with acquittal of abusive employers a forgone conclusion. When blacks went to court charged with crimes their trials sometimes became an extension of vigilantism. Legal executions rather than lynching had the same effect on black observers. Of the relatively few black defendants acquitted in trials, several were shot dead before leaving the courthouse.[7]

NAACP members looked into investigations, trials, and their consequences, and didn't like what they saw. The organization received many appeals for help from peonage victims. Notices of abuse caused William Pickens, an NAACP field secretary, to warn that the sharecropping system turned laborers into slaves. He called tenant-landlord arrangements debt-slavery sanctioned by law. S. B. Argain from Pinckney wrote the NAACP on June 1, 1921, about a method of intimidation used by planter henchmen. They took black men to a river, tied their hands and feet, and dunked them until they told their persecutors what they wanted to hear. Then the kidnappers notified Crittenden County law officers to come get the victims.[8]

Some black residents in the Delta put themselves in great peril when they wrote to the justice department for assistance to help their neighbors. A Mississippi County man wrote that "We as negroes here at this place need protection and must have it. Now listen, we have a man here in our community that I think is treating the negro real brutish and there is no help for it." He whips his workers "some time unmerciful, without a cause. He had a widow woman with him this year

---

[6] *American Nightmare*, 132.
[7] Michael J. Klarman, *From Jim Crow to Civil Rights. The Supreme Court and the Struggle for Racial Equality* (New York: Oxford University Press, 2004), 120.
[8] John H. Bracey Jr. and August Meir, eds. *Papers of the NAACP. Part 10. Peonage, Labor and the New Deal 1913-1939* (Bethesda, Md.: University Publications of America, 1990) S. B. Argain to J. E. Spingarn, June 1, 1921, Reel 16, Group 1, Box C386.

and whipped her until she was sent to the asylum [and is] now whipping her children unconscious at times, without a cause. He and the other two men whipped a negro this summer until he died the next day . . . and castrated him . . . in the presents [sic] of a white lady and his wife. We as negroes cant help ourselves, the white people don't seem to be very much interested about it. Will you send a man for him or to take care of the situation for us, or shall we continier [sic] to beg for mercy. Is it possible that we must continue to cry for help and can't get it."[9]

In another Delta peonage case reported to the NAACP a member from St. Francis County claimed that Charlie Hulett operated a convict farm using black men arrested on trumped-up charges. According to John Callie, Hulett and cronies confronted James Dunlap as he returned home from work. They found an NAACP pin on him, took his money and pistol, shot him, and hauled Dunlap to the farm without telling his pregnant wife where he was. Jim Coleman, an NAACP member, said that Hulett maintained an environment of fear. He "hunts up things . . . to keep us stirred up scared all the time [and] will kill a colored man if he looks too straight and so my members has a hard way to go."[10]

Residing in Peace, Arkansas, Reverend W. H. Booker added to the list of atrocities. He wrote the NAACP in February 1922:

> *We have no law to protect us. The system of debt slavery rules in this county. If a negro is arrested, he is taken to jail kept there a while then he is taken to a big man's farm and put to work without any trial whatever. Whenever a white man kills a negro he is taken and buried and that is all there is to it. If a negro commits a crime against the State, if he promises the white man that he will work for him in the cotton field, that settles that case. One big white man rules the eastern half of the county, and what he says go, law or no law. There are men on some of these farms here that don't know what it is to have a settlement. If they attempt to leave their account is run up so high until the next man will not pay it off.*

---

[9] R. H. to Department of Justice, December 14, 1925. Department of Justice peonage files, Reel 10, 50-9-2.
[10] Jim Coleman to NAACP, May 19, 1922, NAACP Papers, Group 1, Box G11.

Josie Coleman also reported abuse in a letter dated June 12, 1922.

> *White people here have got some of our members under slavery yet telling them they got to chop their crops until they open ready to pick drives an curses our members like dogs. Man carry his pistol over our members do the women like he do the men, drives the women to work without they cooking any dinner. Some days they got to go that field the white agent behind them running them.*

An NAACP letter to the justice department illustrated difficulties turning such peonage reports into prosecutions. The association received two letters alleging violations in St. Francis County and sought a federal investigation of persons allegedly violating peonage laws. These letters came from Jim Coleman of Democrat, Arkansas. The NAACP said that it frequently received such reports, but lacked the necessary funds to investigate the facts before reporting them to the justice department. However, "as far as we are able, we always try to ascertain, if possible, the truth regarding these cases before reporting them to you. Will you be good enough to advise us as to the proper method of procedure in such cases."[11]

Complaints in Mississippi County produced an investigation of collusion between a county judge and planters, which led to a June 24, 1922, report. Federal agents investigated C. S. Driver, G. C. Driver, and Judge G. E. Keck for possible peonage violations. The Driver brothers had a contract with Keck for maintaining prisoners, and G. C. Driver went to Blytheville on Monday mornings to pick them up. That town had three justices of the peace, and many misdemeanor cases went before Justice W. S. Smith. He told an investigator that Keck instructed him to commit all prisoners convicted in Smith's court to the Driver farm. Justice Ed Walker told the same story. Keck refused to be interviewed. Though this case displayed several characteristics of peonage, in other ways it did not. A federal agent found satisfactory living conditions at the Driver farm and no armed guards monitoring field workers. According to the inspection, prisoners appeared to be satisfied with conditions. In an August 7, 1922, letter to the U. S. Attorney General, an Assistant U. S. Attorney in Little Rock made reference to the report. He called this contract between the Drivers and

---

[11] NAACP Papers, Reel 16, Group 1, Box C386.

Keck pursuant to Arkansas laws. It did not appear that the brothers held prisoners after sentence expiration or that they treated anyone inhumanely. Consequently, the U. S. Attorney did not recommend criminal prosecution since the contract did not violate federal statutes.[12]

The klan continued to disregard federal statutes and state laws as well. More than 1,000 members attended a rally in Little Rock during 1922. Leaders claimed a membership of 25,000 from throughout the state. The organization had its share of rabble, but many respectable people as well. A female legislator said that everybody who was anybody and everybody who wanted to be somebody joined. Her boss joined, her friends joined, and she joined.[13] A rally in Helena during 1923 drew about 10,000 persons from several states. The November 11, 1923, *New York Herald* declared the Arkansas klan thriving in rural regions and towns. A reporter pegged state membership at approximately 50,000 persons. The klan gathered renewed strength in the 1920s by combining racial prejudice, ethnic hostility, and moral authoritarianism. The organization accepted native-born white Protestants at least 18 years old willing to adhere to its standards, sometimes preached from fundamentalist pulpits. Its leadership claimed to be lineal descendants of those who opposed Republicans and freedmen during Reconstruction. Members spewed out hatred of "Catholics, Jews, Negroes, foreigners, and radicals." [14] They also attacked bootleggers, prostitutes, adulterers, and crooked politicians. Arkansas must have provided a target-rich environment.

Racism of this sort and financial restrictions contributed to a notable decline of black Delta residents in the 1920s. Chicot County lost 11.3 percent of its black population; Desha, 11.5 percent; Lee, 11.9 percent, and Phillips, 6.9 percent. [15] An Arkansas revenue collector sought to stem the tide. Colonel H. L. Remmel petitioned President Calvin Coolidge to keep black workers in the state, but that attempt failed. Though worried about insufficient labor to make and harvest crops, planters refused to change their ways. Rather than accept

[12] Department of Justice, Mails and Files Division, Reel 19, 50-611.
[13] Michael B. Dougan, *Arkansas Odyssey. The Saga of Arkansas from Prehistoric Times to Present* (Little Rock, Ark.: Rose Publishing Co., 1993), 395.
[14] Charles C. Alexander, "White–Robed Reformers: The Ku Klux Klan Comes to Arkansas, 1921-1922," *Arkansas Historical Quarterly* 22:1 (Spring 1963), 9, 12.
[15] U. S. censuses, 1920 and 1930.

reasonable accommodations with farm workers, landlords and political allies sought to hinder migration. In 1923, Arkansas increased maximum penalties for persons convicted under state enticement laws. In the antebellum South, slave traders arranged for reallocation of labor from areas of abundance to places of scarcity. After the Civil War, recruiters provided this service, and planter attitudes depended on whether a landlord had all the help he needed or needed all the help he could get. Some planters hired black recruiters who knew where to find available workers and could travel in areas less conspicuously than white agents. In an effort to restrict movement, Arkansas and other states required employers to grant discharge certificates to laborers "legitimately" leaving their service. A subsequent employer who hired a worker without this certificate could be prosecuted.

This example of an enticement prosecution occurred in Arkansas County. A justice of the peace there convicted S. H. Moore of enticing a laborer, George Butler, "negro," and the case ultimately landed in the state supreme court on appeal. That court clarified acts of enticement in *State v. Moore* on October 27, 1924. According to the state's evidence, J. A. Price in May 1924 hired Butler to help with the planter's rice crop. After Butler worked for three weeks, Price advanced him $15. Butler went to town and never returned. Moore admitted to Price that he hired Butler to help harvest timber, and a witness for the state testified that Moore said he knew that Butler was working for Price. However, the defendant told a different story. Moore claimed that he employed Butler after the hired hand quit working for Price. An Arkansas County Circuit Court "instructed a verdict of acquittal," and the state appealed. The state argued that the circuit court "was mistaken in its view of the law. Our statute provides that if any person shall interfere with, entice away, knowingly employ, or induce a laborer, who has contracted with another person for a specified time, to leave his employer before the expiration of his contract, without the consent of the employer, he shall, upon conviction, be fined not less than $25, nor more than $100." The state supreme court ruled that the circuit court erred in telling the jury, as a matter of law, that the defendant was not guilty of a violation of the statute." The guilt or innocence of the defendant should have been submitted to the jury as a question of fact to be determined by it. "It follows that the judgment will be reversed, and the cause remanded for a new trial."[16]

The Arkansas Supreme Court's decision in *Simonson v. Butler*, November 23, 1926, touched on the issue. According to C. E. Butler's testimony, he contracted with Katie Moffit Parks and her son to work 15 acres for him. Butler advanced Mrs. Parks $169 for furnish, but in July 1924, Mrs. Parks and her son moved without notice to S. E. Simonson's property. Butler and the boy did not get along, and the planter had slapped the boy. Butler demanded that Simonson pay Mrs. Parks's debt, but the defendant refused. Simonson testified that he told Mrs. Parks that he would not hire her, but would allow them to move into a vacant house he owned. Henry Dean, a witness, verified this account. Additionally, the defendant testified that Mrs. Parks did not move to his property until after she left Butler's land. A jury in Mississippi County Circuit Court rendered a verdict for Butler, and Simonson appealed. The state supreme court ruled that the evidence was not legally sufficient to support a verdict for the plaintiff, and the circuit court erred in not directing a verdict for the defendant. The judgment was reversed, and the cause remanded for a new trial.[17]

Not all Delta residents lacked compassion for workers. Genevieve Grant Sadler, an outsider who came to the region after marrying a resident, describes a heartbreaking scene:

> *It was while some snow was still on the ground that my neighbor called me to the window of her sitting-room, one afternoon when we had been sitting by her fire sewing. "Look out there and you will see something that will make your heart ache," she said. I looked and saw that cotton pickers were picking the cotton in the field close to her house. Men, women and children were there, with their pinched faces and ragged clothes. One very young woman dragged along a little soap box, with heavy disks of wood cut for wheels. In this box was a little boy, just old enough to sit up. The child wore nothing but a short bit of a cotton dress and a tiny ragged cotton sweater. The poor mother wore a thin cotton dress, and had no wrap whatever. There were tears in my*

[16] 166 Ark. 412, 265 S. W. 363.
[17] 171 Ark. 1189, 287 S. W. 1014.

eyes. We were standing by a roaring fire, and I knew how bitterly the wind was blowing outside. But my neighbor assured me that her daughter was hunting up some of her children's old clothes to take out to the girl, and that I needn't cry, for if I did I would be always in tears. "There are lots who are worse off than those you see there. You'll get used to it if you stay in the South." But would I? It was my first inkling of the bottomless pit of misery.[18]

This scene supported historian George B. Tindall's observation that the South suffered from a white plague – cotton. The crop caused a bottomless pit of misery. However, cotton paid for many southern empires, and British mills wrote the checks. Planters continued to be a major supplier to industry in England and New England. To flourish, cotton plants need about 200 days of warm weather and moderate rainfall. Rows run parallel about a yard apart with 12 inches between plants. Flowers form bolls that in the fall pop open releasing fluffy cotton. During those years harvesting by hand usually began in August, and a late crop might require picking during cold Decembers. Cotton gins compressed lint into 500-pound bales shipped to manufacturers here and abroad.[19] Cotton production required intensive hand labor well into the 20th Century. Mexican workers provided a portion of it, and they sometimes filed complaints with their embassy about landlord mistreatment. One involved Lee Wilson's plantation company. A December 4, 1925, Mexican Embassy letter to the U. S. Secretary of State said it received information about a large group of Mexican laborers in a trying situation at Wilson. They claimed that the company failed to follow through on promises when it recruited Mexican families. An agent hired workers in Texas, offering them $1.50 per 100 pounds for picking cotton. When they arrived the price apparently fell to $1 and eventually to 60 cents. Pickers had neither a written contract nor a way of returning to Texas, and they spoke little or no English. Some workers claimed that company foremen intimidated and threatened them. After a stream of letters between the embassy, state department, and justice department an investigation commenced. A federal agent interviewed many Wilson employees who denied being harassed and did not observe threatening behavior. Language barriers

---

[18] Genevieve Grant Sadler, *Muzzled Oxen. Reaping Cotton and Sowing Hope in 1920s Arkansas* (Little Rock, Ark.: Butler Center Books, 2014), 73.

[19] Gene Dattel, *Cotton and Race in The Making of America. The Human Costs of Economic Power* (New York: Ivan R. Dee, 2009), 32.

caused some misunderstandings, and rainy weather produced others. It reduced picking time and anticipated earnings.[20]

Arkansas authorities also investigated the Wilson company. Governor Tom J. Terral authorized the state treasurer, D. H. Blackwood, to look into labor conditions at the company's camps. A Mexican vice consul from New Orleans accompanied Blackwood. The state treasurer's report included the following statements. "I found that there were two or three dissatisfied Mexicans in the bunch, who had caused all the trouble simply because they felt that they were not making enough money, however, I will say that at least two-thirds of the entire population there were perfectly satisfied and told us that they had never been treated any better than Mr. Wilson and his men had treated them." The report declared that "I never found a man or woman in the whole bunch who said that they had been mistreated in any way, and as I have stated before, the only grievance any of them had was just because it rained too much and they could not make enough money." The investigation concluded that Wilson had "doubly fulfilled" his contract. "I will say he has done more than he agreed to do. His agreement was to pay them one dollar and twenty five cents per hundred to pick, furnish a house, wood, water and pick sack, but he furnished them bedding and advanced them food when they were not able to work." As to the complaint that Wilson's foreman carried a gun, "this is all false and unfounded. The only pistol that anyone knew about was one that Mr. Ellison, a foreman, took off of a Mexican. Of course, that Mexican was put off the job and naturally made a big holler." Blackwood decided that "I cannot see where any wrong has been done any of them, and on the other hand they have been treated better than they even expected. Due to the fact of there being no evidence of a violation of the Slave Trade and Peonage Act, this investigation is closed."[21]

Other embassy complaints accused Delta planters of mistreatment. Though the American government agreed to work with Mexican officials, the Francisco Cervantes case indicated limits of cooperation due to higher priorities. A justice department agent reported in August 1924 that a constable removed Cervantes from a train at Wynne and charged him with trespassing on railroad property. A justice of the

---

[20]Department of Justice, Mail and Files Division, Reel 24, 50-636.

[21] Department of Justice, Reel 24, 50-636.

peace fined him $15 and tacked on costs, which raised the debt to $40.90. A man named Sampson paid costs only and put the Mexican to work on a dredge boat under contract with a county judge. Using armed guards, Sampson controlled more than a dozen prisoners, black and white. The Mexican Consul General in New Orleans charged that Sampson held Cervantes in peonage at Fair Oaks and requested a copy of the investigation report. The state department forwarded this request to the attorney general. He advised the state department that while this report did not contain confidential information, "it would be unwise to furnish a copy of said report to the Mexican government in view of the confidence in which all such reports are held, and in view further of the precedent which it would establish and which might later in some other case be embarrassing." Following this suspicious reply, the state department asked the justice department to provide a statement to the consul concerning this case in lieu of a full report. So the attorney general sent a memorandum to the embassy. According to this document, after Cervantes paid his fine authorities released him.[22]

[22] Department of Justice, Division of Records, Reel 10, 50-4-1.

Scenes during the 1927 flood. Top, sandbagging the levee near Lake Village, Arkansas, with Lakeport Plantation in the background. Bottom, flood refugees camped out on the levee at Arkansas City. Library of Congress Prints and Photographs Division.

CHAPTER 12

God and the Mississippi

Some Delta planters found themselves under investigation and under water during spring 1927. "People in the Delta fear god and the Mississippi River," said David L. Cohen in the April 21, 1977, Greenville, Mississippi, *Delta Democrat*. They had good reason. In 1927 the Mississippi River and tributaries flooded about 26,000 square miles in seven states, and misery rose with the river. Willie Williams, who lived in a southern Delta county, recalled its impact. "Oh yeah. The flood of '27. They give us plenty of time to get out after the levee broke. They warned us to get to the hills because they couldn't hold it. And so it broke up here, and you could hear that water roarin'. I was at that time 12 years old. You could hear it comin'. People runnin', going to the hills with wagons and horses and what not. You couldn't tell where the lake [Lake Chicot] started. You could see houses goin' down the lake, floatin'. You could see houses, chickens settin' up on top of them. Dogs barkin' on top of somethin'. Done got up on a house or somethin' and be floatin' down the lake there. Caskets even. I done seen caskets come up out of the ground. Dead bodies in them, floatin' down the lake." Flooding hurt the rich, but devastated the poor. "What could they do," Williams said. "They done lost everything they had." [1]

---

[1] Willie Williams, Lake Village, Arkansas. Interview with Mike Bowman and Greg Hansen, September 20, 2003. Transcript, Lakeport Plantation Collection, Arkansas State University.

Water rushed southward in a path several miles wide and 100 or more feet deep, moving at about nine miles per hour. A *New Orleans Tribune* on February 3, 1927, reported that both the White and Little Red rivers in Arkansas broke through levees and flooded about 100,000 acres. Approximately 5,000 Arkansans lost their homes in this deluge. Major John Lee, in charge of Mississippi River Commission's Vicksburg office, mustered resources to reinforce levees and hold back the rising tide. He commanded about 1,500 full-time levee workers and maintained six contractor camps known to be brutal by those with knowledge of them. At each isolated location one or two white overseers supervised about 200 black laborers. In addition, Lee and local levee boards drafted plantation employees. Levee breaks on one side of the river relieved pressure on the other, which made residents on each side watch for saboteurs. A *Jackson Clarion-Ledger* reported on February 5 an incident in Marked Tree on the St. Francis River. A four-foot-deep gash appeared at the top of a levee, so armed men stood guard at that weak spot. They shot four men trying to plant 105 sticks of dynamite to blow up the levee. Many things can cause levees to collapse: a piece of wood that rots and creates a cavity, burrowing animals, and crawfish nests. The river assaults these weak points until the earth gives way, but the biggest threat to levees is the constant pressure of water against them. It saturates the earth, weakens it, and rips it apart.

In March the oldest levee in Arkansas, Laconia Circle, dissolved into the Mississippi River. The St. Francis, Black, White, and Arkansas rivers approached or reached record levels and overcame levees. Desperation led Arkansas Senator T. H. Caraway to wire Dwight Davis, U. S. Secretary of War, requesting tents, boxcars, and available houses for Phillips County to shelter refugees. In another message to Davis he said that in Forrest City about 5,000 persons needed shelter and food. The Mississippi Flood Control Association wired Davis that about 6,000 refugees in Helena lacked food. As misery mounted so did levee failures. The *New York Times* reported breached levees at Big Lake in northeast Arkansas and at Whitehall Landing on the St. Francis River. On April 13, tornadoes ripped through the region. Under cover of chaos caused by the storm, troublemakers attempted to dynamite another Arkansas levee. An initial explosion did little damage, however, because guards opened fire before all the charges could be properly set, according to the *Greenville Democrat-Times* on April 22, 1927. Amid obstacles caused by man and nature, workers attempted to reinforce levees with mud boxes, plank walls, and sandbags. Plugging weak spots called for thousands of sandbags, each one filled, carried, and stacked by hand. Wet sandbags weighed from 60 to 80 pounds so this process required continuous, back-breaking work in a hazardous environment. Men sometimes slipped, fell into the river, and disappeared, but work went on without them. The Associated Press on April 19, 1927, reported that attempts to save levees on the White River had been abandoned. Levees collapsed that day at New Madrid, Missouri, dooming one million acres in Missouri and Arkansas.

On both sides of the Mississippi River, police patrolled black neighborhoods and commandeered men for levee work. Those who refused were jailed, beaten, or shot. A *Democrat Times* on April 21, 1927, described a scene when water rushed over a levee. Black workers initially ran to the spot, but seeing a hopeless situation they retreated. Armed guards forced them back to the levee at gunpoint. Several hundred of them filled sandbags and heaved them onto the barrier, but water quickly swept the bags away. When this levee broke, water carried off everything in its path, including people. The *Memphis Commercial Appeal* on April 22, 1927, reported that "It was impossible to recover the bodies swept onward by the current at an enormous rate of speed." On April 24, 1927, the *Jackson Clarion-Ledger* quoted refugees from Greenville claiming that "there is not the slightest doubt in their minds that several hundred negro plantation workers lost their lives in the great sweep of water which swept over the country." In Arkansas a levee crew foreman killed a black man named Nathan Nunley near the White River. Nunley told the foreman directing men filling sandbags that he could not help since he was on his way to get a doctor for his ill wife. The overseer killed him anyhow.[2] Arkansas newspapers owned and operated by black journalists publicized the dreadful state of affairs, following a tradition of exposing ill-treatment of black citizens. Tabbs Gross began publishing the state's first newspaper for black people, the *Freedmen,* during 1869. Talbot Bailey published the *Little Rock Sun* in 1885 and became a strong and vocal supporter of equal rights for the races, that is, until he disappeared. Black spokesmen who criticized a society controlled by the white majority needed real backbone. And that, they had.

White residents welcomed arrival of Mississippi National Guard members, but blacks came to dread them. The Guard forced men they

---

[2] *Arkansas Odyssey*, 411.

deemed able-bodied to work or not receive food rations for their families. In many respects levee camps became slave labor sites with guardsmen maintaining order. "The Guard had power of the most elemental kind. They had guns and controlled men in a camp. Even without the complication of race, such power intoxicates, creates arrogance. And there was race." Witnesses described black workers being knocked in the head with guns, thrown down and kicked, denied food, and victimized in other ways. Addie Oliver, who witnessed abuse, said in an interview that blacks were treated "like dogs."[3] Horror stories soon arrived in northern newsrooms and resulted in graphic headlines. A May 6, 1927, *Chicago Defender*: "Refugees Herded Like Cattle to Stop Escape from Peonage" and "Deny Food to Flood Sufferers; Relief Bodies Issue Work or Starve Rule." A *Pittsburgh Courier* on May 14, 1927: "Conscript Labor Gangs Keep Flood Refugees in Legal Bondage." A *New York Tribune* on May 28, 1927: "Peonage Charged. Walter White, Negro Novelist, says Members of his Race Are Being Victimized as Result of Disaster. Negroes are held in peonage in the Mississippi flood area." White declared after touring the region that "Negro tenants are prevented from leaving concentrations camps without the consent of their landlords, and are being charged for flood relief administered to them. In many refugee camps . . . Negroes are released only to their landlords [and] are sent back to the plantation from which they came." A press report out of Memphis confirmed stories of black men being forced to work at gunpoint. Liberty Life Insurance Company inspectors traveling from Little Rock to Memphis saw "a crowd of Negro and white men, most of them in overalls, many of them waiting for the train to take them to various points." Three white men on horses rode up and ordered the black men to get on up the road. "We need you up there." They were forced to go.

A *Houston Informer* reported "awful suffering among black residents . . . how Negro men are kept in virtual slavery in the refugee camps by armed soldiers, at the behest of plantation owners and demagogic politicians, the latter being mere puppets and mannikins [sic] in the hands of these white planters. Negroes are held in abject peonage, a type of slavery more vicious and dehumanizing than [a] human mind can conjure or comprehend." The newspaper also charged that state militiamen assaulted black women in refugee camps. A white

---

[3] John M. Barry, *Rising Tide. The Great Mississippi Flood of 1927 and How It Changed America* (New York: Simon & Schuster, 1997), 315.

soldier died when a husband entered his tent unexpectedly and found the soldier "outraging" his wife. Authorities allegedly assigned husbands of desired women to night shifts so white soldiers could "ravage" these women under cover of darkness.

W. A. Percy, son of LeRoy Percy of Sunnyside notoriety, remembered this crisis differently. He describes numerous problems when Greenville's mayor appointed him chairman of a flood relief committee and local Red Cross board. The mayor charged him with rescuing, housing, and feeding about 60,000 persons and 30,000 head of livestock. [4] Percy became exasperated with planters and black families. Blacks did not want to move from plantations to soggy levees, and landlords agreed. Percy accused planters of thinking about their pocketbooks and not welfare of the black community. He blamed newspaper criticism on an irresponsible press, claiming that the "Negro press of the North" started a campaign of vilification directed at him. Percy disputed charges that he had sewage unloaded in a black residential neighborhood while white patrons played golf at the country club. Percy pointed out that the golf course was under water, and the town's sewerage system never ceased to function. He called it "unfortunate that the Delta Negroes could read Negro newspapers during the flood." [5] Sidney Dillon Redmond, a prominent black physician and attorney from Mississippi, observed treatment of levee workers and declared it peonage. In an April 30, 1927, letter to President Calvin Coolidge he complained about planters holding their employees at gunpoint for fear they would run away. Perry Howard, another prominent black leader, wrote the attorney general on May 4, 1927, about "colored refugees," employees of landlords in the Mississippi Valley being held in a state of peonage in refugee camps.[6]

Despite negative press accounts, abuse of black families continued. This form of peonage persisted due to the "inability of Americans to

---

[4] William Alexander Percy, *Lanterns On the Levee. Recollections of a Planter's Son* (New York: Alfred A. Knopf, 1941), 251. A descendant of slaveholders, Percy was born in 1885 into a prominent southern family. He inherited the Old South's culture and defended southern traditions that supported it. Percy disdained northern liberals and despised a black press that questioned his beliefs and activities.

[5] *Lanterns,* 263-264.

[6] Redmond to Coolidge, April 30, 1927, Department of Justice, File 50-637-2, Rg. 60, National Archives. Howard to the attorney general, May 4, 1927, Department of Justice, File 50-637-2, Rg. 60, National Archives.

believe that anything akin to slavery could continue to exist in the United States. The idea was unbearable and consequently unthinkable." [7] Though Greenville's situation received inordinate publicity, mistreatment of black families existed throughout the region. L. M. Moore, president of the Pine Bluff NAACP chapter, wrote to the organization's headquarters on May 18, 1927, about dreadful treatment by Red Cross workers. The Red Cross denied these charges and demanded unavailable data to support complaints. However, an agency spokesman inadvertently provided this troubling response to a journalist's question. He said that treatment of blacks during the disaster was better than what they received in normal conditions. In charge of disaster services, the politically ambitious Herbert Hoover, U.S. Secretary of Commerce at the time, understood the effect of such criticism on his career. He took the politician's path out of a political storm and created a committee to study which way the wind was blowing. Hoover appointed Dr. Robert Moton, head of Tuskegee Institute, to lead an investigation and tasked the committee with examining treatment of "colored folks" in concentration camps. Though Hoover attempted to get ahead of bad publicity, he could not outrun the press. A May 28, 1927, *New York Times* ran a story describing treatment of people held in camps. The reporter learned of black workers eluding guards and escaping, preferring to forego food, clothing, and shelter rather than being forced back to plantations from which the flood waters had driven them. Moton's committee estimated that of about 637,000 persons forced out of their homes, roughly 94 percent were from Arkansas, Mississippi, and Louisiana. Blacks made up approximately 69 percent of the 325,146 living in concentration camps.[8] To counteract criticism of the Red Cross, committee members said that the organization "is largely built upon chapter units operating on a county-wide basis, which in the final analyses, have immediate control of local administration." Commissioners praised Red Cross achievements and commended Hoover for taking prompt and rigorous action. The committee declared that the tremendous pressure of rescue efforts gave little time or opportunity for addressing racial antagonisms.[9]

---

[7] *Shadow of Slavery*, 171.

[8] Robert Russa Moton, Final Report of the Colored Advisory Commission. Mississippi Valley Flood Disaster, 1927 (Washington, D.C.: American Red Cross, May 21, 1929), 11.

[9] Moton report, 11-12, 14.

To assess devastated regions the commissioners split up and spread out. R. M. Roddy and Dr. L. M. McCoy drew the Delta. Along with H. C. Ray, Arkansas's first black agent for agricultural extension work among black families, they sought out people needing assistance. The three identified 893 such families and aided them. Their Arkansas survey found that except for a few instances, "colored people were being well treated when the full colored state committee entered the field."[10] These representatives revealed that camps with the most satisfactory conditions were those where black families had opportunities to assist in administration. Investigators followed a policy that limited scope of their report and avoided personal revelations of abuse. They declared it impossible to cite individual cases, favorable or otherwise, with specific names and incidents because it would burden the report with a mass of details. However, commissioners recognized systemic problems, verifying unequal treatment due in part to personal and group experiences preceding the flood. Arkansas investigators recommended elimination of armed white guards at black refugee camps, that black social workers conduct health clinics, and that two black men be delegated to visit camps and help direct relief distribution.[11] Pete Daniel says that Moton proposed to Hoover that his committee prepare another report. It would explain how treatment of black families during the flood epitomized life in the South. Moton added that "we were interested in a song that these people sang in the levee camps – that the flood had washed away the old account." They believed that the flood freed them from peonage. Moton pointed out severe discrimination, such as despicable Arkansas planters receiving relief supplies free and charging tenants for them. He said that workers faced one of the greatest labor problems in America, relations between planters and farm workers. Moton wanted his investigation to help relieve the hopeless condition under which these people lived.[12] As was the case wherever peonage flourished, victims admitted being afraid to tell the truth to investigators. According to those who suffered silently, if planters found out, those who talked too much would be killed.

---

[10] Moton report, 26.

[11] Moton report, 19-21.

[12] Robert Moton, Memo for the Committee (Moton Family Papers: Library of Congress, Washington, D. C.) General Correspondence, 48.

Top, on the road looking for work in Crittenden County, Arkansas, 1936. Photo by Carl Mydans. Bottom, tenants evicted from the Dibble Plantation for union activities, 1936. Photo by John Vachon. Farm Security Administration, Library of Congress Prints and Photographs Division.

CHAPTER 13

My Sister's Turn to Eat

Heart-breaking stories made the rounds in rural America during the Great Depression. An often repeated one related that a country schoolteacher told an obviously sick child to go home and get something to eat. "I can't," the girl replied. "It's my sister's turn to eat."[1] A letter came to the NAACP dated September 3, 1930, from Round Pond. The writer said that "people here is catching fish out of these mud holes and boiling them and eating them. The water is about 8 inches deep and there is about as many dead fish in the holes as there are live ones."[2] During the 1930s poor Delta families faced great challenges. And though some black families had moved upward, many whites passed them going the opposite direction.

Planters pulled them down with restrictive laws, unfavorable contracts, financial entrapment, and violence. Difficulties piled up and weighed down white as well as black tenant farmers during the decade. It started with an economic collapse in the late 1920s when the stock market crashed. At that time Arkansas ranked 46th in per capita income and first in per capita indebtedness. The plunging economy

---

[1] T. H. Watkins, *The Great Depression. America in the 1930s* (New York: Back Bay Books, 1993), 57.

[2] Round Pond resident to NAACP, September 3, 1930, NAACP Papers, Reel 16, Group 1, Box C386.

caused 66 banks to close, soon followed by 46 others. Since most Delta farmers borrowed money from banks to make a crop, many went under along with their bank. A Mississippi County bank avoided ruin thanks to Lee Wilson. He heard there would be a run on Farmers Bank and sent for money from Memphis carried in armored trucks to be parked in front of the bank. After an hour or two of withdrawals, customers went home. Since they could get their money if they wanted it, why worry about it. That saved the bank.[3]

Difficulties intensified in 1930 when Delta farmers suffered from a devastating drought. Summer temperatures reached 110 degrees, and rainfall measured the lowest on record. According to an August 12, 1930, *Arkansas Gazette*, the Delta was suffering from the "most severe drought in climatological history." Arkansas congressmen asked President Hoover for assistance to avert human suffering during the coming winter, but the tone-deaf president said that help should come from neighbors and charities, not the government. Senator T. H. Caraway proposed that $15 million be allocated for food loans to Americans in greatest need, and the Red Cross estimated that about 250,000 Arkansans qualified. Though the U. S. Senate approved Caraway's plan, the House of Representatives voted it down. Appalled, the senator made a modest proposal. "If we are going to let them starve, why, I think we should just as well withdraw all relief at once. There is no use to torture humanity by giving them a bite today and a bite tomorrow so as to prolong their agony." Caraway pointed out that the federal government had recently refunded $126 million to corporations for tax overpayments.[4] The Arkansas governor also lacked sympathy for poor farmers. In a letter from Governor Marion Futrell to Arkansas Senator Joe T. Robinson the governor called them "subhuman."

R. E. Lee Wilson criticized the habits of some poor people. He wrote a letter in 1930 giving his views.

To My Employees & Friends –

The laws of human conduct are not changed by an economic upheaval, and it is just as true now that the spender will in the end

---

[3] Snowden, *Appreciating the Past*,125.

[4] Roger Lambert, "Hoover and the Red Cross in the Arkansas Drought of 1930," *The Arkansas Historical Quarterly* 29:1 (Spring 1970), 13.

come to want and the saver reap prosperity as it was before the panic. Fortunes will still be built on thrift and industry in the future as they have been in the past. The man with a little money saved up will be able to take advantage of opportunities that carry him to fortune. The man who has laid up something for his old age will be happy and independent, while the spender will never rise in the world and in his old age will know the bitterness of dependence.

A very wise man once said that the ability to save is the test of character. It takes strength and courage and the ability to deny oneself the things that one wants, but it is fatally easy to spend.

It seems to me that the ability to save is not only a test of character but a test of honesty and fairness and justice, because the spenders know well enough that in their need they are bound to rob the prudent. Somebody is bound to take care of them. Somebody has to feed and clothe them when they are out of work and sick and old.

I have known many spenders, who, while they were making money, indulged themselves in every luxury and who never saved a cent of their earnings. But their evil day came, as it does to us all, and then they grafted off their children or their sisters and brothers or friends, who had denied themselves in order to lay up a little money, and I have thought that these parasites were no better than thieves, for they should have provided for themselves.

So it becomes a matter of principle and character and self respect to save some of the money you earn instead of spending it all as you go along.[5]

Wilson's analysis had an obvious flaw. Many poor Delta residents had nothing squirrelled away because planters cheated them out of their earnings. Despite mistreatment, back-breaking labor, and enormous financial risk, tenants continued to farm. They made up a large percentage of Americans involved in agriculture. A 1930 census recorded that 73 percent of the nation's cotton farmers were tenants. In ten major cotton growing states about 937, 000 were white and 671,000

---

[5] Lee Wilson, "Boss Lee's 1930 Message," *Delta Historical Review* (Spring 1998), 25.

black. Though landlords complained of hard times, a survey of Delta planters reported an average annual net income of $4,743. (About $72,866 in 2019 dollars.) By comparison, doctors earned about $3,300. So the average landlord was hardly poverty-stricken.[6] Unfortunately, too little farm income trickled down to tenants. Protests by the Delta's poor usually ended badly because planters banded together to suppress them. One instance when it ended the other way occurred in 1931. Out of money, food, and patience, approximately 300 farmers, black and white, from Lonoke County marched into England, Arkansas, and refused to take no for an answer. The January 4, 1931, *Arkansas Gazette* reported what happened. The protestors demanded food from town merchants who asked the Red Cross to reimburse them. That agency declined because it lacked requisition forms. As the crowd's impatience grew, merchants reconsidered and distributed $1,500 worth of staples. The national press called this event a food riot. Will Rogers said that "Paul Revere just woke up Concord. Those birds woke up America."[7]

Black penitentiary labor suffered more than others during those lean years. A report about convict treatment in White County led to an investigation and suspicious conclusion. An unknown informant wrote the NAACP that "It is common talk here on the streets that some of the Negro prisoners working out fines under the County Judge have been unmercifully whipped. One man is said to have been lashed twenty times by a powerful boss." The writer identified himself as a white man who could not "stand to see the black folks abused even when criminals." On August 27, 1930, Little Rock Attorney John A. Hibbler wrote the NAACP about this claim. He referred to reported maltreatment of "Colored People" by local authorities around Bald Knob. Hibbler said that he investigated the matter and found nothing to sustain information sent to the justice department. He claimed that "I have been unable to find a single case as yet to justify the report." This conclusion is odd since he claimed not to have found one case, an unlikely situation in the region. Hibbler wrote the NAACP on September 19, 1930, to say that black residents in Searcy did not report a single instance of mistreatment. However, he admitted that "colored people living in smaller towns for the most part are afraid to give out

[6] Donald H. Grubbs, *Cry From the Cotton: The Southern Tenant Farmers Union and the New Deal* (Chapel Hill: University of North Carolina Press, 1971), 12.
[7] Donald Day, ed., *The Autobiography of Will Rogers* (New York: Houghton Mifflin, 1949), 237.

confidential information in reference to their mistreatment."[8] True, since snitching could result in severe beatings and death.

When the Red Cross attempted to help needy people some planters confiscated donations. Local committees often manipulated assistance to prevent workers from receiving aid during harvests, forcing them to work for low wages. After harvests, landlords put families back on Red Cross relief to reduce labor costs during winter months. Despite regulations prohibiting this practice, authorities required them to work for planters in order to receive benefits. The Red Cross announced its goal to provide $2 in monthly rations to each adult and 50 cents for each child. A family receiving $6 per month could buy 25 pounds of meal, 48 pounds of flour, 25 pounds of pinto beans, two gallons of molasses, 10 pounds of lard, 1.5 bushels of potatoes, 10 pounds of salt, one package of baking soda, and one can of baking powder.[9] But relief services in Poinsett County illustrated the ability of planters to subvert charitable efforts. Businessmen controlled county programs, and families who applied to the Red Cross for assistance claimed that administrators withheld benefits until they worked on private projects. Complaints led to an investigation, but the chairman of Marked Tree's Red Cross chapter defended work requirements. John Buxton said that the works program "eliminated the professional bum" and "the street corner daily gatherings of the hundreds who had nothing to do and would group up and talk about how badly they were being treated."[10] The *Arkansas Gazette* on September 25 and 26, 1931, reported a labor shortage in Phillips County and what authorities planned to do about it. Once again, the situation developed from low wages paid cotton pickers, 35 cents per hundred pounds. Coincidentally, Helena Chief of Police Lucian Webster decided to stamp out vagrancy in his town. He promised to make a house-to-house canvas if necessary to supply 1,000 additional workers needed by county planters.

Victims could not get help from elected officials because genuine democracy did not exist in the Delta, according to H. L. Mitchell, co-founder of the Southern Tenant Farmers Union (STFU). Planters and

---

[8] NAACP Papers, 16, Group 1, Box C387.

[9] Gail Murray, "Forty Years Ago: The Great Depression Comes to Arkansas," *Arkansas Historical Quarterly* 29:4 (Winter 1970), 298-299.

[10] Jeanne Whayne, *A New Plantation South: Land, Labor, and Federal Favor in Twentieth-Century Arkansas* (Charlottesville: University Press of Virginia, 1996), 153.

their political allies controlled elections. They bought blocks of poll tax receipts and gave them to people who would vote as directed. Arkansas had a semi-private ballot. Voters received a numbered ballot, and poll workers put the person's name beside that number so they could check who a person voted for. Politicians used this system to control the white vote, and Mitchell claimed that "The only Negro who had the vote in Arkansas was usually a white man's Negro."[11] In 1907, Arkansans passed Amendment No. 9 to the state constitution, which read in part that a 21-year-old citizen, a state resident for 12 months, in a county six months, in a precinct one month preceding an election, and who exhibited a poll tax receipt would be allowed to vote. A Mississippi County resident described methods used by local powers to dominate county politics. He called sheriffs powerful county officers because they issued poll tax receipts and solicited landlords to pay for them.[12] From a prominent Delta family, Hays T. Sullivan described the process of selecting candidates in Mississippi County. Planters and businessmen would meet and decide who they would support for state representative and senator. "That's pretty well the way it was. I can remember groups comin' into my daddy's office on a Saturday afternoon and maybe a Sunday afternoon and wanna know who they was supposed to vote for and how we were gonna vote. In most cases they just followed right along."[13]

By the time Franklin Roosevelt became president in 1933, many Delta day laborers and sharecroppers lived in shacks made from discarded lumber, the insides lined with newspapers to keep out a little of the cold and rain. Fortunate ones survived in shotgun houses. Work days started before dawn. Breakfast on good days consisted of biscuits, red-eye gravy, and maybe fatback. Family members, including older children, walked to the fields after breakfast and worked while supervised by riding bosses. Sometimes deputized, these overseers rode horses among laborers to ensure progress. After sunset the croppers returned to their shacks and a meager evening meal. Federal inspectors called their lives a "picture of squalor, filth, and poverty."[14] These

---

[11] H. L. Mitchell, "The Founding and Early History of the Southern Tenant Farmers Union," *Arkansas Historical Quarterly* 32: 4 (Winter 1973), 348-349.
[12] *Appreciating the Past*, 114.
[13] Hays Sullivan, Interview by author, March 24, 2002. Transcript. Southern Tenant Farmers Museum Collection, Arkansas State University.
[14] Louis Cantor, *Prologue to the Protest Movement: The Missouri Sharecropper Roadside Demonstration of 1939* (Durham, N. C.: Duke University Press, 1969), 14.

desperate people became the subject of books by John Steinbeck and Erskine Caldwell. The author of *Tobacco Road*, Caldwell declared that "Stretching from South Carolina to Arkansas, stench is a complacent nation's shame." He described southern people "subjected to the economic blood-sucking of the land-lord-elders and the politician-deacons," according to the May 10, 1936, *New York Times*. Caldwell said that though peonage was not condoned in theory, southerners found ways to justify it.

Johnny Rye's family sharecropped near Tyronza in the 1930s, and he described the life. They rose before daylight to start at sunup. "I picked a lot of cotton. A whole lot of cotton." Meals were plain, but "My mother was a great provider. She done the best with the least of anybody I seen. We just didn't have nothing." His mother went to the field in the morning and worked until about 11:00 a.m. when she returned home to cook. Like many others, his family attempted to work their way through life's difficulties. While Rye chopped cotton one day the landlord drove by. "I was having a hard time keeping up with the blacks," Rye admitted. The planter said, "Johnny, I know you need the money, but I can't stand to see you working like that." The landlord told Rye to go home. "I was just having to struggle . . . you know, I needed it," Rye exclaimed.[15]

Women hoed and picked tough rows beside men. From 1929 to 1933, economic opportunities for women declined lower than previous lows. A desperate widow wrote to the Red Cross. "I wish if you will please send me some clothes. Just enough to wear to the cotton patch." A depressed woman wrote that "I am near my row's end."[16] Works Progress Administration (WPA) sometimes failed to help. Male agents had trouble placing women in appropriate work accessible to their homes. Plus, they questioned what constituted women's work. Some believed raking leaves too hard on women, including those who plowed fields and picked cotton while pulling babies on their pick sacks. Peonage affecting women spread beyond cotton patches. The National Recovery Administration (NRA), called Negro Removal Act by sarcastic

---

[15] Johnny Rye, Tyronza, Arkansas. Interview by author, May 22, 2003. Transcript. Southern Tenant Farmers Museum Collection, Arkansas State University.
[16] Martha H. Swain, "A New Deal for Southern Women," *Women of the American South: A Multicultural Reader*. Christie Anne Farnham, ed. (New York: New York University Press, 1997), 243.

observers, established wage rates. It caused dismissal of black female workers at the Maid-Well Garment Company in Forrest City. The company employed 194 black seamstresses who did not receive an NRA-required $12 minimum weekly wage. Management paid them only $6.16 per week. Employees refrained from complaining to a local compliance board stacked with friends of company officials, but an anonymous employee notified NRA's Washington office. After learning of a coming investigation, management fired all 194 black workers, calling them too inefficient to be paid a higher wage. Following this NRA investigation the Arkansas director ordered restitution of back wages at $5.84 per week for each week the seamstresses had been unemployed during the investigation. A company executive refused to make restitution and destroyed employee records to prevent NRA from determining amounts owed in back wages.[17]

Another non-agricultural investigation focused on the lumber industry. A May 6, 1934, *Arkansas Democrat* ran a story headlined "Labor Bureau Probes Lumber Camp Peonage." It revealed cruel and revolting conditions in the state's lumber industry. According to the article, sawmill operators and timber cutters bound employees – black and white--in "economic servility which cannot be described in its full significance with the word peonage. It amounted to serfdom," said Harry Malcom, deputy state commissioner of labor. "This is one of the most abominable conditions of present-day civilization."

---

[17] Raymond Wolters, *Negros and the Great Depression. The Problem of Economic Recovery* (Westport, Conn.: Greenwood Publishing Corp., 1970), 123.

Top, a woman drags her cotton sack to be weighed. Photo by Ben Shahn, ca 1936. Bottom, a woman working at home. Photo by Carl Mydans, 1936. Farm Security Administration. Library of Congress Prints and Photographs Division.

Black and white farmers attend an STFU rally. University of North Carolina, Southern Tenant Farmers Union Papers.

A colonist chosen to relocate to Dyess arrives with his family and his belongings. National Archives.

Chapter 14

Planters Who Chisel and Cheat

In a March 1935 *Socialist Call*, Norman Thomas, leader of the national Socialist Party, described the plight of a poor Arkansas Delta family. Near Marked Tree, he "came across a family, a mother with five children, a couple of young hogs, six chickens, two puppies in the children's arms, and a few scraps of furniture. They had just been dumped on the side of the road by a deputy sheriff. The father came walking down the road a little later. He had been beaten up a few days before, arrested and jailed on the nominally untrue charge of stealing a couple of eggs." Thomas said that "The most wretched conditions on any large scale anywhere to be found in exploited America exist in cotton country." It made country roads "somewhat reminiscent of a war zone."[1]

Though the Roosevelt Administration's Agricultural Adjustment Act (AAA) had the goal of helping poor families in the "war zone," it hurt many. The law, which became effective on May 12, 1933, required reductions of planted acres in order to receive cash payments from the federal government. This principle appeared sound since reduced supplies should raise commodity prices. The program called for checks made payable to landlords to be split among tenants pro rata, but in many cases that did not happen. Planters used schemes and devices to keep all or more than their fair share of government money. AAA began

[1] STFU, Reel 1.

in May and required reduction of cotton acres by 25 percent that year and a 40 percent reduction the next. Fewer acres made many tenants unnecessary and unwanted so landlords evicted them or made them day laborers. Regulations allocating money to tenants lacked an effective means of enforcement, and the law's vague language opened the door to abuse. A paragraph from section 7 of this contract revealed possibilities for cheating tenants. "The producer will endeavor . . . to bring about reduction as to cause the least possible . . . social disturbance and . . . in so far as possible he shall effect the acreage reduction as nearly ratable as practicable among tenants . . . [and] shall insofar as possible maintain . . . the normal number of tenants."[2] Directions that allowed planters this much discretion made it rife for abuse, and tenants had little recourse when cheated. In only 11 instances did Arkansas planters have contracts cancelled by September 1934, though tenants filed more than 450 complaints. It is possible that Washington officials never intended for much money to benefit tenants. Secretary of Agriculture Henry A. Wallace assured prominent agricultural leaders that it would not threaten their power. He told them that federal programs would "conform to the wishes of the farm leaders conference."[3]

Tenant vulnerability developed because USDA did not contract with those who actually farmed the land. The agency considered it impractical to bind about one million cotton growers to these agreements. Even when tenants received an AAA check they did not keep it for long. When a St. Francis County sharecropper went to the county agent's office to pick up his parity check he found a room full of plantation riding bosses. They demanded that he put his x on the check and turn it over to his landlord's man.[4] The cropper refused, but the henchmen took it anyhow. County committees established to prevent such practices were composed of planters and their allies. They consistently abused section 8 of the act, which required that "Any change between the landlord and the tenants or sharecroppers . . . shall not operate to increase the landlord's payments." However, this section could be enforced only if county committeemen found a change or

---

[2] Van Hawkins, *Plowing New Ground. The Southern Tenant Farmers Union and Its Place in Delta History* (Virginia Beach, Va.: The Donning Company, 2007), 81.
[3] Henry A. Wallace, *New Frontiers* (New York: Reynal & Hitchcock, 1934), 164-165.
[4] H. L. Mitchell, *Mean Things Happening in this Land: the Life and Times of H. L. Mitchell, Cofounder of the Southern Tenant Farmers' Union* (Montclair, N. J.: Allanheld, Osmun, 1979), 120-121.

reduction unjustified. As a result of such opportunities for landlords to cheat, an act established to help poor farmers actually hurt many of them. Howard Kester, a community activist and advocate for farm laborers, studied the regulation's impact and said that AAA policies "intensified the already deepening misery of the southern sharecropper." Kester accused the agency of attempting to bail out a sea of misery with a tiny bucket.[5] Reports of abuse and desperation led an Arkansas congressman to investigate. Brooks Hays described in a 1934 memorandum to the Federal Emergency Relief Administration (FERA) what he saw. "I had seen many dilapidated tenant houses, but I could hardly believe that people lived in the one that I found on this country road. This home was about 10 feet by 20, and was made of corrugated tin and scraps of lumber. It was flat upon the ground, and had only one or two small openings."[6]

Farm program administrators apparently worried more about irritating planters than advocating for tenants. Cully Cobb, head of AAA's cotton section, instructed investigators in a May 5, 1934, memorandum how to approach tenant complaints. "The work to be done must be carried on in close cooperation with those who have had charge of the cotton adjustment program in the states and counties and in close cooperation with the county cotton adjustment committees in the various counties. Nothing must be done which might cause them to feel that their actions are being questioned, and nothing must happen which might create an impression that the committeemen and others have not been fair and just. Also, the impression must not be created that there has been widespread efforts to chisel, cheat or be unfair."[7] Planter arithmetic became legendary through anecdotes about settling up. One widely repeated story concerned a schoolboy's lesson. A rural schoolteacher asked a farm boy, "If a landlord lends you $20, and you pay him back $5 per month, how much will you owe him after three months?" The boy answered, "$20." The teacher responded, "You don't understand arithmetic." The student replied, "You don't understand our landlord."

---

[5] Howard Kester, *Revolt Among the Sharecroppers* (New York: Arno Press, 1969), 54.
[6] Brooks Hays, Memorandum for Paul Porter, 1935. Landlord-Tenant Section, Rg. 145, National Archives.
[7] C. C. Davis, Administrator, AAA, to District Agents and Others Who are to Assist with Landlord-Tenant Problems, May 5, 1934, 10. STFU records, Southern Historical Collection, Wilson Library, University of North Carolina at Chapel Hill.

One might assume the Delta to be poor ground for raising socialists, but two lived in Tyronza when the economy collapsed. H. L. Mitchell operated a dry-cleaning shop and Clay East a gas station in adjacent buildings on the town square, called Red Square by critics. The location became an informal meeting place for abused and displaced farm workers considering what to do next. During a visit to the town by Norman Thomas, he proposed that the two socialists organize a farm workers union. A tipping point came when Hiram Norcross, owner of Fairview plantation in Poinsett County, evicted 23 sharecropper families. It led 11 white men and seven black men to form the Southern Tenant Farmers Union (STFU) in July 1934. Remarkable for that time and place, the organization brought together both races and included women in lead roles. East criticized the AAA in interviews, pointing out that it caused cotton to become scarce when poor people went without adequate clothing. He became a socialist after reading Upton Sinclair's *Letters to Judd.* The author accused capitalists of controlling poor people with a "subtle and perfect machine of exploitation."[8] When Thomas visited the Delta he toured a plantation barn that had running water and a concrete floor. Thomas observed that livestock lived in better conditions than Delta tenants.

Verification of planters refusing to share AAA money appeared in a USDA report prepared by C. C. Davis, AAA program director. In a May 1934 directive issued to field agents he provided examples. "It is reported that in certain cases planters, operators, landowners, or landlords have inserted special clauses in rental contracts . . . or have adopted supplemental special agreements by which their tenants surrender claim to any portion of rental and parity payments." Davis admitted that planters warned tenants against reporting contract violations to a county committee, county agent, or the administration. Landlords used other means of defrauding tenants as well. They created leases requiring more rent to indirectly obtain a larger portion of parity payments. Though he suggested that agents investigate such abuses, Davis stressed that they "must be dealt with in such a way as not to unduly disturb the cotton adjustment program and in such a way as not to arouse additional controversy and ill feeling between landowners and tenants."[9] STFU complaints about landlord chicanery led the

---

[8] Upton Sinclair, *Letters to Judd, an American Workingman* (Pasadena, Cal.: 1932), 5. East interviews were conducted in 1987 and 1992.

[9] STFU Records, Reel 1.

USDA to send E. A. Miller to undertake what turned out to be a sham investigation. After interviewing planters and avoiding displaced tenants he reported that no eviction problems existed.

The union pushed for an unbiased federal investigation and continued to publicize mistreatment of working men and women. By joining black and white farmers in its cause, planters could not play one race against the other. However, completely integrated locals proved elusive. The union maintained segregated chapters on some plantations, but it made important decisions at integrated meetings.[10] Though AAA created deplorable unintended consequences, by 1934 several New Deal programs brought relief to the Delta. The Farm Credit Administration (FCA) financed mortgages and prevented foreclosures. Commodity Credit Corporation loans protected growers from sinking prices. The Works Progress Administration (WPA) constructed hospitals, schools, and public buildings while paying good wages. Civilian Conservation Corps (CCC) workers completed important public projects. These men lived in more than 100 camps throughout the state and received $30 per month to create or improve parks and bridges. Planters disliked these programs because they contributed to labor independence, which threatened peonage. Lorena Hickok from the Roosevelt Administration traveled throughout the nation recording the effects of government assistance. Her reports revealed the callousness of southern businessmen. In a June 1934 letter to the White House she disclosed a wealthy Memphis cotton merchant's opinion. "He thinks that tenants are lazy and should be treated as serfs." In another letter to Washington, Hickok said that the rural South retained the goal of enslaved labor. After the Civil War landlords established forms of peonage as close to slavery as possible, and they eventually bound vulnerable white families as well. Planters initially supported federal programs, but after learning that benefits reduced the amount of cheap labor, they opposed them. She said that landlords "are raising a terrific howl."[11] This mindset caused an observer to call the South an "economy of the Middle Ages without the cathedrals."[12] And southern

---

[10] *Cry From Cotton*, 68.

[11] Richard Lowitt and Maurine Beasley, eds., *One Third of a Nation, Lorena Hickok Reports on the Great Depression* (Urbana: University of Illinois Press, 1981), 186-187, 277.

[12] H. C. Nixon, *Forty Acres and Steel Mules* (Chapel Hill: University of North Carolina Press, 1938), 19.

planters attempted to dominate their workers like Medieval lords treated their serfs.

Several hundred farm tenants and laborers seeking to escape the clutches of abusive landlords got their chance when the federal government established a resettlement colony in the Delta. William R. Dyess led the WPA and FERA in Arkansas, and he used political contacts to obtain federal money for purchase of about 16,000 acres for a model rural community. [13] Dyess received support from Harry Hopkins, a powerful Roosevelt advisor, who expressed an urgent need to help struggling farmers. Hopkins claimed that about 40 percent of approximately 5.1 million families on relief resided in the country and small towns.[14] Work began on the colony during spring 1934 when crews cleared the land for houses and cultivation. This project became an important source of employment for Delta workers trucked in from nearby towns, with unskilled laborers earning $1.60 per day. Employees lived in barracks and ate in mess halls. The colony developed 61 three-room houses, 233 four-room models, and 206 five-room homes. Additionally, 334 farms had 20 acres, 64 had 30 acres, and 102 contained 40 acres.[15] With colony financing, settlers purchased houses and farms with favorable terms. Prospects came from every Arkansas county.

The most famous family to win a coveted spot turned out to be Ray and Carrie Cash and their children, including three-year-old Johnny Cash. At first his mother doubted the move. Johnny recalled that while a government truck carried them toward Dyess sometimes his mother "would cry and sometimes she'd sing, and sometimes it was hard to tell which was which."[16] After arrival the family made a home along with several hundred others. What the Cash family discovered at Dyess may seem small now, but it was huge then. They found an opportunity for

---

[13] Van Hawkins, *A New Deal in Dyess. The Depression Era Agricultural Resettlement Colony in Arkansas* (Jonesboro, Ark., Writers Bloc, 2015), 12.
[14] Harry Hopkins, September 27, 1935. Hopkins press highlights, WPA press clippings, Box 5, Arkansas State Archives.
[15] Records Section, Rehabilitation Administration Management Division, "Dyess Project Book." National Archives, Rg. 96, Farmers Home Administration. Copy in Everett Henson Collection, Historic Dyess Colony, Record 2016-33-031.; Letter from Lawrence Westbrook to Harry Hopkins, July 10, 1937, Everett Henson Collection, Historic Dyess Colony, Record 2016-33-025.
[16] Johnny Cash, *Cash: The Autobiography*, with Patrick Carr (New York: HarperCollins, 1997), 15.

poor people to replace desperation with hope. William Dyess exposed the magnitude of Arkansas's labor problems when he spoke to FERA members at a 1935 conference:

> *We have 35,000 men and women now on work projects of the Relief Administration, and we must either get these projects approved as federal projects or get new projects in their place and absorb the works into the Works Progress Administration. In addition, we have 20,000 other relief clients not on the work program. If they are able-bodied, we must develop additional projects to absorb them, and if they are not able-bodied, we must forget all about them and tell the State of Arkansas that they are the responsibility of the newly created State Welfare Department. That is the picture.*[17]

Dyess Colony organizers were not blind to the injustice of limiting the project to white families, but a government report addressing the issue reeks of hypocrisy.

> *In none of our projects are we sanctioning any discrimination in regard to nationality, race or creed. However, in localities where there exists deep-rooted prejudices they cannot be ignored. It is not our function to attempt to reform in a day age-old attitudes of the people in the localities from which we are drawing our families, though we cannot dodge the responsibility of following enlightened social practices. We need to give consideration to homogeneity within the group and harmony both within the group and between the group and the outside neighborhood.*[18]

This explanation may have been clouded with platitudes, but its meaning was clear. Dyess was a white-only opportunity.

---

[17] Background Section, Final Report and Physical Accomplishments of the Arkansas Work Projects Administration (March 1, 1943), Everett Henson Collection, Historic Dyess Colony.

[18] John P. Holt, An Analysis of Methods and Criteria Used in Selecting Families for Colonization Projects, Social Research Report No.1, 1937. Farm Security Administration and the Bureau of Agricultural Economics. National Archives, Rg. 96. Copy in Everett Henson Collection, Historic Dyess Colony, Record 2016-33-004.

Formal dedication at Dyess Colony came in May 1936. The project contained 500 farm houses, an administration building, cannery, cotton gin, commissary, community building, post office, café, and hospital. Records indicate that at that time 487 families made homes there, but the town may have had more critics than residents. A March 31, 1936, *New York Times* reported that the Republican National Committee accused Roosevelt of sponsoring farm communities communistic in conception. The committee claimed that the federal government established farms in the Russian pattern. Planter power centers such as the American Farm Bureau Federation and extension services objected to federal assistance since it weakened their control of workers. Extension agents, employed jointly by USDA, a college of agriculture, and the county they served, existed to assist farmers, but agents answered to county officials often allied with planters. Dan T. Gray, director of Arkansas extension services, accused the Resettlement Administration (RA) of doing things in Arkansas that people connected with the college of agriculture could not endorse. Agents complained that certain ideas did not harmonize with the spirit of the people. Which people? It was true that poor farmers gaining financial independence did not harmonize with planters and their allies.[19]

Travelers going from surrounding farms into Dyess Colony witnessed a dramatic transition. Two reporters, Jonathan Daniels and Phil Kinsley, put the community into perspective after their separate visits. Both saw run-down tenant shacks while driving to Dyess, and after entering the colony, Daniels said that "I crossed the colony line like a man moving across a frontier." When Kinsley entered Dyess he observed that "The unprepossessing homes of sharecroppers gave way to broad roads bordering neat homes with front yards flaming in purple feathery flowers that wave like banners of dignity and freedom. The houses are painted, and there are barns and out buildings, glimpses of corn and gardens, hay and beans, cows, pigs, and chickens."[20]

Though colony organizers feared the consequences of racial integration, STFU leaders did not. Combining blacks and whites in one organization with equal status for both advanced an interracial

---

[19] Sidney Baldwin, "The Resettlement Administration," *Poverty and Politics: The Rise and Decline of Farm Security Administration* (Chapel Hill: University of North Carolina Press, 1968), 116.
[20] *New Deal in Dyess*, 29.

understanding that represented one of its "greatest legacies."[21] Mitchell warned that if the union failed to integrate, planters would use racial divisions to divide and conquer as they had in the past. In a November 1935 letter to a Widener member he stressed the importance of removing that weapon from the landlord arsenal. "It is very important that we organize the whites as well as the negroes. For many years the [planter] class has succeeded in keeping the two races divided, and at the same time robbed both the negroes and the whites equally. Nothing will win the battle quicker than by having workers of all races, creeds, and colors united in one strong union. The Southern Tenant Farmers Union is founded on these principles."[22] Planters formed their own union in 1935 to combat the STFU, but Abner Page, a Methodist preacher, turned out to be an unfortunate choice for the group's spokesman. An April 16, 1935, *New York Times* reported Page saying that "It would have been better to have a few no-account, shiftless people killed at the start than to have all this fuss raised up. We have had a pretty serious situation here, what with the mistering of the niggers and stirring them up to think the Government is going to give them forty acres." This planter union, called Marked Tree Cooperative Association, could not recruit enough members to survive. Still, Page's vicious attitude dominated landlord actions. On April 17 the *Times* reported a Delta tenant's complaint and the consequences of making it. C. G. Fletcher's charges led to a USDA investigation. Unfortunately, the agency ruled that Fletcher had no right to AAA money, and the landlord then took away his house and livelihood.

Membership rolls expanded in several states, and the STFU grew faster among black residents. Observers credited this response to previous organizing experiences developed in church groups and fraternal associations. In 1935, Mitchell led several black and white STFU members to Washington, D. C., to meet the secretary of agriculture and protest farm program abuses. Wallace directed them to underlings who proved barely civil and largely unhelpful. Columnists Drew Pearson and Robert S. Allen illustrated how politicians blocked reform. They reported that U. S. Secretary of Labor Frances Perkins proposed sending an arbitrator to Arkansas to resolve differences between planters and the STFU. Cabinet members agreed, as did the president, but Vice President John Garner objected. He stressed that it

---

[21] *Cry From Cotton*, 66.
[22] STFU, Reel 1.

might embarrass Joe Robinson, a powerful Arkansas senator, and nothing should be done without discussing it with him. That is "a very delicate situation in Arkansas," Garner warned. Roosevelt dropped the idea, according to Pearson and Allen in a column that ran in the March 17, 1936, *Florida Times Union.*[23]

Negative publicity eventually caused Wallace to authorize a report about tenant treatment, and he sent Mary Connor Myers to investigate. This administrative law attorney travelled throughout the Delta with STFU members and observed appalling conditions. Myers sent a telegram to the justice department that excoriated planters. "Have heard one long story human greed." She disclosed that "Section Seven only one section contract being openly and generally violated." Myers called sharecroppers a higher class than she expected and "all pathetically pleased" that the federal government sent someone to hear their grievances.[24] After conducting her investigation, Myers wrote a memorandum to Chester Davis, chief of USDA's production division, titled "Tenants on Cotton Plantations in Northeastern Arkansas." Davis read the memo and discussed its inflammatory contents with Myers. She had concluded that affidavits of tenants provided enough evidence to warrant a full-scale investigation, but Davis suppressed the report to protect AAA and identities of persons interviewed, or so he said. Myers gave him all but one copy and called this episode the most humiliating professional experience of her career. USDA received requests for copies of her report, but to no avail, and the highly critical document disappeared.[25]

Herbert Barnes wrote in a February 15, 1935, *Farmers National Weekly* that "It is clear that Wallace has no intentions of taking any steps likely to conflict with the interests of the planters." As landlord abuses increased, so did STFU membership rolls. At its first convention in 1935 about 1,400 persons attended. Their mission statement said

---

[23] David Eugene Conrad, *The forgotten Farmers. The Story of Sharecroppers in the New Deal* (Urbana: University of Illinois Press, 1965), 174.
[24] Myers to Frank, January 18, 1935, STFU, Reel 1. A successful Boston attorney, Myers joined the AAA's legal department at the request of Henry Wallace. Her assignment in Arkansas may have come about because of Myers's conservative reputation. Still, Cobb didn't trust her and believed Myers to be a radical who knew nothing about farming. His views bore a remarkable resemblance to Leroy Percy's attitude about his Yankee woman lawyer critic.
[25] Myers to Chester Davis, March 8, 1935, Department of Agriculture, Folder 467, Solicitor's File, Rg. 145, National Archives.

that the organization sought to improve living conditions and gain higher wages for farm labor. These goals threatened peonage as practiced in the Delta, so nightriders harassed members during meetings and threatened organizers with violence. After a speech by Ward Rodgers, a political activist and union ally, authorities arrested him for conspiring to overthrow the government and using profane language. A jury found Rodgers guilty of anarchy.

To protect its leaders from physical harm, in 1935 the union moved its headquarters to Memphis. Relocation became necessary because of attacks such as those aimed at A. B. Brookins. More than 70 years old and the union chaplain, he barely escaped being lynched by riding bosses. According to Brookins, after that plan failed, nightriders fired into his house nearly killing his daughter. The *New York Times* on April 15, 1935, verified threats and violence aimed at union members. The article described their deplorable living conditions, "if the hand-to-mouth existence they have led since the war between the states may be called a living at all. Attempts to better their lot through organizations such as the Southern Tenant Farmers Union have taught them that they have few rights under the laws of Arkansas. Scores have been evicted or run off the place for union activity, and masked nightriders have spread fear among union members, both white and negro. In some communities the most fundamental rights of free speech and assemblage have been abridged." Despite harassment and threats, the STFU mounted an effective cotton picker strike in 1935. Planters established a 40 cents per pound cotton picking wage every year, which earned a good hand about one dollar a day. The union demanded one dollar per pound. Carrie Dilworth, a union organizer, explained how STFU prepared for this strike by handing out notices the night before. "I was riding in my car. Marie Pierce, a student from Memphis, was riding in the back seat with Mr. Bolden. Mrs. Burton and I sat in the front. I was laying down on my stomach holding the door cracked open, and I'd push the leaflet through the crack and spread them out in the street. You pick up speed and that'd just make them things go flying all over the yards. White folks thought it was a plane that distributed fliers."[26] Negotiations reached a 75-cents-per-pound compromise, but

[26] Sue Thrasher and Leah Wise, eds. "Southern Tenant Farmers Union," *Southern Exposure* 1:3 (Winter 1974), 25-26.

the potential strike forced planters to negotiate terms rather than dictate them.

On June 26, 1935, Kester spoke at NAACP's 27th annual conference and described the effects of peonage, giving it an identical meaning with slavery.

> *Peonage is a phrase that has relatively little meaning except to people who dwell in college walls and are somewhat sophisticated, and therefore, I do not particularly cherish the word. The word which has tremendous significance and meaning to men and women who are in peonage or enslaved is the word slavery, and I want to change my subject tonight from that of "The Struggle Against Peonage" to "The Struggle Against Slavery."*
>
> *The word, sharecropper, has, I believe, in the last several months, probably within the last couple of years, become more or less a household word to many Americans. It is a word that expresses the most exploited, the most degraded, the most brutalized group of workers in America; and it is about the sharecroppers, the tenant farmers, that I wish to speak to you tonight. If I seem to parade before you the sins of Arkansas, I want you to know that in picking on Arkansas I am picking on the South.*
>
> *During the last year I visited numerous schools in northeastern Arkansas. I have seen children crowded into schools three and four times as many as the seating capacity could take care of. Some of them I have found seated in one corner of the room eating corn pone and molasses. In another corner was a larger group seated quietly watching the other group eat, because they had nothing to eat. I have seen children come to school with no baskets at all. I have seen them come to school barefoot, with one piece of clothing on, and with no books. After asking them why they came to school the answer was, 'We came to school to get warm,' because of no warmth at home.*
>
> *Hundreds of thousands of Negro and white tenant farmers and sharecroppers in the deep South today have less value upon their heads than a good mule or a good horse. Labor is plentiful. If a man grows sick and dies, there is another ready and willing to take his place; and so you find my people and your people suffering untold agonies because they have neither the money nor*

the good will of the master, or the landlord, to secure for them medical care.

These people are disfranchised. These people are brutalized. These people are lynched – lynched in body, lynched in spirit. These people are your people. These people are my people. And until we identify ourselves with these disinherited, oppressed masses; until their pain becomes our pain; until their sorrow becomes our sorrow; until their suffering becomes our suffering; until their longing for a decent world becomes our longing; we, too, will remain enslaved, brutalized, lynched.

When some planters attempted to work with union labor other landlords pulled them back into line. Mitchell claimed that during spring 1936 a Delta planter named C. H. Dibble considered a collective bargaining agreement with the STFU. But several neighbors explained that if he contracted with the union his operating credit would be denied. Dibble then sent eviction notices to union families on his land. He put their names on a "black list" and passed it along to other planters to freeze them out of the job market. Expelled families lived in a tent colony, and after a union supporter from Memphis observed their conditions he wrote a letter to Mitchell. "I have never been so nauseated as on this trip. The utter brutality and callousness with which the planters are throwing off families is beyond belief."[27] When Norman Thomas returned to the Delta he attempted to speak to farmers in Birdsong. Opponents and authorities broke up the meeting, telling Thomas that no "gawd-damn yankee bastard" was welcome in Arkansas. Many black tenants felt unwelcome as well and continued to head north. By the 1930s, almost every child in Milwaukee, Wisconsin's, North Side grade schools was from Mississippi, Tennessee, or Arkansas.[28]

---

[27] STFU, Reel 1.

[28] Isabel Wilkerson, *The Warmth of Other Suns. The Epic Story of America's Great Migration* (New York: Random House, 2010), 245.

STRIKE -:- STRIKE -:- STRIKE

GENERAL STRIKE CALL!

Stop All Work – Stop Every Hoe – Stop Every Plow – Strike On Every Plantation and Farm!

SHARECROPPERS-TENANTS-DAYLABORERS

Every One Out of the Fields — Refuse to Do Another Day's Work
Force the Owners and Bosses to Deal With Your Union!

Do not return until your demands are won. By using the only power you have—the strength you show when all work stops—you can win a victory—that will never be forgotten. The Federal Government will be forced to act, in behalf of justice, when all work stops. Use your power, stop all work on every plantation and farm. Strike a blow that will be remembered forever.

STRIKE FOR:

The Right to Live Like Human Beings.
For a Fair Day's Wage for a Fair Day's Work.
For Decent Contracts for Sharecroppers and Tenants.
For the Right to Bargain Collectively with the Owners.
For Arbitration of Wage and Contract Disputes.

STRIKE AGAINST:

Forcing of Men to Work at the Point of Guns.
Against the Illegal and False Imprisonment of Honest Workers.
Concentration Camps or Stockades Erected to Force Strikers to Labor.
The Breaking Up of Meetings of Workers, and Jailing and Mistreatment of Leaders of Their Organizations.

By calling out every one from the fields and keeping them out we can force disarmament of plantation thugs. We can force resignation of brutal yellow curs who hold peace officers' commissions. We can put a stop to terrorism and intimidation. We can make Arkansas a fit place to live. Use your power—strike on every farm and plantation . . . shut down the works.

Pass This Leaflet On — Spread the Word — For Every One to Come Out

CENTRAL WAGE COMMITTEE

SOUTHERN TENANT FARMERS' UNION

1936 STFU poster calling for an agricultural workers strike. University of North Carolina, Southern Tenant Farmers Union Papers.

Chapter 15

Where Once Perhaps Were Eyes

Justice

That Justice is a blind goddess
Is a thing to which we black are wise:
Her bandage hides two festering sores
That once perhaps were eyes.

Langston Hughes

The STFU caused major problems for a powerful Delta planter when it shared accusations of AAA injustice with a *Washington Post* reporter. The union claimed that Lee Wilson & Company received large set-aside payments in 1934 and 1935, refused to share the subsidies with tenants, and evicted them. During a federal investigation, AAA suspended 1936 payments to Wilson and those for several future years. However, in 1941 the suspension was lifted, and the planter received some back payments.[1]

In addition to stirring up trouble for Wilson, union officials announced a picker strike in 1936 to increase wages, but this time landlords were ready for it. Authorities arrested strikers for vagrancy,

[1] Jeannie M. Whayne, et al, *Arkansas: A Concise History* (Fayetteville: University of Arkansas Press, 2019), 274-275.

and thugs beat pickers refusing to work. *March of Time* made a film about the strike. Producers released their documentary, *Land of Cotton*, in about 6,000 theaters throughout America. Despite visual evidence in the film, Governor Marion Futrell claimed that peonage did not exist in Arkansas. [2] Union members became involved in an investigation related to the strike. A September 28, 1936, FBI report focused on events in St. Francis County. The synopsis of facts section stated that planters Henry Craft and Charles Dabbs forced "negroes" to work in Craft's cotton fields during the strike by use of firearms. The planters said workers requested their protection after shots were fired over the field, supposedly by Josh Turner and Nathaniel Smith, both "colored" employees and STFU members. Sheriff Jack Curlin of Marion held Turner and Smith in the county jail awaiting indictments. Curlin said that he possessed signed affidavits from the two prisoners that they did the shooting, but the sheriff told FBI agents that after the accused met with an attorney they recanted.

In the FBI report, Turner said that when they arrived at the jail, Deputy Sheriff C. C. Culp and Dabbs questioned them about the shooting. "When they first told me that I did the shooting, I said that I didn't, and Mr. Culp told me that I was a damned liar. I was afraid of Mr. Culp and was afraid Mr. Culp would hurt me, so I told him that I did the shooting to save myself from getting a beating." Smith gave the following statement. "After being taken to the jail, the law told us that if we didn't own up to this shooting they were going to kill us." Smith said that he signed the confession "because I was scared. I did not do the shooting and do not know who did it." Craft and Dabbs signed a joint statement. Dabbs said that he and Deputy Sheriff G. D. Trusty, both armed, had been present when shots were fired. After an investigation by planters and authorities they took the two STFU members to jail, and both voluntarily admitted everything after they arrived. The joint statement said that "at no time have I ever forced either day workers or share croppers to labor in the fields, nor has Mr. Craft to my knowledge." Following interviews with other people who had knowledge of these events, investigators ruled that "no further investigation was desired."[3]

---

[2] *Mean Things*, 92.

[3] Department of Justice, Criminal Division, Reel 24, 50-643.

In a December 15, 1936, Commonwealth College *Fortnightly*, Edward Norman explained how southern employers manipulated races against each other during work stoppages. If a walkout occurred among white workers in the cotton patch or on the factory floor the boss "will simply throw out the white workers, saying that he had all the time wished he might use Negroes, who would work for less. But he had felt obligated to use those of his own race, which was no longer so. He wins the Negroes to strike breaking by asking them what they owe the white trash. He will tell them, 'Stick with your jobs and I'll see you get a square deal.' Who can blame them if they break the strike? Whose fault is it that the white workers have to take the wage cut or longer hours? Certainly not the Negroes!" On the other hand, if "Negroes strike the boss gets his white strike breakers by bellowing about the superiority of the white race and his desire to have white rather than Negro laborers. The boss will say, 'Why should you be squeamish about scabbing on a bunch of niggers, and besides, if you will help me break the strike I will do as you have been asking and kick all the niggers out and hire white men instead.' The strike is broken and down go wages again. The boss plays one race against the other to his benefit and their common detriment."

Deputies Paul D. Peacher and Everett Hood became notorious strike-breakers. They led gangs of bullies who threatened union members with ball bats and guns. In May 1936, union members gathered at a church near Earle. When Hood and Peacher broke in, James Ball grabbed his gun, and Hood beat him. The deputies took Ball to jail and charged him with attempted murder. Hood and Peacher returned to the church, shot two men, and arrested three others. After Willie Hurst admitted witnessing their actions and planned to testify against them, two masked men murdered him. A judge sentenced Ball to seven years, but the state Supreme Court reduced it to one year. The court reprimanded Hood for violating the STFU's right of free assemblage.[4] Peacher continued to ignore the law. Sherwood Eddy, a union supporter from Mississippi, wrote U. S. Attorney General Homer Cummings that "I have today witnessed a most flagrant violation of the federal peonage act by P. D. Peacher in the lawless county of Crittenden, near Earle, Arkansas. I interviewed 13 negro prisoners in a stockade unlawfully arrested, torn from their homes and imprisoned by Peacher, who threatened us and refused to answer all questions." An STFU press

[4] Fowler, Brief for Appellant James Ball.

release charged that Peacher struck a union attorney and arrested Aron Gilmartin, an investigator, for disturbing the peace.[5] Peacher had negotiated a contract with Earle Special School District to clear a parcel of land, sell its timber, and cultivate new ground. He then searched for people to do the work and arrested about 20 men for vagrancy. T. S. Mitchell, mayor of Earle and justice of the peace, found all of them guilty and sentenced the men to 30 days of labor on Peacher's farm.

Armed guards watched over these prisoners, and living quarters resembled a chicken house with barred windows. In trial testimony Peacher called black workers "loafers and a honky tonk bunch," though most of those arrested were of independent means and did not have to do farm labor. But as usual, when southern authorities learned that planters needed more black manpower, vagrants materialized. Planters provided about $5,000 for Peacher's defense, according to the November 26, 1936, *Memphis Commercial Appeal*. Fred A. Isrig, a U.S. Attorney for eastern Arkansas, reviewed the case and ruled out peonage since mistreatment involved convicts. He admitted that "This situation, while not at all admirable, is one that is used in a great many states." Isrig chose to base charges on an 1866 slave-kidnapping law. The government contended that Peacher rounded up black workers, charged them with vagrancy, arranged convictions in a kangaroo court, and took them to his newly acquired farm for slave labor.[6] He went on trial during December 1936, and Judge John E. Martineau advised jurors that circumstances pointed to Peacher's guilt. With respect to the judge, Peacher said that "He don't scare me none. That jury will turn me loose." A serious miscalculation. On December 7, 1936, *Time* magazine reported that Peacher received a two-year suspended sentence, a $3,500 fine, and lost his marshal's badge. Allies helped pay his fine. A December 9, 1936, *Christian Century* called Peacher's conviction an encouraging indication of changes taking place. It said that "the significant thing about Peacher's case is not that he was guilty, but that he was convicted or even brought to trial."

In 1937, Erskine Caldwell and photographer Margaret Bourke-White co-authored *You Have Seen Their Faces*. In it the *Tobacco Road*

---

[5] STFU, Reel 2.

[6] Record of grand jury testimony at Little Rock, Arkansas, September 24, 1936, Eastern District, pp 5, 35, Rg. 60, Box 2084, Department of Justice, National Archives.

author expresses his views on abuse of farm labor. "Peonage, like lynching, is not condoned in theory; but conditions, usually best described as local, are sometimes called upon to justify it in practice. And when a plantation owner feels the urge to beat and whip and maul a Negro, there are generally several within sight or sound to choose from. Keeping a Negro constantly in physical bondage would be an unnecessary expense and chore; the threat of physical violence is enough."[7] Threats of violence and other abuse kept farm workers on the move. A presidential committee in 1937 concluded that poor farm families moved from place to place without setting roots in communities, and about 500,000 of them lived on land too poor to provide a livelihood.[8]

An FBI investigation of mistreatment in early 1937 targeted the Wilson plantation. A March 7 report disclosed complaints by W. B. Curd of St. Louis, Missouri. Curd wrote the U. S. Attorney General about information supposedly told him by a friend. He claimed that plantation managers made employees work more than 12 hours per day for $1.50 per day and retained some of their earnings. Nearly all remaining wages went for food and lodging. Curd said that if a laborer slipped away and got caught, plantation managers gave the worker a "clubbing" and returned him to the plantation. Investigators interviewed Sheriff Hale Jackson of Mississippi County. Jackson said that he knew many black employees who had worked on the plantation for more than 20 years and were well-treated. The sheriff called allegations of floggings ridiculous. Deputy Sheriff Webb Greer concurred, certain that "negroes have not been forced to work or beaten." This report went to a U. S. Attorney in Little Rock who admitted being acquainted with conditions at Wilson. Since the original complainant could not be located and no peonage violations proven, a federal attorney declined prosecution.[9]

Many peonage cases that appeared to have merit never made it past a grand jury. A March 27, 1937, FBI report typified contradictory versions of events that made prosecutions difficult. A black farm tenant,

---

[7] Erskine Caldwell and Margaret Bourke-White, *You Have Seen Their Faces* (Athens: University of Georgia Press, 1937), 10.
[8] Farm Tenancy, Report of the President's Committee (Washington, D.C.: Government Printing Office, February 1937), 16.
[9] Department of Justice, Criminal Division, Reel, 20, 50-654.

Jake Dunwoodie (spelled Dinwoody in some instances) accused J. T. Wall of peonage on his plantation about nine miles from Helena. The tenant farmer told this story to federal investigators. "I farmed 32 acres for Mr. Wall in 1936, and I made 21 bales of cotton that year. I have kept on trading at his stores. I went to Mr. Wall about March 12, 1937, to get a statement as he had told me I owed him twenty-five dollars. I had gone to see Mr. Solomon, who runs a grocery and hardware store in Helena . . . and he had advised me to get a statement. Mr. Solomon had sent down sixty dollars by his truck driver to pay my account and the account of Wes Brown, a colored man, working for Mr. Wall, but Mr. Wall refused to take it." Dunwoodie said that on March 15 "Mr. Wall sent for me, and in front of his manager's house he and his manager, a new man whose name I don't know, drew pistols on me and my wife and on Ida Brown, wife of Wes Brown. He cussed me, hit me with the pistol and broke two teeth. He told me he had learned I was planning to move on Mr. R. C. Nichol's place near Wabash . . . and that he would kill me before he let me work for anybody else. He told me that I was going to make a crop for him this year or else he would kill me and send me to Hell. He made me get in his automobile and go to his store and get a month's supply of groceries."

Despite these threats, Dunwoodie ran off and said that Solomon told him to notify U. S. agents about the abuse. Federal authorities charged Wall with peonage. This complaint led to Wall's arrest, but the FBI found no corroboration of an alleged threat or that Wall hit Dunwoodie. Solomon confirmed that he offered to pay Dunwoodie's account and that of Wes Brown, and that the landlord refused to accept his payment. But he denied advising Dunwoodie to contact authorities. An agent questioned David M. Norton, a manager with Wall during the disputed attack, and he denied that the planter struck anyone. Norton did say that if anyone tried to "speak so smart" to him he would have "felt justified in hitting him." Ida Brown told authorities that Wall talked to them, but did not threaten the couple or say that they could not leave. Wall persuaded them to remain on his place for another year. Other interviews produced differences about money owed, agreement terms, and other matters. As proved to be the case in many peonage disputes, it came down to a black tenant's word against a white planter, and black witnesses afraid to testify. A federal grand jury in Little Rock returned a no bill in the Dunwoodie case.[10]

An FBI report dated May 29, 1937, disclosed an unusual case of peonage charges lodged against a white husband and wife. Gaston L. Therrell, a Mississippi farmer, claimed that E. L. Hale and his wife from Armorel committed peonage. They removed a black cook named Lizzie Crump Brooks against her will from Therrell's residence in Mississippi and returned her to Armorel. Mrs. Hale's first trip to get Brooks failed after Brooks supposedly told Therrell's wife that she did not want to return to Arkansas. On a second attempt Mrs. Hale drove away with Brooks. Therrell filed a complaint saying that the Hales would not hesitate to beat Brooks. However, Therrell destroyed his case when he told a federal agent that he filed criminal charges against the Hales "only because of their high handed method in taking Lizzie Brooks away and their total disregard of his feelings in the matter." When questioned, Brooks said that she left Therrell's farm of her own accord. Her husband worked for the Hales, and she had cooked for them. Brooks feared flooding at Armorel and went to the Therrell farm where her father worked. She said that "Mrs. Hale didn't make me come back to Armorel. I came because I wanted to." The FBI report concluded that "Inasmuch as peon does not substantiate the complaint as alleged, this case is being closed."[11]

---

[10] Department of Justice, Criminal Division, Division of Records, Reel 20, 50-9-3.
[11] Department of Justice, Criminal Division, Reel 24, 50-666.

CHAPTER 16

Suffering and Fear

Just when Delta farmers thought their problems could not get worse, they did. Flooding began in 1937 when Mississippi River tributaries covered much of the region. Rising water and plunging temperatures created extensive suffering and fear. A man described the terror of living near advancing flood waters. "You just can't sleep in a house – even if it is your house – within four blocks of a wild, deep river which threatens to break through weak, soggy levees into your house. You lie awake because you are afraid of the worst that would come with raging flood waters. You imagine you can hear alarms from the guards on the river; you think you hear autos speeding through the streets to the levees to empty its men into a crew" to stack sandbags.[1] Johnny Cash's mother and siblings joined other Dyess residents headed for high ground and returned only after water subsided. Cash described their home place when they returned. Water had washed away their beehives, and the cow drowned. Chickens and pigs took over the house, even though water rose up to the floor. "We went back to the most terrible mess you can imagine. The couch was covered with eggs where the hens had laid. You can imagine what kind of mess [pigs] made all over the house, but we still had them."[2]

---

[1] Don Hamilton, "Jonesboro and Arkansas During the Flood of 1937," *Craighead County Historical Quarterly* 9:1 (Winter 1971), 5.
[2] Johnny Cash, excerpt from interview conducted by Ed Salamon, program director, WHN Radio, New York. Johnny Cash Silver Anniversary Radio Special aired on Mutual Broadcasting System, July 4, 1980.

Despite flooding, financial woes, and planter resistance, the STFU survived. It did so in large part due to its women members. They marched beside men in picket lines, and though thugs had orders to stop protests, they hesitated to assault female union members. Several women made prominent leaders. Henrietta Green, president of a Howell local, led a successful boycott that raised tenant shares from one-third to one-half. Mitchell called Myrtle Lawrence of Colt, Arkansas, one of the union's best organizers. Evelyn Smith managed STFU's Memphis office and wrote a union songbook and most issues of its newsletter, *Sharecropper Voice*.

Even with effective leaders such as these women, union efforts to raise wages for cotton pickers and eliminate peonage became increasingly difficult because planters anticipated them and prepared accordingly. At a local meeting in Armorel, Lee Wilson's plantation manager and about 40 planters with riding bosses allegedly drove away members. Blytheville's Chamber of Commerce offered a $50 reward for the arrest of labor agitators.[3] Amid widespread abuses, peonage charges against Jay May and Tom Brown were outrageous even by Delta standards. An FBI report dated July 9, 1937, stated that Mrs. W. H. Breedlove from Lepanto claimed that a planter, Tom Brown, "bought John Baldwin, colored," from Jay May, city marshal of Osceola and a Poinsett County deputy sheriff. Brown supposedly paid $35 for him. This allegation generated four FBI reports and a mass of contradictions. In a summary of one account, the dispute began when Lucien Coleman, a local attorney, accused Baldwin of breaking into his house. But after May picked up Baldwin, Coleman could not positively identify him. His charge could have been based on an irrelevant belief that Baldwin was "considered to have a bad reputation." Though May did not charge Baldwin with a crime, the deputy allegedly sold him to Brown for $35. Learning of a federal inquiry into the matter, May returned the $35 to Brown. The planter then paid Baldwin $19 for work on Brown's plantation.

Agents interviewed Justice of the Peace George Nowlin (an unclear spelling in the report) at Lepanto, but he was "too intoxicated at the time" to provide much information. The agents said he disliked May since the deputy would not bring cases into Nowlin's court. Lepanto Mayor C. E. McCellan testified that he had endeavored to improve the

---

[3] News release, May 28, 1937, STFU papers, box 8.

town and supported May's padlocking of beer joints. However, some residents sought to keep Lepanto "wide open" and were attempting to oust the mayor and May. Brown claimed that May approached him and asked if he still "wanted the nigger around until he could make an investigation, whether this nigger had broken into the house or knew anything about it. He said that the nigger had caused him putting out a lot of time and money, about $35, in fooling with the case. I should take him up to my farm and make him think that he was working out this $35 expense. After he made his investigation and found that he couldn't find anything about the nigger he told me I should go ahead and pay him for his work." Brown testified that "I have never paid Jay May any money, in other words I didn't buy the nigger off of him." May claimed that "Mr. and Mrs. Breedlove wanted to oust him because of his activities making Lepanto a "law abiding town." Mrs. Breedlove had gone so far as to file a charge of rape against him. May said that he took Baldwin to Brown's plantation, but "no money was ever exchanged in this transaction."

After being returned from Pittsburgh, Pennsylvania, Baldwin gave agents the following account of May's efforts to frame him. May told him, "'Now John listen, we want the truth, if you don't tell me I'm going to put you in jail.' He told me to remember what happened to Willie Key. He was a colored boy who was killed by a mob crowd." May said that "if I could get $35 and give it to him, Jay May, he would drop the case. At that time I had only $3.92 in my pocket and although I could get $35 from my friends still I didn't do anything wrong and so would not pay it." May and Brown might have used a middleman for the payment to evade detection and thus swear that they had not exchanged money. An FBI report stated that Tom Brown's account in the Stuckey Brothers store journal in Lepanto showed $35 to order of Jay May. However, after reading the reports a U. S. Attorney wrote the attorney general that "We could not secure a conviction on this case on a charge of peonage. Therefore, there will be no prosecution."[4]

The FBI continued Delta peonage investigations during the 1930s despite few prosecutions. A November 1, 1937, report charged Guy Courtney and Charles C. Hemingway Sr. with peonage. Authorities had arrested Lawrence Williams, James Johnson, and Wilmer Lee, "all colored," for vagrancy and trespass. Hemingway, a justice of the peace,

---

[4] Department of Justice, Criminal Division, Reel 24, 50-672.

sentenced each man to 30 days and a $10 fine. Courtney, a planter living near McGehee, contracted with Desha County to work prisoners at 75 cents per day after he paid the court fines and costs. In this case costs of $9.15 went to Hemingway and a deputy. When interviewed by the FBI, Hemingway "did not recall specific cases and further did not remember them having been searched in his presence; that he could not state definitely that any money had been found on their person." This story became more suspect when investigators interviewed Mrs. Courtney, who kept the plantation books. She admitted that they did not credit prisoners for Sunday confinement; did not allow them credit for sick days, and any sick days were added to their release date. Additionally, her records indicated that these three men owed $5 more than the court recorded. Mrs. Courtney called the discrepancy an error, but it meant that the three worked beyond their release date. The FBI forwarded this case to a U. S. Attorney, but despite accounting irregularities causing involuntary servitude he declined to prosecute and closed the file.[5]

The STFU became directly involved in a Delta peonage investigation described in a March 10, 1938, FBI report. Union President J. R. Butler charged that authorities arrested Harry Swift, "negro," of Gesick several times on trumped up charges. A court assessed fines and required Swift (identified as Thrift in some interviews) to work out debt on E. E. Bullard's property. Bullard contracted with St. Francis and Cross counties to work convicts. Butler told agents that on three occasions white people picked up Swift at the behest of Bullard, who fined him and required the prisoner to work off his alleged debt. Butler could not gain access to Swift, but a black preacher named James Hayes did. The prisoner told Hayes that he sharecropped for more than a year along with other prisoners. When he got into a fight with another sharecropper, Bullard fined him and added that amount to his debt to be worked out. When Swift had almost paid off the amount he owed, the "boss man" threatened to beat him. Swift struck the man, and Bullard doubled the fine. When he asked Bullard for a crop settlement the planter put him on a chain gang. A justice of the peace and Parkin city marshal told investigators that a court convicted Swift of stealing cotton, assault and battery, and disturbing

---

[5] Department of Justice, Criminal Division, Reel 24, 50-697.

the peace. This explained multiple arrests, they said, and a U. S. Attorney declined to prosecute.[6]

Another Bullard-related case with STFU involvement produced an FBI report dated May 27, 1938. Butler charged Bullard with peonage, claiming that he did not release prisoners when directed by a court order. A synopsis of facts section included the following. Edmond T. Norfleet, a Forrest City deputy prosecuting attorney, charged Henrietta McGehee, Alberta Vaughan, and William Vaughan with "enticing labor." A justice of the peace found them guilty and fined each $250 and costs. The court released them to Bullard under hiring bonds to work out their fines at 75 cents per day. Butler and C. A. Standfill, an attorney who represented the union, filed a petition alleging that authorities held the three defendants several days without trial and prevented them from employing counsel. They called the trial a mockery. A circuit court ordered Bullard to release the three prisoners pending appeal. FBI agents obtained a case file, and it contained a letter by Judge W. D. Davenport to the Forrest City Circuit Court clerk saying that the judge heard that Bullard did not intend to obey the court order until told to do so by the sheriff. Davenport stated that Bullard should be advised to release the three or he would be held in contempt. FBI agents reported that Norfleet and Deputy Sheriff J. R. Campbell said that Butler and other union members had caused a "great deal of labor trouble" in St. Francis County, inducing "a good many negroes" to leave their employers. The FBI report indicated that the three convicted STFU members attempted to increase picking wages from 75 cents per hundred to a dollar. The deputy sheriff and deputy prosecutor accused STFU members of threatening workers with violence if they did not support the union demand. They told "ignorant negroes that if they did not leave their employ, an army that was at their disposal would occupy the territory, and they would be treated in a very severe manner." Norfleet said that Standfill did not appear at the hearing. However, the sheriff admitted that a "considerable crowd" surrounded the courthouse, and "various parties" assaulted Standfill. The attorney asked Campbell for assistance, and the deputy sheriff asked Standfill if he wanted to remain there or leave. Standfill departed. Butler was unpopular as well. Prior to the trial, he had been in town handing out union materials, and on that occasion a resident "forcibly compelled" Butler to eat a hand-bill. Bullard released the three prisoners, but a

---

[6] Department of Justice, Criminal Division, Reel 24, 50-700.

difference of opinion existed as to whether he delayed their release beyond the order date. Federal authorities did not pursue the peonage charge against Bullard. A U. S. Attorney declined prosecution because he did not believe the facts constituted a peonage violation.[7]

Bad publicity about such abuses caused Governor Futrell to create a commission. It produced vague ideas for improvements in farm life, but no realistic steps to achieve them. Roosevelt also established a committee to study tenant problems. He appointed Arkansans to this panel, and participants found clear cases of denied civil liberties when groups attempted to organize for bargaining power.[8] When this report went to Congress it entered a "political labyrinth" devised by southern politicians and exited a skeleton. Congressmen drastically reduced funding allocated for poor farmers to purchase homesteads. With no help coming from congress or southern state legislatures, peonage continued unabated, particularly with respect to vagrancy laws.

The FBI reported one such charge on March 18, 1937. Albert Garrett, "negro," notified the agency that while in Pine Bluff during the first part of February 1937, sheriffs arrested him for "no reason whatever." A Little Rock resident, Garrett went to Pine Bluff to get his brother and go with him to Grady and attend a funeral. After a walk in Pine Bluff, Garrett stopped in a vacant lot. "My asthma was bothering me, and I took out some of my asthma powder and lit it and began inhaling the fumes to relieve me." A car drove up with two men in it, and one of them motioned for Garrett, another man, and a boy to approach the car. A deputy sheriff exited and searched Garrett. He then questioned him and "the colored boy and the white man who had been talking with me." The deputy ordered all three to get into the car, and he took them to jail. Garrett said that they spent the night in jail then went to court where a judge did not sentence or fine him. But "a man took me out to the County Farm with some other prisoners." The "colored boy" and white man arrested with him were not taken to the farm. Garrett sent a note to his brother who hired an attorney, M. L. Reinberger, and he arranged Garrett's release. After returning to Little Rock, Garrett contacted a U. S. Attorney and filed a peonage complaint. An agent interviewed Reinberger, and his statement confirmed that

---

[7] Department of Justice, Reel 24, 50-700.

[8] James G. Maddox, "The Bankhead-Jones Farm Tenant Act," *Law and Contemporary Problems* 4 (October 1937), 45.

Garrett had been arrested for vagrancy and released after posting a bond. But Reinberger declined to assist with the peonage charge. Records verified Garrett's conviction for vagrancy and a municipal court fine. A deputy sheriff admitted his practice of arresting "strange negroes who were loafers in order to eliminate burglaries, etc." Another deputy confirmed this practice and referred to the recent attempt by a "strange negro in Pine Bluff to attack a white girl." He said that authorities arrested strangers only to protect citizens from petty thefts and other offenses that occurred when people appeared in the city unable to give "a good account of themselves." Court records indicated a $10 fine and court costs of $19.60. According to the FBI, a U. S. Attorney decided that facts did not justify further investigation, and he would not authorize a prosecution.[9]

While black citizens experienced unlawful discrimination in towns such as Pine Bluff, country folks faced it as well. Landlords banned the use of radios by workers; opened employee mail in order to destroy critical material; linked employment to housing; threatened to seize personal property for payment of debt, and discouraged railroad and bus companies from selling tickets to working families wanting to leave the region. A planter openly advertised his peonage practices in the Yanceyville, North Carolina, *Caswell Messenger*. He ran this warning: "NOTICE: I forbid anyone to hire or harbor Norman Miles, colored, during the year 1939.—A. P. Dobbs, Route 1, Yanceyville." A neighbor explained the impact of such notices. "Few landlords will risk incurring the wrath of some good Christian, Democratic freeholder by hiring his hand after he has warned us not to."[10] Though hampered by this and many other roadblocks, the STFU pressed ahead, and members avoided danger as best they could. John Handcox, a black recruiter, recalled the day when that job almost cost his life. "I was in the river shelling, and I hear my mother call. I thought my kids, that something had happened to them. So I got back as fast as I could row the boat to where she was, and she said, 'John, you better get away from here.' Said that this fellow was standing at the store. He had a rope and limb, and all he wanted was me. I said, I ain't going nowhere. I'm gonna shoot it out. She said, 'Oh, John, no. If you just get one of them they'll kill us all.' And she was right. So that's the way it was." He walked about four miles to a friend's

---

[9] FBI report of March 18, 1937. Department of Justice, Criminal Division, Reel 24, 50-6-53.

[10] *Lost Promise*, 67.

house and caught a bus to STFU headquarters in Memphis. The union arranged for him to stay in the city.[11] Due to the efforts of Handcox and other organizers the STFU gained locals in Missouri, Mississippi, Oklahoma, and Tennessee by the end of 1938. Mitchell claimed the union had about 30,000 members, probably an inflated number since he expanded membership rolls for publicity purposes. Unlike the STFU, many unions excluded black workers and even called strikes when necessary to eliminate them from preferred jobs. Some union leaders considered black men potential scabs because they crossed picket lines manned by unions that excluded them. Booker T. Washington admitted that black labor "was not inclined to trade unionism. [12] An NAACP official verified lack of support for black workers by organized labor. William Taylor, chairman of the NAACP's legislative committee, described union hostility toward black employees. "Organized labor is hostile to colored people," he declared. "Practically every labor organization in the country denies Negroes the right of membership therein." Unions that admit "colored people restrict their employment to the least desirable work, and, because of the race or color of the darker members of the union, deny them the right to the skilled and, in some instances, the semiskilled positions, regardless of their training, skill, or experience."[13]

Black job seekers received little help from Washington either. America's black population in the 1930s consisted of disproportionately concentrated unskilled agricultural and domestic labor. Helping them proved to be difficult because southern Democrats dominated the U. S. Congress and controlled more than one-half of its congressional committees.[14] The president made it clear that he would not alienate southern congressmen needed for legislative priorities. He admitted that it is "not the purpose of this Administration to impair southern industry by refusing to recognize traditional differentials," meaning

---

[11] John L. Handcox interview with Michael Honey and Joe Glazer, "Songs, Poems, and Stories of the Southern Tenant Farmers Union." Produced by Mark Jackson, West Virginia University Press Sound Archive, December 13, 2000.

[12] James Gray Pope, "Contract, Race, and Freedom of Labor in the Constitutional Law of Involuntary Servitude," *Yale Law Journal* (May 2010), 41.

[13] Juan F. Perea, "The Echoes of Slavery: Recognizing the Racist Origins of the Agricultural and Domestic Worker Exclusion from the National Labor Relations Act," *Ohio State Law Journal* (2011), 14.

[14] Harvard Sitkoff, *A New Deal for Blacks. The Emergence of Civil Rights as a National Issue: The Depression Decade* (New York: Oxford University Press, 1978), 34-35.

lower wages for black workers.[15] Southern legislators devised cynical means to achieve discrimination in government assistance. Since they sought benefits for southern whites, but not blacks, they used race neutral language in legislation. Most southern black workers labored in agriculture and domestic services, so eliminating assistance to those categories blocked funding. Racism seeped into legislation such as the National Industrial Recovery Act (NIRA), Social Security Act (SSA), and Fair Labor Standards Act (FLSA). In addition to statutory exclusions, southern congressmen often delegated control of benefits to local administrators rather than federal agents. Some politicians chose not to hide their intent. Senator Cotton Ed Smith of South Carolina harangued fellow legislators during debates about a version of FLSA without discriminatory provisions. He complained about black participation in political matters and its effect on American culture. "I shall not attempt to use the proper adjective to designate" FLSA. "Any man on this floor who has sense enough to read the English language knows that the main object of this bill is, by human legislation, to overcome the splendid gifts of God to the South." Other southern legislators also defended God's "splendid gifts" to the South. Representative Mark Wilcox of Florida warned that this FLSA draft would not work in the South. "You cannot put the Negro and white man on the same basis and get away with it." He considered the bill a "political gold brick for the Negro."[16]

Many southerners believed that inclusive assistance and services would erode race and class distinctions embedded in their culture. So final drafts of federal legislation contained exclusionary provisions. What happened with the National Labor Relations Act (NLRA) demonstrated the process. Though a first draft contained inclusive language, the final draft did not. It stated that the term employee "shall not include any individual employed as an agricultural laborer, or in the domestic service of any family or person at his home."[17] Such exclusions blocked assistance to black working men and women who often held these positions. President Roosevelt went along with racist federal programs, saying that "I did not choose the tools with which I must work. Had I been permitted to choose them I would have selected quite different ones. But I've got to get legislation passed by Congress to save

---

15 "Racist Origins," 5.

16 Congressional Record, 75th Congress, 2nd Session (1937), 82:1404.

17 National Labor Relations Act, 49 stat. 449, 450, 1935.

America." The president made clear that if he opposed southern legislators "they will block every bill I ask congress to pass to keep America from collapsing." [18]

In another subterfuge adopted by white racists, so-called legal executions replaced lynchings. The NAACP reported that national statistics from 1930 forward showed many more blacks than whites being legally executed. An NAACP Legal Defense Fund brief clarified matters. It said that people sentenced to die were poor, powerless, socially unacceptable, and black in disproportionate percentages. National data confirmed racial discrimination in capital punishment, according to commissions and individuals studying administration of the death penalty in America. [19] The problem dated back to years following the Civil War when southern states provided legal frameworks within which differential applications of the death penalty could prevail. So lack of fair trials for black citizens joined other Civil Rights issues vying for federal attention. After Frank Murphy's appointment as U. S. Attorney General in 1939, he established a special unit to prosecute Civil Rights violations. It became known as the Civil Rights Section (CRS) with peonage one of its first issues for review. Assistant Attorney General Brian McMahon uncovered only three successful prosecutions between 1936 and 1939. Lack of peonage prosecutions and definitional issues led Attorney General Francis Biddle to issue instructions to all U. S. attorneys that they should prosecute peonage using the Slave-Kidnapping Act instead of the Anti-Peonage Act. He reached this decision after a review of department files on alleged peonage violations. They disclosed wholesale instances of prosecutions declined by U. S. attorneys when debt was not an issue. Biddle advised federal attorneys to use involuntary servitude in its stead. Despite increased federal attention paid to peonage claims and Civil Rights violations, STFU organizers continued to meet illegal resistance. An April 16, 1939, union news release reported one outrage. A marshal and thugs beat up three union organizers in Crawfordsville. Jim Thompson, the town marshal, seized D. A. Griffin, E. G. Creasey, and L. H. Van Ryan when they stopped in the town for groceries. Kidnappers took them to Mayor Mosby's office, where he told the three that town residents had no respect for state or federal laws and were

---

[18] *New Deal For Blacks*, 35.

[19] William J. Bowers, et al., *Legal Homicide. Death as Punishment in America 1864-1982* (Boston, Mass.: Northeastern University Press, 1974), 68.

bound only by community laws. Mosby warned that they would be killed and their bodies thrown in the bayou if they returned. After the mayor walked out of his office, Thompson beat the three with a blackjack and refused to let Mosby back in. The mayor called Howard Curlin, a county sheriff, who released the men. When STFU members investigated the incident, Curlin said that he knew nothing about this violence. A May 11, 1939, FBI report referred to the kidnapping and assault, but not disposition of the case.[20]

Another May FBI report contained sworn statements from three black women about mistreatment while working at the Wilson plantation. Mary Elizabeth Hicks, Cassie Neal, and Katie Lee Benimon told similar stories to investigators. Neal said she lived in Memphis when Mattie Knox, "a colored woman," talked to her about working for Wilson. According to Knox, the plantation paid $1 per day for cotton chopping and provided three meals and good lodging. So the three women agreed to work for Wilson. According to Neal, managers put her, Katie Lee Benimon, and Mrs. Benimon's husband Dennis in a room with four other people and one bed. Knox told her recruits that they would work from six a.m. to six p.m. Instead, choppers started work at 4 a.m. and worked without food until 3 p.m. A manager named Joe McFadden gave each person $1.50 worth of food to last a week and paid them with plantation doodlum. Neal said that "I told Mr. McFadden I couldn't work that way and he told me I had to work and that no one could leave the plantation; that if I tried to leave I would be whipped and that if I did leave and get back to Memphis he would send someone over to do away with me." Despite his threat Neal returned to Memphis the following day when McFadden and his "sneakers" were not around. Knox had recruited Mrs. Benimon using the same story about working conditions and wages. However, Mrs. Benimon said that plantation managers locked the door to her sleeping quarters that first day and did not open it until the next morning in time for work. Her husband quit after three days. Mrs. Benimon continued to work there and said that she wrote Dennis after he left, but they would not let her mail letters and told her that Knox would take it to him when she went to Memphis. But Mr. Benimon did not receive any letters. His wife said that plantation managers did not threaten her, but other employees indicated that if she did not do what they wanted, bosses would tie a

---

[20] Department of Justice, Reel 23, 50-72-1.

sack of rocks to her and throw her into a river. After she worked for about two weeks Mr. Benimon came for her despite a "colored boss" warning her that they would "kick me if I tried to leave." She heard that Knox earned $2.50 for each person brought to the plantation. This FBI report made no mention of the case's resolution.[21]

Little Rock's labor department office set in motion another peonage investigation in 1939. A letter from agents there to the U. S. Attorney General enclosed a report about a peonage charge. This investigation focused on alleged abuse of Jessie Paul, a young black man held against his will on the Stimson Mill Co. plantation. He started a crop there, but abandoned it due to what he called family trouble. Management claimed that Paul owed $8. Joe Breedlove, a constable, jailed Paul on authority of a verbal complaint rather than a warrant. Andy Stimson told Paul that he would be freed after working out his debt. The young man went back to work, but as in many peonage cases, the debt increased. Breedlove assessed a $14.75 fine without a trial, and Stimson paid the money to Breedlove. Paul remained on the farm for about six weeks, threatened with arrest if he ran off. During this period his debt increased to $19.93. A state labor department investigator interviewed Paul and told him that he did not have to stay on the plantation. If arrested again for nonrepayment of debt he should have family or friends notify the labor department. In his letter to the U. S. Attorney General the state labor commissioner said that the "Legal Department of the Federal Government in this state [believed] that it was doubtful as to whether a conviction could be had, due to sectional prejudice existing in some sections of this state." The commissioner advised that "In the section where this act occurred, there has been other cases not quite so pronounced a possible violation of the peonage law. It was our opinion unless there is some attempt to call attention to the fact that slavery was abolished some years ago, I am a little fearful that such violations will assume a more pronounced violation of the peonage law." Federal authorities declined to prosecute and closed the case.[22]

---

[21] Department of Justice, Criminal Division, Reel 23, 50-72-1.
[22] Department of Justice, Division of Records, Reel 19, 50-767.

Top, a young black migrant from the South machines aircraft engine parts for the war effort. Photo by Ann Rosener, 1942. Farm Security Administration Collection. Library of Congress Prints and Photographs Division. *Bottom, Mexicans pick cotton in Arkansas.* University of Texas-El Paso.

CHAPTER 17

Wars Here and There

During the 1940s, many Delta men had to fight planters or Nazis, and some chose Nazis. Before Japanese forces attacked Pearl Harbor on December 7, 1941, the federal government prepared men for military service. The Civilian Conservation Corp (CCC) recruited them for its training program and paid $30 per month along with room and board. CCC served as a source for military recruits, and its officials handed out material encouraging them to join the National Defense Program. Government jobs and those at manufacturing plants put many families on an upward path toward higher incomes and better living conditions. Concerned about their trajectory, planters attempted to divert them. A Georgia landlord sought to extradite from Chicago four former workers, but an unlikely ally interceded. William Huff, an attorney and prominent Georgian, defended the four to stop extradition. Huff despised peonage "with all my heart, soul, and mind" and called it "Hitlerized bestiality." Along with like-minded people in Chicago and New York, Huff helped establish the Abolish Peonage Committee of America. He contributed money to the four runaway employees of William T. Cunningham in Georgia, but in February 1940 the justice department announced that despite evidence supporting peonage charges against Cunningham it would not prosecute. Huff wrote a friend that "the Department of Justice as now constituted just simply does not intend to prosecute white persons for anything they do to Negroes!"[1] Though some peonage prosecutions took place, many southern employers ignored laws designed to stop this crime. Criminal surety remained a popular device in the Delta, and in one case it produced perplexing results. Milton R. Konvitz, an NAACP counsel, wrote an association member about a man who received a life sentence, but was paroled on condition that he work on a designated farm.[2] A U.S. Attorney explained that when a "good working negro" neared the end of his sentence, authorities rearrested him and sentenced the man to additional time, often to be served in a cotton patch.

Though cotton production in some ways resisted mechanization, by 1940 many growers used tractors to plant and cultivate their crops. The mechanical revolution spread rapidly when the Rust brothers, John D. and Mack, developed spindle cotton pickers. Soon big business took over. In 1942, International Harvester Company sold mechanical pickers, and Allis Chalmers soon joined the competition. One machine could harvest about 190,000 pounds per day, and an excellent manual picker only 500 pounds. Some drivers earned a princely sum of $22.50 per week. Though planters preferred hand labor for chopping and picking, the age of machines had arrived.[3] Unfortunately for Delta cotton producers who still depended on hand labor, the region's black population declined at a steady clip. By the 1940s, black families urbanized more rapidly than the white population. They grew tired of fighting battles with planters and their proxies.

FBI agents revealed an egregious example in a report dated February 28, 1941. It developed from a complaint filed by Albert Wright. A decision not to prosecute seemed suspicious given numerous corroborating witnesses. According to the synopsis of facts, this black farm worker from Hurlbert said that his employer, K. P. Robbins, did not pay him for work. The planter claimed that Wright owed him money and could not leave his plantation without paying the debt, an obvious example of peonage. Wright moved anyhow, and his wife and child were jailed for several hours to make her tell where Wright went. His wife said that Robbins threatened to kill her husband if he found him, so she refused to cooperate. Other "colored" sharecroppers confirmed

---

[1] Huff to General W. Smith, October 15, 1942, Department of Justice, File 50-837, Rg. 60, National Archives.

[2] Milton R. Konvitz to L. S. Perry, July 8, 1943, NAACP Papers, 13c, Reel 12:608-609.

[3] James H. Street, *New Revolution in the Cotton Economy* (Chapel Hill, University of North Carolina Press, 1957), 115, 133, 167.

that Robbins would not pay them and threatened to keep their personal property if they left his plantation, and the FBI completed a second report with additional interviews on April, 28, 1941. Wright also claimed that Robbins violated crop set-aside rules. The planter plowed up one-half of the tenant's acres and none of his own in order to meet AAA requirements. Wright then had only four acres, not enough to pay debts, so he abandoned the crop. Wright worked as a day laborer on a local plantation until he secured work on the Miller & Rembert plantation in Crittenden County. Frank Miller, a plantation manager there, sent a truck to the Robbins plantation to bring back Wright's wife, two children, and a few household items.

After Wright advised his landlord that he would surrender his remaining acres, the planter told Wright that if he tried to move, Robbins would put him in jail. When Wright asked for an itemized statement of expenses, Robbins told him that he didn't have time to prepare one. Wright said that two "colored" men knew about this mistreatment – Will Logan and A. D. Stewart. Wright's wife testified that Robbins asked Pat Clark, city marshal of Hughes, to put her in jail, but the marshal refused. However, he gave the jail keys to Robbins, who locked her up along with her one-year-old child. Other sharecroppers verified mistreatment on the Robbins plantation. Ethel Stewart, "colored," said that in recent months "practically all of the negro sharecroppers" had moved because of the planter's treatment of them. She never heard Robbins threaten to physically harm dissatisfied tenants, but the planter told them that if they left he would lock up their houses and refuse to let them take any of their personal property. She said that most of the "colored" sharecroppers had moved away in the middle of the night. Tim Rucker, another Robbins tenant, called doodlum allocated to families on the plantation insufficient to feed them. Though he never heard Robbins threaten violence against those leaving the plantation, Rucker said that the planter would withhold all of a family's furniture and clothing. Other tenants who escaped Robbins confirmed the planter's behavior: insufficient furnish to support their families, manipulated debt balances, reduction of tenant crops for AAA payment compliance, and threats to punish croppers who left without paying their alleged debt. Though some tenants did not claim to have heard threats of violence, Will Logan said that Thomas House, a plantation foreman, told Wright that if he did not get back to work the foreman would "hit him in the head with a hammer." The nature of

Robbins's abuses, most connected to alleged debt, and numerous witnesses verifying his behavior made the decision not to prosecute the planter a puzzling conclusion. But on May 21, 1942, an Assistant U. S. Attorney General sent a memorandum to the FBI stating that the file was being closed because "appraisal indicates that the case is not strong enough to warrant presentment to a grand jury."[4]

The case of G. W. Underwood revealed another alleged kidnapping by planters and substantially different versions of what happened. Underwood complained to NAACP's Houston branch about a Forrest City planter, Pugh Hodges (identified as Hugh Hodges in some instances). That branch contacted its national office in New York about Underwood's claims of peonage and kidnapping. Members there notified the justice department, which led to a July 17, 1943, FBI report about involuntary servitude and slavery. The synopsis of facts included the following. Underwood sharecropped on the Pugh Hodges plantation, but he left after a year, refusing to work for existing wages. Underwood claimed that after being threatened, Janie Underwood, his wife, moved with their five children to the farm of Ray Hodges, brother of Pugh Hodges. Underwood visited his family there and became dissatisfied with that arrangement so he planned to relocate his family to Marianna. Ray Hodges refused to allow them to move their possessions until the sharecropper paid debts he supposedly owed the planter. Another FBI report dated August 23, 1943, provided additional information about the controversy and contradictory accounts. Underwood claimed that Ray Hodges seized the family's War Price and Ration Board ration books as well as their personal property and sold a portion of it. After Underwood refused to return to the Pugh Hodges plantation he had to "dodge a mob" and escape to Houston, where he secured employment through the NAACP.

While in Houston, Underwood received a letter from his wife saying that Ray Hodges had moved her and the children back to his farm after threatening to "put the government on her." According to W. J. Clanton, a Delta landlord, Janie Underwood was moved while her husband was away and, "so far as the informant knew, this move was made voluntarily by Janie Underwood and no force or threats were employed by anyone to get her to make this change." An Underwood aunt told the FBI that as far as she knew, no one threatened G. W.

---

[4]Department of Justice, Criminal Division, Division of Records, Reel 20, 50-9-4.

Underwood's family or moved Janie Underwood against her will. The aunt expressed "little faith in the veracity and integrity of G. W. Underwood and stated that he was not liked by members of his own race locally." Janie Underwood told John E. Jackson that she moved to the Ray Hodges farm because she needed food, and Hodges never forced her to move or threatened her. According to Jackson, "Mr. Hodges tried to get G. W. to work on the farm and was going to pay him but G. W. didn't want to work and hid from Mr. Hodges." When the War Price & Rationing Board investigated claims that Hodges seized the family's ration books the planter said that "You have been misinformed about the books. I am not holding no books for a debt. They went off owing me a debt and left their furniture [and] if the books is in it, I do not know. No one has called to see. If they call and books are here the books will [be made] available." After agents discussed the case with an Assistant U. S. Attorney he declined prosecution, stating that the facts in the case did not warrant action.[5]

Though Delta planters attempted in every way possible to stop them, employees steadily headed north during the war. About 11 per cent of the state's population departed from April 1940 to November 1943. They found employment where they earned better wages and put food on the table without begging planters for furnish. Their children went to school rather than a cotton field. This exit during the 1940s contributed to "one of the most significant demographic shifts in American history."[6] Planters chafed as leverage shifted. They wanted tall cotton, high prices, and low wages, but some federal policies threatened this trifecta. Tasked with routing labor according to need, the War Manpower Commission (WMC) established a United States Employment Service (USES) to place them. Lack of control incensed landlords, particularly when WMC decided that the Delta had surplus labor. Planters became outraged when WMC, cooperating with FSA and STFU, sponsored a program to move workers into other regions during layby season. More than 90 percent of these workers returned in time for cotton harvest, but planters resented even this temporary loss of

[5] Department of Justice, Criminal Division, Division of Records, LR file no. 50-9-10.

[6] James Patterson, *Grand Expectations. The United States, 1945-1974* (New York: Oxford University Press, 1996), 19.

control during a slack period.[7] U. S. Secretary of Agriculture Claude R. Wickard pointed out that farm laborers on average earned 30 cents an hour compared to industrial wages of 80 cents, and this disparity should be reduced. He believed that wages should be nearer to $2,400 per year. His attitude and intent produced an alliance between planters and the American Farm Bureau Federation to block Wickard's goals. They began with passage of Public Law 45 in 1942 that created an Emergency Farm Labor Supply Program to implement Farm Bureau recommendations. Successful lobbying added a Pace Amendment, which prohibited use of federal funds to establish minimum wages and maximum hours, regulate housing, or recognize collective bargaining by farm workers. Pace prevented use of federal expenditures to assist with transportation of laborers to other regions without a county agent's release. This amendment became a big win for landlords.[8]

Public Law 45 offered deferments to farm workers from military draft, and planters gained a new motto: work, fight, or go to jail. County agents denied releases to workers for travel to new jobs and threatened them with the draft. This device failed in some instances when men chose to fight Nazis rather than planters. Military service and manufacturing jobs posed the same problems for landlords that existed in World War I. First, they lost an employee. Second, servicemen and factory workers sent checks home to family members, which weakened planter control. Some Delta landlords insisted that employees sign five-year contracts or be drafted. They presented tenants with labor contracts, claiming they were AAA payment forms, and refused to allow tenants to read them. A Florida company recruited in Arkansas by using misleading practices. United States Sugar Company (USSC) agents preyed on patriotic American youths, claiming that jobs on its plantations were national defense work. New hires believed this because of the company's name. USSC flyers solicited "colored farm workers" wanting to enjoy Florida sunshine during winter months. The company displayed several peonage features. After charges for transportation and purchase of work tools, employees found themselves in debt. The company lied about wages, leaving workers unable to pay out. Managers warned that those attempting to leave

[7] Nan Elizabeth Woodruff, "Pick or Fight: The Emergency Farm Labor Program in the Arkansas and Mississippi Deltas during World War II," *Agricultural History* 64:2 (Spring 1990), 77.
[8] "Pick or Fight," 79.

would be jailed or murdered. Employees endured brutal work, filthy living conditions, and food unfit for human consumption. Guards prevented mail from coming in or going out, and management located camps amid imposing terrain. Though they blocked commercial transportation, some workers escaped, and told their stories to relatives and friends who demanded a justice department investigation.[9]

By 1940 more peonage victims contacted federal authorities directly requesting help. Previously, lawyers looked for test cases to prosecute crimes in federal courts, but as letters from victims poured into the justice department a new approach emerged. "Instead of being acted upon as objects in labor and law, peons asserted their agency in both the coerced labor relationship and the legal process by complaining to the federal government."[10] An important response to numerous peonage complaints came from Attorney General Francis Biddle in 1941. Circular No. 3591 provided new guidance about peonage prosecutions. It began with an observation that a summary of department files on alleged violations disclosed numerous instances of declined prosecutions by U. S. attorneys, the chief reason being absence of debt. Biddle said that these prosecutorial decisions were reached after considering facts at hand only in accordance with case law. He stressed that it is the "purpose of these instructions to direct the attention of the United States Attorneys to the possibilities of successful prosecutions stemming from alleged peonage complaints which have heretofore been considered inadequate to invoke federal jurisdiction." He recommended building cases around involuntary servitude and slavery, "disregarding the element of debt." The circular added that if a claimed debt was the basis of intimidation to compel services the indictment should be a separate count.[11]

Vulnerable American workers found a questionable ally, an unwanted one no doubt, in Germany. Nazi propaganda attempted to fan resentment and foment rebellion among black victims of

---

[9] *Lost Promise*, 1-2.

[10] Risa L. Goluboff "Won't You Please Help Me Get My Son Home: Peonage, Patronage, and Protest in the World War II Urban South," *Law and Social Inquiry* 24 (Fall 1999), 782.

[11] U. S. Attorney General Francis Biddle, Circular No. 3591, Office of the Attorney General (Washington, D.C.: December 12, 1941), 1-2. Re: Involuntary Servitude, Slavery, and Peonage. https://en.wikisource.org/wiki/Circular No. 3591, accessed Sept. 23, 2016.

discrimination. Writing to a U. S. Attorney in Texas about a dropped peonage case, U. S. Assistant Attorney General Wendell Berge warned about enemy propagandists using such incidents in international broadcasts. They charged the United States with insincerity about minorities and called Nazis their real allies. As a result, President Roosevelt ordered that lynching complaints be investigated as soon as possible and the government's efforts be fully publicized.[12] The black press demanded additional prosecutions and pointed out the hypocrisy inherent in America's anti-Nazi rhetoric and treatment of black citizens. However, feigned Nazi sympathy for black Americans did not exist inside the German border. Hitler's speeches contained tirades against blacks, warning his countrymen of "racial bastardization" of German culture and German art being "negrified."[13] Many American newspaper editorials rejected comparisons between the Nazi persecution of Jews and lynching of black citizens. They pointed out that lynching was a crime, while the German government supported the murder of Jews. But newspapers failed to point out that southern states rarely prosecuted murderers of black people. A student newspaper at the University of Arkansas, *Arkansas Traveler*, on November 29, 1938, pointed out this hypocrisy. It connected the refusal to grant the "Negro equal rights" and Hitler's ideas about Jews. A December 2, 1938, *Arkansas Democrat* rejected this comparison and blamed the student's misplaced fervor on the negative effects of higher education.

Some laborers during the 1940s endured an arduous journey from Mexico to the Delta, and they were not the first to do so. In 1917 and 1918, more than 300 Mexican workers came to Arkansas, constituting the first sign of large-scale Mexican migration to the state.[14] After the American and Mexican governments finalized a labor agreement in 1942, word spread through radio, newspapers, and word of mouth. When this program got underway both governments scrambled to manage crowds of people at the U.S. Embassy in Mexico City. Applicants hoped to get a contract for one of 1,000 jobs north of the

---

[12] Berge to Steve M. King, Aug. 8, 1942, Department of Justice, File 50-74-4, Rg. 60, National Archives.

[13] Johnpeter Horst Grill and Robert L. Jenkins, "The Nazis and the American South in the 1930s: A Mirror Image?" *The Journal of Southern History* 58:4 (November 1992), 671.

[14] Justin Castro, "Mexican Braceros and Arkansas Cotton: Agricultural Labor and Civil Rights in the Post-World War II South," *Arkansas Historical Quarterly* 75:1 (Spring 2016), 29.

border. It became known as the bracero program, since the term bracero came to mean people who performed manual labor. Braceros who won a coveted 90-day work permit found that the Delta differed in several ways from northern and western states participating in the program. Differences included politics, types of crops, and a legacy of slavery.[15] Delta weather shocked Mexican migrants, too. Many came during fall months wearing sandals and short-sleeved work shirts. They immediately bought heavier clothes, an unexpected expense. Rainy weather reduced take-home pay since braceros earned wages based on how much cotton they picked, not for hours worked. Delays impacted their families in Mexico who depended on checks from the United States. During the 1940s, braceros found relationships with black and white people contingent not only on race, but also on class. Many Arkansans found Mexicans exotic and harmless. Others considered them an economic threat. Some made a distinction between working-class braceros and so-called higher-class Mexicans, but even the higher-class Mexicans experienced problems. When a Mexican consul arrived in Pine Bluff to investigate bracero conditions, local officials attempted to divert him away from the town's only hotel. They suggested that he stay at a campground because the hotel did not want him there, but he refused, and a room became available.[16]

[15] Rocio Gomez, "Braceros in the Arkansas Delta,1943-1964," *Ozark Historical Review* 39 (Spring 2010), 8.
[16] Julie M. Weise, *Corazon De Dixie. Mexicanos in the U.S. South Since 1910* (Chapel Hill: University of North Carolina Press, 2015), 91, 93.

Top, Japanese Americans interned at the Rohwer Relocation Center are shown harvesting a cucumber crop. Bancroft Library, University of California-Berkeley. *Bottom, German prisoners of war arrive at Camp Joseph T. Robinson in North Little Rock during WWII.* Arkansas State Archives.

CHAPTER 18

Some Lost Everything

While braceros came to the Delta voluntarily, other people did not. By executive order in 1942, the war department relocated people of Japanese ancestry from the Pacific Coast. Officials cited national security as the reason for removing thousands of Japanese American citizens from their homes, but racial prejudice contributed.[1] Though their plight might seem entirely different from that of peonage victims, Japanese Americans suffered under similar conditions. Authorities required them to clear inhospitable land, dictated wages, and limited freedom of movement. Two of the ten internment camps in the country were located in Arkansas. The Rohwer Camp had 10,161 acres, and Jerome consisted of 10,054 acres. In September 1942, internees arrived in Rohwer and lived there until November 1945; in Jerome from October 1942 to June 1944. Confined workers earned wages varying from $12 to $19 per month plus furnished necessities. Unfortunately, they suffered an incalculable loss of wealth due to their removal. Some lost everything they had, and many lost most of what they had. Additionally, it was difficult to measure the suffering and humiliation these Americans endured.[2] Though internees did not experience physical violence they suffered

---

[1] C. Calvin Smith, "The Response of Arkansans to Prisoners of War and Japanese Americans in Arkansas, 1942-1945," *Arkansas Historical Quarterly* 53:3 (Autumn 1994), 341.

[2] William Cary Anderson, "Early Reaction in Arkansas to the Relocation of Japanese in the State," *Arkansas Historical Quarterly* 23:3 (Autumn 1964), 197.

legislative attacks. The *Arkansas Gazette* reported on January 13, 1943, that a bill under consideration prohibited both alien and citizen Japanese from owning land in the state. Senator B. Frank Williams, sponsor of the bill, said that he wanted to make sure "no Japs can stay in this state." He claimed that white people could not profitably compete with Japanese. A discriminatory statute passed in the state senate by a vote of 30 to one.

As Japanese Americans struggled with this new form of peonage, authorities dealt with the old forms. Sometimes accusations emerged when planters competed for the same employees. A March 7, 1943, FBI report uncovered a case on point. C. E. Lawler, a manager on the George Hornor plantation, filed charges of involuntary servitude and slavery against Percy Magness. Lawler claimed that Magness caused the prosecution of black farm hands to prevent them from moving to the Hornor plantation in Phillips County. Lawler also accused Magness of having him assaulted because Lawler contracted with some employees to work for Hornor. When he arrived to transport them, Lawler learned that they had been sent to jail for petty thefts, which he believed they had not committed. The Hornor manager stated that Magness and local officials schemed to prevent him from relocating workers and that authorities would not allow Lawler to pay their fines. Hornor confirmed the threats and abuse experienced by his managers, including Dave Norton. In January, Norton went to Parkin, and three men who he recognized as Magness farm managers attacked him. When Lawler drove through Parkin, people ordered him to leave town and advised Lawler to keep away from Magness property or he would be charged with trespass. In several reports the FBI provided testimony with different versions of events related to the Magness-Hornor controversy. In a May 29, 1943, memorandum to the FBI, an Assistant U. S. Attorney advised that the file be closed, "inasmuch as no basis for successful prosecution is presented."[3]

A December 2, 1943, FBI report revealed an instance when a mother attempted to help her son allegedly held in a state of involuntary servitude. Sephirina Stanley, "colored," from North Little Rock told the FBI that W. S. Rodie, a white planter, would not allow her son to leave his plantation. Rodie recruited Cephus Holmes to work on his property near Grand Lake. Stanley received a letter from her son

---

3 Department of Justice, Division of Records, Reel 20, 50-9-7.

which said that he wanted to return home, but Rodie would not allow it. The planter supposedly told Holmes that if he attempted to leave, Rodie would put him in jail. Holmes admitted that the landlord gave him whatever he wanted, except for cash. Stanley received another letter dated November 16, 1943. In it her son said that he would be home for Christmas and would continue to work for Rodie to earn money for the trip home. Though this letter suggested that Rodie had a change of heart, the timing is suspect. The planter agreed to Holmes's departure shortly after the FBI investigation began. Regardless, agents closed the case.[4]

During the war, planters claimed that patriotism required them to keep tenants on their farms hard at work supporting the troops, but greed mattered. Mississippi State University's Frank Welch published a 1943 report titled "Plantation Land Tenure System." Head of the school's agricultural economics department, he verified continuing abusive treatment of tenants by landlords. Welch's charges included familiar ones: cheating on rent at settlement time, use of oral contracts rather than written ones to void terms that proved less profitable, and blocking tenants from reviewing crop records. To combat these practices, justice department attorneys sought applicable federal jurisdictions. U. S. Attorney Fred Folsom dusted off an 1866 slave kidnapping law to prosecute cases of forced labor. He described an enslaved person as someone "so far subjected to the will of another that he is held to labor or service against his will."[5]

In a November 1, 1944, FBI report about alleged slavery, Ruther Mae Bailey claimed that Arthur White, "an elderly white man," held her sister, Millie Jackson, "colored," against her will in Wilmot. Jackson worked for Arthur, his brother Robert, and their sister Minnie, doing housework and sharecropping cotton. A couple drove Ruther and her husband Horace from Arkansas City to the White home when Jackson supposedly wrote them to come get her. After the Baileys arrived, Arthur refused to let Jackson go, calling her "under contract," and Robert threatened them with a pistol. Ruther apparently wanted Jackson to return to Arkansas City and care for their elderly aunt. In an FBI interview with Jackson, she admitted being unable to read or write and had Minnie write the Baileys to advise that she would not be willing

---

[4] Department of Justice, Division of Records, Reel 20, 50-9-12.
[5] *Lost Promise*, 146.

to go to Arkansas City until after Jackson gathered her crop and helped the Whites harvest theirs. Jackson advised the Baileys that she would send for them when ready to move. After the crop had been harvested, Jackson had Minnie write another letter asking the Baileys to come for her. Jackson told investigators that she worked 12 years for the Whites and did not consider them indebted to her, and neither was she indebted to them. In a second report Jackson denied that Arthur had ever prevented her from leaving his farm. She said that during her 12 years employed by the Whites, she tilled four acres of cotton, her "own crop," and did housework. The Whites furnished her food and clothing. According to Jackson, "not once" did the Whites refuse to pay her for work or for crop shares on her four acres. After interviews and fact gathering the justice department concluded that available information did not warrant criminal proceedings and declined prosecution.[6]

Despite many peonage files marked "declined prosecution," several 1944 court decisions proved decisive. A federal appeals court upheld conviction of an employer who purchased goods and billed them to an employee without the worker's permission. This created a contrived debt to control the employee. The court found that in peonage prosecutions neither amount of the debt nor means of coercion mattered. It was sufficient to prove that a person was held against his will and forced to work for repayment of a debt.[7] An important U. S. Supreme Court decision also involved contractual debt. In this case attorneys prosecuted an employer using the 1867 peonage act.[8] A man named Gaskin operated a turpentine camp in Florida and forced James Johnson back to the camp after he escaped. The operator claimed that Johnson owed $20. Despite Gaskin's threat to kill him, Johnson ran off again. The first attempt to secure a federal indictment against Gaskin failed, but a second succeeded. The justice department developed this case to determine if seizure of a victim who escaped before forced to labor resulted in a crime. The U.S. Supreme Court's decision made it a criminal act to arrest a person with intent to hold him in peonage, even though intent was never realized. In 1944, U. S. Supreme Court Justice Robert Jackson wrote that protection from peonage came in two forms, a shield and a sword created by the U. S. Congress.[9] The shield "enabled

---

[6] Department of Justice, Criminal Division, Reel 20, 50-9-15.
[7] *Pierce v. United States,* 146 F. 2d 84 (5th. Cir., 1944).
[8] *United States v. Gaskin*, 320 U. S. 527 (1944).
[9] *Pollock v. Williams*, 322 U. S. 4 (1944).

a person whose freedom is endangered to invoke the Constitution by requesting a federal court to invalidate the state action that is endangering his rights." The sword wielded by the federal government "takes the initiative in protecting helpless individuals by bringing criminal charges against persons who are encroaching upon their rights."[10]

Some Delta workers lacked access to either protection Jackson described. The government housed more than 425,000 prisoners of war (POWs) in the United States during World War II. Arkansas held about 23,000 of them, mostly Germans. They proved to be a valuable source of manpower for farms, factories, and civic projects in a time of significant labor shortages due to military needs.[11] Main camps – Chaffee, Robinson, and Dermott – supported small work sites scattered across Arkansas with many in the Delta. Dermott occupied about 960 acres near Jerome, which housed troublesome prisoners called Nazi fanatics. Geneva Convention terms governed their treatment and prohibited dangerous or unhealthy working conditions. The guidelines required enlisted men to work, but not officers or non-commissioned officers (NCOs). POWs received 10 cents a day if idle and 80 cents for each day of contract labor outside the camp. Officers and NCOs received more money whether they worked or not, and each prisoner earned scrip redeemable at a camp canteen. Some of this sounds familiar – imprisoned workers, pitiful wages, and the equivalent of plantation store doodlum. POWs became increasingly important as military needs and industrial jobs outside the state reduced available Delta workers. Despite employer efforts to meet this shortfall, a widening gap between labor supply and demand could not be bridged with available American workers.

When the war department announced that POWs could work outside the fence, Arkansas employers lined up. Planters applied to participate through their agricultural extension service. However, the War Manpower Commission (WMC) had to verify shortages of civilian labor that made POWs necessary, and planters had to pay prisoners a prevailing wage. Each worker received 80 cents per day, and the federal

---

[10] Robert K. Carr, *Federal Protection of Civil Rights: Quest for a Sword* (Ithaca, N. Y.: Cornell University Press, 1947), 5.

[11] Merrill R. Pritchett and William L. Shea, "The Afrika Korps in Arkansas, 1943-1946," *Arkansas Historical Quarterly* 37:1 (Spring 1978), 3.

government took the rest. Washington officials set up about 30 work camps around the state, with 26 in the Delta. Always on the lookout for cheap labor, 25 Mississippi County planters formed Chickasawba Farmers Association to build a POW camp at Blytheville. A March 31, 1944, *Arkansas Gazette* reported the results. "Blytheville will have a prison camp to house 600 German prisoners and 120 Army guards. It will be located on 20 acres at the west side of the city. The recently organized Chickasawba Farmers Association will finance part of the project, with the government bearing the remainder of the cost. It will be the second camp in Mississippi County. Another at Victoria, 18 miles southwest of Blytheville, houses an undisclosed number of German prisoners who are farming land of the Lee Wilson Company. The Bassett and Keiser communities also are seeking such camps and approval of projects is expected soon. Prisoners probably will be quartered here in time to chop the 1944 cotton crop." POWs and guards arrived in Blytheville during July 1944, and association members employed the workers.

Many Germans abhorred chopping and picking cotton, refused to pick their daily quota, and ignored complaints about it. German prisoners performed well when handling machinery, but not hoes and pick sacks. Despite some problems, Delta planters admitted that POWs saved cotton crops by helping harvest them before ruinous winter weather arrived. Germans considered Arkansans backward, and Arkansans considered Germans arrogant, probably true in both cases. But for the most part they got along. At the behest of planters, President Harry Truman delayed repatriation at the war's end due to severe agricultural labor shortages, but by May 1946 the last prisoners headed home. POW labor in the South may have "helped to extend the life of an exploitive plantation economy."[12] This also may be attributed to the efforts of planters to break the rules and avoid the penalties. Though landlords called prisoner labor necessary due to a shortage of other sources, to some extent they dissembled. The federal government and STFU conducted studies indicating that sufficient labor existed if landlords paid decent wages. Responding to complaints, WMC referred to its prevailing wage requirement. This did not appease H. L. Mitchell who believed that regardless of the rules, planters would break them and get away with it. According to an STFU bulletin, county farm labor

---

[12] Jason Morgan Ward, "Nazis Hoe Cotton: Planters, POWs, and the Future of Farm Labor in the Deep South," *Agricultural History* 81:4 (Fall 2007), 471.

committees included planters and allies who determined need and set prevailing wages. The STFU chose Crittenden County to make its point. According to a union newsletter, the county contained about 1,000 POW farm workers, which allowed planters to fix wage rates and force Americans to accept them. WMC admitted that in some instances county agents established wage rates by polling planters.

Edwin Peltz, a German POW, said that on the first day he picked cotton "There were aches and pains across my back and arms. I was half dead. By noon my sack was full and so heavy I had difficulty pulling it between the rows of cotton plants." POWs were supposed to pick 120 pounds of cotton each day, and his friends explained to Peltz that they made their quota by putting stones and other heavy objects in their sacks to increase weights. Germans who protested picking "tree wool," their name for cotton, sometimes pulled sacks through mud and water to increase weights, though it lowered grades and values.[13] Despite being held prisoner, Germans possessed some advantages that black workers lacked. They could not be evicted from homes or denied food if they refused to work since Geneva Convention requirements protected them. An army manual issued to planters advised that landlords might "find it unwise and at times impossible to use all of the supervisory techniques you may have used to advantage in supervising the work of free American labor."[14] Treatment of POWs displayed white privilege in the Delta. Pastor F. W. A. Eiermann reported an Osceola planter to federal authorities for forcing Germans to work ten hours a day in the parching sun. He feared that some might experience sun strokes and should not be worked on schedules fixed by plantation owners who normally employed "Negro labor." Subjecting white men, even enemies, to grueling physical toil became a sensitive issue. Disparity between race and class did not go unnoticed among Germans. Hein Severloh, a POW, expressed astonishment at the plight of black workers in the Delta. He questioned how they endured such wretched conditions.[15]

---

13 William L. Shea, ed. "A German Prisoner of War in the South: The Memoir of Edwin Pelz," *Arkansas Historical Quarterly* 44:1 (Spring 1985), 53.
14 United States Army Service Forces, Handbook for Work Supervisors of Prisoners of War Labor (Washington, D. C.: Army Service Forces Manual M-811, 1945), 3.
15 Handbook for Work Supervisors, 1.

Though Delta planters used POWs and other opportunities to avoid raising wages during the war, eventually they gave up some ground. Assisted by the STFU, field workers won picking wage increases. However, Mitchell overbid his hand in 1945 by proposing an increase to $3.50 per hundred, assuming planters would fold again. They did not and asked political allies for help. Landlords sought a federally imposed limit on picking wages of $2.05. They claimed that escalating labor costs would drive them out of business and reduce their patriotic efforts to support American soldiers. The USDA scheduled hearings and voting on the matter, and landlords dominated them. Vote tallies gave planters a wage cap of $2.05 per hundred. In the Delta only 2,757 persons voted against the cap, and 9,356 cast ballots for it, a peculiar tally given that the region's poor vastly outnumbered the rich. Mitchell claimed that planters prevented most farm workers from casting ballots.[16] Some workers refused to pick for such low wages, and a January 1, 1945, *Delta Farm Press* criticized them. This planter-friendly periodical railed at women in a shameful article. It claimed that "The government has been very liberal with its people. Your husband goes off to war and Uncle Sam sends you a check. If you quit work and live on that check you are not helping the government which is helping you." This lack of patriotism, claimed the writer, aided the enemy, and if "your husband or son is in the army and he comes home with one leg or arm broken, it may have been your fault."

Despite some favorable court rulings and justice department instructions to expand the bounds of peonage, planters continued to assert their control over vulnerable employees. In a 1945 Arkansas case, George Canady planned to go to work for J. J. Michaelis, a Palestine, Arkansas, landlord. According to an FBI synopsis, when Michaelis sent his son to move the sharecropper to his farm, his previous employer, Jessie Heustess, would not let Canady leave. Heustess claimed that Canady owed him $50 for house rent and wood used to supply fuel in his home and could not leave unless it was paid. Michaelis said it was "not customary" for farmers in that region to charge sharecroppers for house rent or wood they used as fuel in their homes, but he paid the alleged debt on Canady's behalf "to avoid further trouble." FBI director J. Edgar Hoover forwarded the field agent's report to Assistant Attorney General Tom C. Clark, asking for advice on whether Heustess should be prosecuted for holding Canady. Clark advised Hoover that

---

[16] *American Congo*, 212.

"from the information presently available it appears that the institution of criminal proceedings is not warranted."[17]

Among FBI peonage investigations at the war's end, one stands out because an Arkansas deputy sheriff supported a black farm worker, Roy Hill, and not the planter. A September 7, 1945, FBI report presented Hill's charges of involuntary servitude and slavery. The problems began when St. Francis County authorities issued three warrants for Hill, charging him with rape, two counts of grand larceny, and burglary. The accused lived in Phillips County, and Deputy Sheriff Edgar P. Hickey from that county called the warrants false and that they had been issued in order to compel Hill's return to Grady Trainer's farm where the accused previously resided. Three women supposedly witnessed the rape, one man the grand larceny, and Trainer supported a second grand larceny charge. A December 6, 1945, FBI report stated that a St. Francis County circuit court found Hill guilty of carnal abuse and sentenced him to one year and a day in the state penitentiary. However, the court suspended his sentence and released Hill to L. C. Jolly, who posted a $1,000 bond. Other charges remained pending. When Hickey arrested Hill, the tenant called these charges trumped up because he moved his family and a few personal items to Lafe Solomon's farm. Trainer claimed that Hill owed him $250, which Hill denied. Hickey brought this matter to the FBI's attention because he believed Trainer sought Hill's arrest to force the tenant back to Trainer's plantation. But after reviewing the reports and charges against Trainer, an assistant attorney general refused to prosecute him.[18]

In another FBI investigation that fall, A. J. Friedley and his wife Annie accused Emmett Speck of involuntary servitude and slavery. These charges appeared in an October 18, 1945, report that illustrated the lengths a planter would go to control black tenants. The report contained a statement signed by A. J. Friedley and his wife that supported their charges. Friedley contracted with Speck to sharecrop and in 1945 farmed 25 acres of cotton and 15 acres of corn. When Friedley, a World War I veteran with stomach problems, went to the Memphis Veterans Hospital for a checkup, his three sons and their mother tended the crop in his absence. But Speck sent them home and brought in four day laborers to lay by the crop. Speck told Mrs. Friedley

[17] Department of Justice, Criminal Division, Reel 20, 50-9-16.
[18] Department of Justice, Criminal Division, Reel 20, 50-9-17.

and her boys that he had no work for them and continued to use hired hands. After Friedley came home he told the day laborers that his family had not surrendered the crop. Speck disagreed and stopped the family's furnish, which caused Friedley to take a job in Memphis. Speck told Friedley that he could move, but only after he paid the landlord $250. When a Gilmore planter arrived to pick up the Friedley family, Speck told him that the alleged debt had to be paid first. After that relocation failed, Banks & Danner plantation agreed to hire the Friedleys, but Speck warned those planters about the debt repayment. When the sons went to work for Buddie Watson, Speck arranged to have them fired. He successfully froze the family out of the Delta farm labor market and forced them to work on his plantation. Unfortunately, the justice department sent a November 14, 1945, letter to J. Edgar Hoover declining to prosecute.[19]

In an unusual development, a planter lost his peonage case in Cross County. Prosecutors charged Albert Sydney Johnson with the crime, and U. S. Attorney General Francis Biddle in *Safeguarding Civil Liberties Today* described the planter's treatment of laborers. Johnson terrorized black and white workers, threatening to kill them if they tried to run away. He carried a gun and brass knuckles to back up his threats. Tenant families so feared him that they slipped away at night, leaving their possessions and standing crops.[20] A sheriff reported that Johnson held 14 persons in peonage for about two and one-half years. At a time when more than one-third of rural black families made less than $500 per year, Johnson claimed that William Reddick accrued a debt of $600 in a single year and Corrie Duckett owed almost $300 for a six-month furnish. Sometimes accounts were so high "as to be ludicrous," said Biddle.[21] After an FBI investigation, Johnson pled guilty to peonage charges and accepted a prison sentence.

In his *Civil Liberties Today* article, Biddle mistakenly claimed that convictions had been effective in breaking up at least the direct practice of peonage. Unfortunately, they eliminated some symptoms, but not the disease. The plague of Delta peonage that still exists began with freedmen who found their way into Union camps despite the danger if slave chasers found them first. Black families endured Jim Crow's many

---

[19] Department of Justice, Division of Records, Reel 20, 50-9-18.
[20] *Federal Protection*, 180.
[21] *Lost Promise*, 63.

humiliations and overcame the barriers he erected. They fought for the rights and opportunities the Constitution promised them despite planters who seized the fruits of their labor. During the Great Depression, blacks joined vulnerable white people who also were cheated out of assistance promised them by their government. Many refused to back down in the face of powerful adversaries. Men and women, black and white, withstood the racism, greed, and cruelty that contaminated the region. Sometimes these brave people stood alone, sometimes arm in arm with others like them, but all of them stood fast and would not give in. Perhaps that is this story's greatest legacy.

Top, a black tenant tilling his field near Tyronza, Arkansas. Photo by Curtis Duncan. Bottom, cotton pickers weighing their sacks. Photo by J. C. Coovert. Memphis and Shelby County Room, Memphis Library.

EPILOGUE

In a peonage report prepared by Assistant Attorney General Charles Russell, he declared it impossible to confirm the number of persons held in peonage. He said that "while it would be discouraging to think that we have not thus reduced the evil to much smaller dimensions, I regret to say that cases are still being discovered or reported."[1] Russell used the word evil, and many victims chose that word as well to describe their tormentors. Though out of fashion, the word deserves brief reflections in this context. Dr. M. Scott Peck calls evil a force either inside or outside of human beings that seeks to destroy life.[2]

In his book about evil, author Lance Morrow addresses the issue of moral evil. In attempting to explain why people make immoral choices he mentions several reasons that are characteristics of peonage:[3]

It gives them power – Evil in the antebellum South remained constant through use of the lash. Its presence confirmed Peck's belief that evil appears when one imposes his will upon others.[4]

They are afraid of their victims – At Elaine and in many other locales, fear of worker unions brought harsh treatment and murder. Planters also rejected voting rights, education, and land ownership. They feared all things that might bring freedom to oppressed people.

---

[1] Russell supplement, 8.
[2] M. Scott Peck, *People of the Lie. The Hope for Healing Human Evil* (New York: Simon & Schuster, 1983), 43.
[3] Lance Morrow, *Evil. An Investigation* (New York: Basic Books, 2003), 334-35.
[4] *Of the Lie*, 74.

They think that the evil they are doing is good and necessary – A common racist trope held that planters were doing black workers a favor by providing jobs and punishing them when necessary to instill discipline.

They are indifferent to the suffering of others – Writing for the *New York World* about convict labor, Samuel D. McCoy said that when people heard screams from whipped convicts some protested, and some were ashamed. But others closed their eyes, shrugged their shoulders, and turned away.

It is customary and not to do it would breach community tradition – Bertram Wyatt-Brown says that racial domination helped preserve community solidarity.[5]

These oppressors were not crazy. That may be the most troubling realization. Thomas Merton says that a psychiatrist testifying at the Nazi war criminal's trial called Adolph Eichman perfectly sane. If all Nazis were psychotic, "their appalling cruelty would have been in some sense easier to understand." [6] But what about the perfectly sane torturers and murderers. The explanation for this eluded Hanna Arendt, who covered Eichman's lengthy trial for *New Yorker* magazine in February 1963. At its end she asked, "Why did it happen?" The question applies to peonage as well, and it hangs in the air, unanswered, like Othello's question to Iago.

Othello: "Will you, I pray, demand that demi-devil

Why he hath thus ensnared my soul and body?"

Iago: "Demand me nothing. What you know, you know."[7]

What we know is that somehow in many Delta hearts a dark hole formed that swallowed goodness and mercy and spewed out ignorance and hatred. Those who watched but did not throw the rope over a tree

---

[5] Bertram Wyatt-Brown, *Southern Honor: Ethics and Behavior in the Old South*, (New York: Oxford University Press, 1966), 12.
[6] Thomas Merton, "Devout Meditation in Memory of Adolph Eichman," *Raids On The Unspeakable* (New York: New Directions, 1964), 45-46.
[7] William Shakespeare, "Othello," *Arden Shakespeare* (Walton-on-Thames Surrey, Great Britain: Thomas Nelson & Sons, 1997), 327.

limb may feel safe, but perhaps they should not. Malachi Martin, a Catholic priest who wrote about evil, warns about complacency. "Evil has power over us. And even when defeated and put to flight, it scrapes you in passing by. If you don't defeat it, evil exacts a price of more terrible agony. It rips a gash in the spirit with a filthy claw, and some of its venom enters the veins of the soul. A warning that it will return again."[8]

---

[8] Malachi Martin, *Hostage to the Devil* (New York: Harper Collins, 1992), 454-455.

Appendix A

Glossary of Frequently Used Agencies, Organizations, and Programs

Agricultural Adjustment Act (AAA): a federal law enacted in 1933 that reduced agricultural production by paying farmers subsidies not to plant part of their land, thus reducing supply and increasing demand.

Arkansas Emergency Relief Administration (AERA): Federal Emergency Relief Administration's state division headed up by W. R. Dyess.

Arkansas Rural Rehabilitation Corporation (ARRC): a separate corporation established under the AERA with initial responsibilities for Dyess Colony.

Civilian Conservation Corps (CCC): one of Roosevelt's first New Deal entities, CCC was a public work relief program to provide employment for young, unmarried men.

Civil Rights Section (CRS) of the Justice Department: unit set up in the 1930s to prosecute Civil Rights cases.

Emergency Farm Labor Supply Program: operated during wartime to assist farmers in producing vital crops when and where needed most.

Farm Credit Administration (FCA): established in 1933 to help farmers refinance mortgages with longer amortizations and lower interest rates than those available from commercial lenders.

Farm Security Administration (FSA): New Deal agency created in 1937 to combat rural poverty.

Farmers Home Administration (FHA): established in 1946 to provide credit for agricultural and rural development; it replaced FSA.

Federal Emergency Relief Administration (FERA): provided states grants and loans to operate relief programs.

Resettlement Administration (RA): set up in 1935 to relocate out-of-work families to communities planned by the federal government.

Rural Rehabilitation (RR): a division of FERA that enabled poor families to purchase land and capital assets using long-term loans.

Southern Tenant Farmers Union (STFU): an integrated farm laborers union established in 1934 in response to landlord abuses.

U. S. Employment Service: established in February 1907 to direct flow of immigrant labor to job openings and collect information valuable to this distribution process.

War Manpower Commission (WMC): created by federal government in April 1942 to ensure sufficient workers for war and essential industries.

Works Progress Administration (WPA): the largest of New Deal programs; it employed millions of people for public works projects.

APPENDIX B

Report on Peonage and Involuntary Servitude
Charles W. Russell, Assistant U. S. Attorney General
(Abridged)

Mr. Attorney General:

In my report of February 14, 1907, concerning peonage prosecutions in which I had been personally concerned during a stay of four months in the South, under instructions to investigate conditions and, by talks with prominent people and otherwise, to better them, I said:

In a supplementary report I shall take the liberty of explaining more in detail the information I have obtained concerning peonage and concerning the labor-agent system in New York.

For the convenience of some of the representatives of our Department who have not as yet had occasion to prosecute for this offense, I deem it well to set forth some matters of fact and law with which you are already acquainted.

What Peonage Is, Legally Speaking

Under the criminal law as now in force the offense of peonage may be defined as causing compulsory service to be rendered by one man to another on the pretext of having him work out the amount of a debt, real or claimed. That is Mexican peonage proper, as defined by our highest court in the Clyatt case (197 U. S., p. 201). But, as fully explained in my report of October, 1907, and January, 1908, where there is no indebtedness either real or claimed, a conspiracy to cause compulsory service of citizens of the United States is punishable; and so, also, according to the only court that has directly passed upon the question, is the carrying or enticing any person from one place to another in order that he may be held in compulsory service.

I use the words compulsory service as equivalent to the constitutional phrase "involuntary servitude" because the Supreme Court so treats them in the Clyatt case, and I say that a mere claim of debt is sufficient because several inferior courts have so decided, and because in the Clyatt case the indictment, to which no objection seems to have been made, alleged a mere claim of indebtedness.

"Service" does not necessarily mean labor, as pointed out by Federal Judge Locke of Florida; that is to say a man may be in peonage if he is held to make him work, though he may escape before he has begun to work. So he may be in peonage if held by threats as well as if held by force and whether by threats of prosecution or by threats of bodily harm. Federal Judge Niles of Mississippi charged that a holding by threat of prosecution under even a valid law is peonage, the validity of the law not justifying its use for the criminal purpose of causing compulsory service by intimidation.

******

The Chief Support of Peonage

I have no doubt from my investigations and experiences that the chief support of peonage is the peculiar system of State laws prevailing in the South, intended evidently to compel service on the part of the workingman.

From the usual condition of the great mass of laboring men where these laws are in force to peonage is but a step at most. In fact, it is difficult to draw a distinction between the condition of a man who remains in service against his will, because the State has passed a certain law under which he can be arrested and returned to work, and the condition of a man on a near-by farm who is actually made to stay at work by arrest and actual threats of force under the same law. The actual spoken threat of an individual employer who makes his laborer stay at work against his will by fear of the chain gang and the threat of the State to send him to the chain gang whenever his employer chooses to have him arrested are the same in result and do not seem to me very different in any other way.

This Congress may have vaguely understood when it passed revised statutes declaring void all laws under color of which peonage should be maintained. But Congress omitted to provide any punishment for enforcing such laws. Void or not, until repealed or Congress provides a special punishment for officers and others who use them for this criminal purpose of producing involuntary service, they are in the way as the main strength of peonage.

****

Extent of Peonage

I have been asked by persons desiring to publish articles about peonage and others for statistics of the number of persons held in peonage. These questions show a misapprehension of the nature of peonage or of the facilities of this Department for investigating it.

We have discovered cases of peonage, and others have been brought to our attention; we have examined into many and obtained indictments and convictions. But how many cases are in existence is the same kind of a question as though the crime were pension fraud, or counterfeiting, or public land fraud, or fraud on the revenue.

Where we have found several cases we may conclude that there are, or have been, or are likely to be, others; but this is speculation. Sometimes we feel confident that our pounding away for nearly two years has frightened into inactivity those who were practicing peonage in the same State with persons convicted and sentenced; we hear now and then of workmen being " turned loose" when prosecutions are going on; but while it would be discouraging to think that we have not thus reduced the evil to much smaller dimensions, I regret to say that cases are still being discovered or reported in various directions.

Unfortunately, we cannot prevent others from generalizing or from exaggerating with the result that the real truth, which is bad enough, may be obscured, and the further result that disinterested persons may think it patriotic to defend the guilty under the wrong impression that they are the victims of slander.

But I hope to be able to say before many months that southern juries have been willing to convict, that public opinion in the South has come to the aid of the prosecution, and that there is no longer any neighborhood in the South where a workingman, if unjustly treated, will not be protected by the State and Federal courts.

******

Construction Camp Peonage

The temporary suspension of a great part of the railroad building in the South, owing to causes affecting the general business affairs of the country, has suspended much of peonage of a kind frequently complained of that of railroad construction camps.

An advantage the railroad constructors have for maintaining peonage, in addition to the large force of foremen and remoteness from settled communities, is that as a rule the camps are broken up and the work transferred to another locality before the peonage is thoroughly known and can be prosecuted. Moreover, it is comparatively easy in work of the kind to transfer and scatter workmen and replace them with others whenever the Government's representatives begin investigations and prosecutions dangerously near.

Several times it was reported to me in the South that men in peonage were being released under those circumstances. But of course definite information concerning peonage thus abandoned cannot be given; still less can much that is definite be stated concerning peonage prevented by neighboring prosecutions.

******

Convict Camp Peonage

In Georgia and Florida I have investigated to some extent the connection between peonage and convict leasing, but not as fully as some other aspects of the subject of peonage or involuntary servitude because I was desirous of assuring myself concerning the simpler and more easily proven forms of the evil, intending to take up the others afterwards, and among them the involuntary servitude of Greek and other boys in our large cities. I devoted considerable attention to a case of peonage in a State in which, according to one of our attorneys there, it is made more difficult to convict for the reason that the districts have been cut up into such small divisions that the method prescribed by section 802 of the Revised Statutes for getting an impartial jury is practically nullified. That section authorizes the judge to have jurors returned from such parts of the district as the court shall direct so as to be most favorable to an impartial trial. A high law officer in Mississippi remarked upon the same situation there.

******

Labor Agencies

Until we began our work in October, 1906, the chief supply of peons came from the slums, i. e. foreign quarters of New York, and from Ellis Island through the operations of licensed labor agents of New York. These were reaping a rich harvest from the price per head for laborers supplied to employers at a distance, and the temptations to fill all orders and outdo rival agents by a total disregard of truth and honesty in dealing with both laborer and employer was too great for a number of these brokers.

The representatives of the Department, and chiefly Mrs. Quackenbos and Mr. Posner, have succeeded in procuring from the license commissioner the revocation of several licenses; and the knowledge that the Department intends to continue a similar policy is believed to have had a very good effect.

These agents know, what the southern people are slow to learn, that these supposedly ignorant and insignificant foreigners fill American newspapers printed in their own languages, and the mails for Europe, and consulates and embassies with accounts of any mistreatment they receive – accounts which, according to the usual way with human nature, are not confined to a plain statement of the facts, but adorned with high coloring, hearsay reports, and expressions of intense feeling. Not only so, but many of them return to their European homes and their stories lose nothing from the effect of distance. Lately the fact has begun to dawn upon those practicing peonage that foreign governments have been learning the facts about it and expressing opinions concerning those who practice it.

Under the labor agents' license law of New York a printed slip must be given to each workman sent to a distant employer, on which must be written in a language he can read, a few simple things for his guidance and protection, as follows:

Whenever such licensed person or any other acting for him agrees to send one or more persons to work as contract laborers in anyone place outside the city in which such agency is located the said licensed person shall file with the mayor or commissioner of licenses within five days after the contract is made a statement containing the following items: Name and address of the employer, name and address of the employee, nature of the work to be performed, hours of labor, wages offered, destination of the persons employed, and terms of transportation. A duplicate copy of this statement shall be given to the applicant for employment in a language which he is able to understand.

All manner of frauds were resorted to in order to circumvent the object of this law. For example, in one case with which I am familiar the slips were not given to the men until they were on board the boat on which they left New York; in another instance they were delivered just as a crowd of men were being piled into a van to go to the boat. Then, when the statement was delivered and called for pay at $1.26 per day the strangers were told in one case that this wage was for the first week only and would be increased to $2 and soon to $3. When the work was stated as day labor making a railroad or as a sawmill worker a man was asked his trade, and when the answer was bookkeeper he was told that there was a pressing demand for a bookkeeper at the place to which he was destined and that it was providential that a bookkeeper should be among the workmen applying. If he answered that he was a machinist, the wisdom of Providence was similarly recognized. As for the place of destination, the strangers were told that it was so many days or hours by boat and so many by train when it was twice or three times as far. A man supposedly bound for Pittsburg would sometimes find himself in Georgia.

They were told in the O'Hara case that while $1.26 per day might seem small, they would have to work but four hours a day and would get $1.26 even when doing nothing. Many of the men cannot read in any language, and by the time their statements are explained to them by their companions they have all been hurried to the boat or train, and, once on it, all are too ignorant of the geography of the country, of the language, the laws and their legal rights – in fact, of everything about them, to know what to do. Many people in the South have wondered that white men need care and protection instead of protecting themselves. If those who so wonder were suddenly set down in the middle of Russia without money or friends they would be almost as helpless. Many of these people are not accustomed to firearms; and in one of our cases (that of the Raleigh Lumber Company in West Virginia) some nineteen athletic young Italians were so flustered at the exhibition of a pistol by a law officer that they all acted as though they expected instant death, and some even fainted at the sight. I have no idea that these people had less natural courage than men in general.

******

Concluding Remarks

I have seen some bitter complaints by Southern employers about the deceptions practiced upon them by the labor agents and pretended philanthropic promoters of colonizing schemes, who sent them laborers from New York. All that the labor agent or philanthropist wanted was the per capita commission; and he was as willing to deceive the distant employer about the laborer as vice versa.

The vice-president of a mining company involved in the peonage prosecutions in West Virginia remarked to me concerning a somewhat cruel foreman or watchman, 'I suppose you believe I selected the man because of his brutality.' I answered, 'No; what I think is that your superintendent wanted to make to you a satisfactory report of the mining operations, and this foreman wanted to satisfy the superintendent by helping him do that, and that from these motives they had been led into practicing peonage.'

He did not expressly assent to this, because he did not care to admit that peonage had been practiced, but he raised no objection to what I said. Such are, I think, very commonly the motives of peonage, which is rather a mining, lumbering, construction, and manufacturing than an agricultural phenomenon.

A friend of a man tried for peonage said that the motive in putting pressure on the men to remain at work was that the firm's time limit in its contract to build a railroad had almost been reached. Pressure was resorted to, and special efforts were needed.

In conclusion, I have the honor to say that I have written this report with the understanding that those of October-January last and of February 14, 1907, would be read in connection with it, and that all three would be considered as one document.

Respectfully,

Charles W. Russell

Assistant Attorney General

APPENDIX C

Speech by Howard Kester
27th annual NAACP conference
June 26, 1935
(Abridged)

It is a very great privilege and pleasure for me to be with you on the occasion of your Twenty-sixth Annual Convention. I am very glad to stand before you tonight and raise my voice not against peonage but against the slavery that is practiced in the southern states, against not only my Negro brothers but against my white brothers.

Peonage is a phrase that has relatively little meaning except to people who dwell in college walls and are somewhat sophisticated, and therefore I do not particularly cherish the word. The word which has tremendous significance and meaning to men and women who are in peonage or enslaved is the word slavery, and I want to change my subject tonight from that of "The Struggle Against Peonage" to "The Struggle Against Slavery."

In 1857 Chief Justice Taney in writing the majority opinion in the Dred Scott Case said that the Negro had no rights which the white man was bound to respect. I say that for the masses of Negroes today in America, particularly in the deep South, that opinion is still the majority opinion – that the Negro has no right which the white man is bound to respect. I want to go further and say that there are great masses of white men as well as great masses of Negroes who have no rights and who are slaves today together. A few weeks ago I was in Memphis and while there the cotton carnival was in progress; one of the greatest pageants, one of the greatest displays of wealth, that the South has seen in many a day. During this pageant they crowned cotton king. King Cotton! I did not see any of the slaves at the carnival, though I have seen thousands of them scattered throughout the deep South. There were slaves in ancient times and there were kings. There are kings in our modem times and there are slaves. There are no slaves in the world that are more oppressed, more degraded, more proscribed, than the slaves of King Cotton.

If I judge southern society correctly, it seems to me that southern society is a civilization apart from the rest of America. It is a civilization which has all of the subterfuges, all of the anachronisms, of modern-day imperialism. It is a society which has a hangover from feudalism and which is in some respects feudalistic, which has adopted all the stereotypes of imperialism and the brutalities of feudalism, in the actions of the Roosevelt administration, particularly the AAA which has driven the already enslaved Negro and white masses into greater despair than they have ever known since Emancipation.

The word sharecropper has, I believe, in the last several months, probably within the last couple of years, become more or less a household word to many Americans. It is a word that expresses the most exploited, the most degraded, the most brutalized group of workers in America; and it is about the sharecroppers, the tenant farmers, that I wish to speak to you tonight. If I seem to parade before you the sins of Arkansas, I want you to know that in picking on Arkansas I am picking on the South and I am also parading before you the sins of the South and the sins of America. What has happened in Arkansas is no different from what will happen in every southern state where the economic crisis continues and where those who are oppressed and enslaved begin to gather themselves together into organizations for their own protection and to march toward economic freedom and security. The situation is no different in Arkansas from what it will be in other southern states and for that matter in other states of the Union where these conflicting forces meet and grapple with one another.

The present system of farm tenancy and of sharecropper grew up naturally out of the debacle of the Civil War. There was a civilization that was hard to face. There were great plantations with landlords but no laborers; great masses of laborers, but no land upon which to work. The landlord said to the sharecroppers and the tenants: "Come to me; work on my land; pay me a part of the crop and I will furnish you with your upkeep." By 1880 that process, that economy, had fundamentally become a part of southern life. Since 1880 sharecropping and tenancy have rapidly increased.

How significant is agriculture to Negroes in America? 97.8% of all land farmed by Negroes in America is in the South. More than 80% of the Negro farmers in the southern states are tenant farmers or sharecroppers. 78.7% of the population lives in the southern states. 56% of the population is rural. Of the approximately nine million Negroes living in the southern states, five million are living in the black belt and some three million in the border states. Of the total population, 36.1 %, according to the 1930 census, are engaged directly in agriculture. More than one-third of the rural population is, therefore, tied up industrially with conditions that prevail on the farm; and since the great masses live in the southern states, they are intimately affected by the prevailing economy in these southern states.

The terms sharecropper and tenant farmer I shall use interchangeably. A sharecropper is an individual who has only his labor to sell. He has neither tools nor animals. He may have a few household goods, a few broken chairs, a bed and some clothes; but outside of his labor he has nothing with which to earn his living. He therefore rents himself out to the landlord, so to speak, who furnishes him with his care during the growing season, in return for which the landlord receives a fourth, a third, a half and sometimes all that he produces. In recent months we have had many visitors from various parts of America and from various parts of England in northeastern Arkansas. A distinguished British novelist and historian said conditions in northeastern Arkansas are worse than conditions she had seen anywhere in the peasant areas of Europe. A former professor of mine at Vanderbilt came through Arkansas the other day. He had spent some fifteen years in the interior of China, and he said that conditions which he saw on the cotton plantations of northeastern Arkansas were worse than conditions in the interior of China.

Let me picture, if I may, something of the life of the Negro or of the white tenant farmer or sharecropper in the cotton country. You ask a tenant farmer or a sharecropper how long he works. He says, "I work from can to can't." He means he rises before the sun is up and works until the sun goes down. What about the homes in which these people live? The self-respecting farmer in Missouri would not permit his pigs or his cattle to live in some of the hovels and shanties which sharecroppers and tenant farmers live in Arkansas. What kind of food do these people exist on? Do they have the same delicacies, the same sustaining foods that we have? Rupert Vance of the University of North Carolina in his *Geography of the South* says the tenant farmers of the South live on the three M's, meal, molasses and meat – a pellagra producing diet; a diet that turns the system sour. The meat they eat we call sow belly, a name that should be descriptive for an audience like this; a meat that turns your system sour.

These people raise more than 55% of the cotton in the world, and yet they go in rags. The kind of underwear that the men and the women, particularly the women and children, wear is conditioned by the kind of flour sacks they happen to buy their flour in. They do not have store-bought underclothes like we do. They get the flour sacks, rip them up, wash the print out, and make underclothes. Cotton is king but his slaves go in rags.

What about the schools? I understand you are going to be shown some pictures of schoolhouses in cotton countries. During the last year I visited numerous schools in northeastern Arkansas. I have seen children crowded into schools three and four times as many as the seating capacity could take care of. Some of them I have found seated in one corner of the room eating com pone and molasses. In another corner was a larger group seated quietly watching the other group eat, because they had nothing to eat. I have seen children come to school with no baskets at all. I have seen them come to school barefoot, with one piece of clothing on, and with no books. After asking them why they came to school the answer was, "We came to school to get warm" because of no warmth at home. I have seen men walk four, five and six miles bringing wood back over their shoulders to burn, not in stoves, because they are too poor to have stoves. An oil can with one end knocked out provided the only stove that thousands and thousands of the slaves of King Cotton tried warming themselves by and get their miserable meals upon. They raise cotton and yet they and their children go in rags.

When the sharecropper signs himself out to the landlord he not only signs his own life to the landlord but the labor of himself, his wife and his children. The N. R. A. may have driven child labor out of some industrial communities, but child labor goes on as great today as ever in the South. Children of school age, from six to sixteen, may be found in the cotton field laboring along with adults. King Cotton makes little choice concerning the kind of slaves he takes his toll from.

What about the medical care of these people? Do they have physicians when they become ill? I want to make a statement here for which I think I could present a good argument if I had time. Millions of your fellow men in the South today are in a worse condition than those who lived in slavery prior to the Emancipation Proclamation. If a slave was fortunate enough to have a beneficent master he had a fairly decent house to live in; he had clothes for his back and his family's; he had good food, and when he got sick he had a doctor to care for him. But hundreds of thousands of Negro and white tenant farmers and sharecroppers in the deep South today have less value upon their heads than a good mule or a good horse. Labor is plentiful. If a man grows sick and dies, there is another ready and willing to take his place; and so you find my people and your people suffering untold agonies because they have neither the money nor the good will of the master, or the landlord, to secure for them medical care.

These people are disfranchised. These people are brutalized. These people are lynched - - lynched in body, lynched in spirit. These people are your people. These people are my people. And until we identify ourselves with these disinherited, oppressed masses; until their pain becomes our pain; until their sorrow becomes our sorrow; until their suffering becomes our suffering; until their longing for a decent world becomes our longing; we, too, will remain enslaved, brutalized, lynched.

Year after year in the deep South the oppressed Negro farmer has come together in organizations for his own protection. The South is covered with the graveyards of union organizations born into this world to give protection to agricultural workers and smashed the moment the landlords get wind of them because they feared that in them were the seeds of destruction of their system and an uprising of the oppressed ones. Until July of 1934 outside of the state of Alabama there was no significant movement among these oppressed groups of sharecroppers and tenant farmers. In July 1934 the Southern Tenant Farmers' Union was organized, an organization not of Negro workers alone but of Negro and white workers. For the first time in the history of the South since the Civil War, Negro and white workers came to the conclusion, to the fundamental and inescapable conclusion, that they were one; that color made no difference; that they ate the same food, lived in the same kind of houses; that they worked the same kind of land, raised the same kind of crops, worked for the same kind of landlord; that together they must be saved or together they must be lost. And so we have in the South, not only in Arkansas but in Texas, in Oklahoma, and rapidly spreading to other southern states, an organization of Negro and white sharecroppers and tenant farmers, a new thing under the southern sun, a thing that should give every man and woman and child who has the interest of America at heart the greatest concern and the greatest encouragement.

There were only fifteen of these sharecroppers who first came together in July less than a year ago. Gradually the organization began to spread and take in membership until practically all of northeast Arkansas was organized; and when it became organized, those who had been living on the sweat and very life blood of those agricultural works became fearful. They saw that a death blow had been struck at their system of exploitation and tyranny. No longer were they ableto take the white sharecropper and play him up against his Negro brother on the same plantation. They knew they were united together in one solid unit. Men who had ten years ago been members of the Ku Klux Klan, economically deprived of leadership of intelligent men, forgot their superiority complex and they stretched out the hand of comradeship, of friendship, of brotherhood to their Negro brothers; and from that day to this the Southern Tenant Farmers' Union has been on the move. As the organization grew in power and in prestige and turned the spotlight on the entire question, upon what was going on in the cotton belt, those who were attacking the organization of these exploited workers, the landlords themselves, began to organize, began to use the courts, began to use all the instruments of tyranny and oppression known to the ruling class, to break up this one hope for the oppressed and exploited.

I want to tell you something of the nature of the tyranny and the oppression through which these men and women have lived during these last eleven months. The first thing they began to do was to invade our meetings and break them up; landlords and their riding bosses, deputy sheriffs, everyone whom they could call into their service. Then they began to falsely arrest and imprison our leaders. One young man, a Methodist minister, was arrested, imprisoned and sentenced to jail for six months and to pay a fine of five hundred dollars on the absurd charge of anarchy. The real reason was that he was teaching illiterate Negro men and women and illiterate white men and women how to read and write; teaching them something of the fundamentals of economics; trying to tell them what was happening to them in this world that has gone crazy, and making the mistake of calling a Negro "Mr." There were numerous arrests, numerous false imprisonments. Then they began mobbing our meetings, breaking them up with the law. We have in our possession a rope which was taken from a number of men who went out to lynch some of the organizers. We have in our possession part of a machine gun which was used in shooting up the home of E. B. McKinney, Vice President of the Union. Within the last three weeks three members of the Union have been shot and those who shot them have been cleared. One of our members, a minister and organizer, was found with a chain about his neck and rocks bout his feet, floating on the banks of a river in Mississippi. The sheriff said that as an organizer of the Union the planters considered him a dangerous man and therefore got rid of him. I have seen men, women and children beaten with guns, beaten with wash lines. I have seen their homes shot to pieces. I have seen them driven from their homes by night and day. I have seen churches burned, schools packed with hay. All of these things done to keep the Union from spreading, to spread terror among those who were members of the Union. Despite all of the oppressive acts, despite all of the tyranny, the Union has continued to move steadily forward.

I wonder what a significance the movement of this mass of oppressed and disinherited workers in America has for us here tonight. About three weeks ago three of us went from Memphis into Arkansas. We knew before we left that we might never return, because if the sheriffs discovered we were there, a price being on our heads, we might never come back. The Negro member of our party, John Allen, who had worked on a notorious plantation since 1922, had been driven out because of his Union activities. He spent nights and days walking a distance of some eighty miles, hiding in homes and under bushes, trying to escape officers and planters, in his attempt to get to a haven. For months he had not seen his wife. He wanted to go back, and we decided to go with him. And so we went back, and we sent word to Mrs. Allen to come and meet her husband; and there on the banks of the St. Francis we saw a man who had been driven from his family and away from everything which he held dear in life meet his wife. There was no emotion, no tears, only expressions of love and a friendly talk; and as the moment came for us to depart, I heard these words fall from the lips of John Allen: "The Union is the thing for which 1 must live, for which, if necessary, I must die. The Union is the thing which you must live for and, if necessary, die for." Words which came soberly, thoughtfully, not from the lips of an arm chair philosopher, but from the lips of a man who has given years and years of service to King Cotton, and who in his last years of life, now past sixty, walks out from it all, from all of his friends, from everything that has any significance to him, and throws his life into something that is new, and that something is an organization of Negro and white workers.

The struggle which is going on in northeastern Arkansas and spreading to other states is a struggle that involves not only those men and women who work in the fields of King Cotton. It involves every man, woman and child in America. It involves you as the representatives of a great organization. I want to see the N.A.A.C.P. become sharecropper conscious. I want it to become slavery conscious. And I am not indulging in extravagant words when I say the conditions under which the mass of Negro and white farm workers live in the deep South is slavery. I want the N.A.A.C.P. to become so aware of the conditions under which these people live that when the voice of the sharecropper is raised in distress it immediately and forthright becomes the voice of every Negro in America. I want the N.A.A.C.P. to become a sounding board upon which the cries of these exploited workers can be sounded from Johannesburg to the White House. The struggle is here, my friends. The struggle is theirs. The struggle is yours.

We have been on the move, and we are still moving. We are on the move toward a new society, a society not only of free men and women, but a society of equals, a society in which there shall be economic, political and social equality for every man, woman and child who wants it; a society in which a man can call another man brother and mean it. There is no place in the society of which I am forced to be a part to call a man brother and mean it, because my whole society cuts across everything that brother means; and that society is the society that I am not particularly keen about dying for; it is a society that I want to live to see buried. And I invite all of you to join with the disinherited in Arkansas and Mississippi and Alabama in our struggle toward a society of freedom, of peace, and of plenty, for one and for all.

APPENDIX D

Office of the Attorney General
Washington, D. C.
December 12, 1941 Circular No. 3591

TO ALL UNITED STATES ATTORNEYS:

RE: Involuntary Servitude, Slavery, and Peonage (Abridged)

A summary of the Department files on alleged peonage violations discloses numerous instances of 'prosecution declined' by United States Attorneys, the chief reason stated as being the absence of the element of debt. It is apparent that these determinations were reached after considering the facts at hand only in accordance with the case law under Section 444, Title 18, U.S. Code, which holds that debt is the "basal element" of peonage. It is further disclosed that only in a negligible number of instances was consideration given these complaints in light of:

(a) Section 443, Title 18, U.S. Code, which punishes for causing persons to be held in involuntary servitude, regardless of the existence of a debt.

(b) Section 51, Title 18, U.S. Code, which punishes for conspiracy to deprive citizens of rights secured to them by the Constitution, particularly the right to be free from slavery and involuntary servitude.

(c) Section 52, Title 18, U.S. Code, which punishes persons vested with official authority who aid or cause others to suffer deprivation of rights secured to them by the Constitution, particularly the right to be free from slavery and compulsory servitude.

(d) Section 88, Title 18, U.S. Code, the general conspiracy statute, which may be employed in combination with Section 443 or Section 52.

It is the purpose of these instructions to direct the attention of United States Attorneys to possibilities of successful prosecutions stemming from alleged peonage complaints which have heretofore been considered inadequate to invoke federal jurisdiction. It is requested that the spelling out of peonage under Section 444 be deferred in favor of building the cases around the issue of involuntary servitude and slavery under Sections 443, 51 and 52, disregarding entirely the element of debt. If it is found that a claimed debt is the basis of intimidation to compel one to the service of another, a separate count under Section 444 should be included in the indictment. Evidence of such debt may likewise be employed as an additional circumstance to prove intimidation under the counts based on Sections 443, 51 and 52.

In any event the Government should henceforth emphasize and depend upon the issue of involuntary servitude and slavery in lieu of peonage (debt plus involuntary service) in prosecuting this type of case.

The United States Attorneys are instructed to consider such complaints in accordance with the following statutes and authorize prosecutions where any one or more of the following conditions exist, regardless of the existence of debt real or claimed:

(a) Section 443, Title 18, U.S. Code
Carrying or enticing of any person from one place to another in order that he may be held in slavery or involuntary servitude; causing another by force, fraud or intimidation to enter and remain in another's employment; causing one to be held by threats, as well as by force, and whether such threats are of prosecution, arrest or imprisonment or by threats of bodily harm; holding another by threats of prosecution, even under a valid law; the validity of the law not justifying its use for the criminal purpose of causing compulsory service by intimidation; where one does not stay in his employment of his own free will but only in accordance with the will of his master or employer, involuntary service exists. Service does not necessarily mean labor, i.e., a man may be in that state if he is held to be made to work but escapes before he has begun such work; by falsely accusing another of crime and carrying him before a magistrate in order that he may be convicted and put to hard labor in consequence of which such person is convicted and put to hard labor, the false accuser at the time having the purpose or design to hire such person or to enable some other person to hire him.

(b) Section 51, Title 18, U.S. Code
If two or more persons conspire or combine to do any of the acts outlined above they are guilty of a conspiracy to deprive the person, if he is a citizen of the United States, of the free exercise or enjoyment of the right and privilege secured to him by the Constitution of the United States to be free from involuntary servitude, and are indictable accordingly.

(c) Section 52, Title 18, U.S. Code
This section is applicable to public officers, judges, sheriffs local constabulary, etc., who act under color and in the name of their authority in perpetrating any of the acts listed above in violation of a person's rights to be free from involuntary servitude and slavery as secured to him by the Thirteenth Amendment to the Constitution.

For a discussion of the applicability of this Section to official action, see Circular No. 3356, Supp. 1. In the matter of control by one over the person of another, the circumstances under which each person is placed must be determined i.e., the subservience of the will of one to the other. Open force, threats or intimidation need not be used to cause a person to go involuntarily from one place to another to work and to remain at such work; nor does evidence of kind treatment show an absence of involuntary servitude.

In the United States one cannot sell himself as a peon or slave. The law is fixed and established to protect the weak-minded, the poor, the miserable. Men will sometimes sell themselves for a meal of victuals or contract with another who acts as surety on his bond to work out the amount of the bond upon his release from jail. Any such contract is positively null and void and the procuring and causing of such contract to be made violates these statutes. It is not necessary that the defendants be themselves charged with holding a person in a condition of compulsory servitude, a showing of aiding in holding or returning one to that condition is sufficient.

Procedure

1. The United States Attorneys should contact local law enforcement officials by letter, circular, conference, or any other means found effective for seeking state wide cooperation and advise them that the practices outlined above will be prosecuted by the Federal Government.

2. In those states where legislatures have enacted criminal statutes to enforce labor contracts, United States Attorneys from various districts therein should promptly notify the local magistrates, sheriffs, and other law enforcement officers that such laws are repugnant to the provisions of the Thirteenth Amendment to the Constitution of the United States and that action to enforce such statutes may subject the local officials to federal prosecution.

3. In the interest of consistency and uniformity in the method of investigation, the Federal Bureau of Investigation has been requested to direct all original complaints in this field to the Civil Rights Section of the Criminal Division of the Department for clearance and instruction before embarking upon a formal investigation. No investigation or prosecution of these cases should be commenced through the offices of the various United States Attorneys without Departmental sanction. Because of the importance of unified and consistent prosecution policy in these cases it is further requested that no indictments under these statutes be sought without obtaining authority from the Department.

4. To assure emphasis on the issue of involuntary servitude and slavery in considering these cases on the one hand and to minimize the necessity of relying upon the element of debt to fix jurisdiction on the other, the Federal Bureau of Investigation has been requested to change the title on its reports from Peonage to read Involuntary Servitude and Slavery. Henceforth, Peonage will be considered as secondary to involuntary servitude and slavery investigations.

Selected Bibliography

Books:

Adams, Jessica. *Wounds of Returning: Race, Memory, and Property on the Postslavery Plantation.* Chapel Hill: University of North Carolina Press, 2007.

Aptheker, Herbert, ed. A *Documentary History of the Negro People in the United States 1910-1932.* Vol. 3, from the NAACP to the New Deal. Secaucus, N. J.: Citadel Press, 1960.

Ayers, Edward. *The Promise of the New South: Life After Reconstruction.* New York: Oxford University Press, 1992.

Baker, Ray Stannard. *Following the Color Line: American Negro Citizenship in the Progressive Era.* New York: Harper & Row, 1964.

Baldwin, Sidney. *Poverty and Politics: The Rise and Decline of the Farm Security Administration.* Chapel Hill: University of North Carolina Press, 1968.

Barry, John M. *Rising Tide: The Great Mississippi Flood of 1927 and How It Changed America.* New York: Simon & Schuster, 1997.

Baskett, Tom, Jr., ed. *The Arkansas Delta: A Landscape of Change.* Helena, Ark.: Delta Cultural Center, 1990.

Becker, Gary. *Economics of Discrimination.* Chicago: University of Chicago Press, 1971.

Berlin, Ira. *Slaves Without Masters: The Free Negro in the Antebellum South.* New York: Pantheon Books, 1974.

Bernstein, David E. *Only One Place of Redress: African Americans, Labor Regulations, and the Courts From Reconstruction to the New Deal.* Durham, N. C.: Duke University Press, 2001.

Blackmon, Douglas A. *Slavery by Another Name.* New York: Random House, 2009.

Bogart, E. L. and C. M. Thompson, eds. *Readings in the Economic History of the United States*. New York: Longmans, Green, and Co., 1916.

Bowers, William J., with Glenn L. Pierce and John F. McDevitt. *Legal Homicide: Death as Punishment in America, 1864-1982*. Boston: Northeastern University Press, 1974.

Bracey, John H. Jr. and August Meir, eds. *Papers of the NAACP. Part 10: Peonage, Labor and the New* Deal 1913-1939. Bethesda, Md.: University Publications of America, 1990.

Caldwell, Erskine and Margaret Bourke-White. *You Have Seen Their Faces*. Athens: University of Georgia Press, 1937.

Canonici, Paul V. *The Delta Italians*. Madison, Miss.: Creative Designs, 2003.

Cantor, Louis. *Prologue to the Protest Movement: The Missouri Sharecropper Roadside Demonstration of 1939*. Durham, N. C.: Duke University Press, 1969.

Carr, Robert K. *Federal Protection of Civil Rights: Quest for a Sword*. Ithaca, N. Y.: Cornell University Press, 1947.

Cash, Johnny, with Patrick Carr. *Cash: The Autobiography*. New York: HarperCollins, 1997.

Cash, Wilbur J. *The Mind of the South*. New York: Alfred A. Knopf, 1941.

Cobb, James C. *The Most Southern Place on Earth*. New York: Oxford University Press, 1992.

Cohen, William. *At Freedom's Edge: Black Mobility and the Southern White Quest for Racial Control*. Baton Rouge: Louisiana State University Press, 1991.

Collins, Ann V. *All Hell Broke Loose: American Race Riots from the Progressive Era to World War II*. Santa Barbara, Calif.: Praeger, 2012.

Collins, Janelle, ed. *Defining the Delta: Multidisciplinary Perspectives on the Lower Mississippi River Delta*. Fayetteville: University of Arkansas Press, 2015.

Conrad, David Eugene. *The Forgotten Farmers: The Story of Sharecroppers in the New Deal*. Urbana: University of Illinois Press, 1965.

Constitution of the United States, 14th Amendment and 15th Amendment. Washington, D. C.: Cato Institute, 1998.

Cortner, Richard C. *A Mob Intent on Death: The NAACP and the Arkansas Race Riot Cases*. Middleton, Conn.: Wesleyan University Press, 1988.

Daniel, Pete, ed. *Index To The Peonage Files of the U.S. Department of Justice.* Frederick, Md.: University Publications of America, 1989.

__________*The Shadow of Slavery: Peonage in the South, 1901-1969.* Urbana: University of Illinois Press, 1972.

Dattel, Gene. *Cotton and Race in the Making of America. The Human Costs of Economic Power.* New York: Van R. Dee, 2009.

David, Jay. ed. *Black Defiance: Black Profiles in Courage.* New York: William Morrow & Company, 1972.

Day, Donald, ed. *The Autobiography of Will Rogers.* New York: Houghton Mifflin, 1949.

Dougan, Michael B. *Arkansas Odyssey: The Saga of Arkansas from Prehistoric Times to Present.* Little Rock, Ark.: Rose Publishing Company, 1993.

Du Bois, W.E.B. *Black Reconstruction in America.* New York: Free Press, 1997.

__________ *The Souls of Black Folk: Essays and Sketches.* New York: Barnes and Noble Classics, 2003.

Dunaway, Louis Sharpe. *What a Preacher Saw Through a Key-Hole in Arkansas.* Little Rock, Ark.: Parker Harper Publishing Co., 1925.

Egerton, Douglas R. *The Wars of Reconstruction: The Brief, Violent History of America's Most Progressive Era.* New York: Bloomsbury Press, 2014.

Escott, Paul D., et. al., eds. *The New South: Major Problems in the History of the American South.* Vol. II. New York: Houghton Mifflin Company, 1999.

Farmer-Kaiser, Mary. *Freedwomen and the Freedmen's Bureau: Race, Gender, and Public Policy in the Age of Emancipation.* New York: Fordham University Press, 2010.

Farnham, Christi Anne, ed. *Women of the American South: A Multicultural Reader.* New York: New York University Press, 1997.

Faust, Drew Gilpin. *Republic of Suffering: Death and the American Civil War.* New York: Alfred A. Knopf, 2008.

Finley, Randy. *Slavery to Uncertain Freedom: The Freedmen's Bureau in Arkansas, 1865-1869.* Fayetteville: University of Arkansas Press, 1996.

Flint, Timothy. *A Condensed Geography and History of the Western States, or the Mississippi Valley.* Vol. 1. Gainesville, Fla.: Scholars' Facsimiles and Reprints, 1970.

Foner, Eric. *Reconstruction: America's Unfinished Revolution, 1863-1877.* New York: Perennial Classics, 1988.

___________*Story of American Freedom.* New York: W. W. Norton, 1998.

Franklin, John Hope. *From Slavery to Freedom.* New York: Alfred A. Knopf, 1956.

Fraser, Walter J., Jr. and Winfred B. Moore, Jr., eds. *From the Old South to the New.* Santa Barbara, Calif.: Praeger Publishing, 1981.

French, Samuel G. *Two Wars: An Autobiography.* Nashville, Tenn.: Confederate Veteran, 1901.

Gantt, Edward W., ed. *A Digest of the Statutes of Arkansas.* Little Rock, Ark.: Little Rock Printing and Publishing Co., 1874.

Genovese, Eugene D. *Roll Jordan Roll: The World the Slaves Made.* New York: Vintage Books, 1976.

Godden, Richard and Martin Crawford, eds. *Reading Southern Poverty Between the Wars, 1918-1939.* Athens: University of Georgia Press, 2006.

Goluboff, Risa L. *The Lost Promise of Civil Rights.* Cambridge, Mass.: Harvard University Press, 2007.

Gordon, Fon Louise. *Caste and Class: The Black Experience in Arkansas, 1880-1920.* Athens: University of Georgia Press, 1995.

Grossman, James R., ed. *Black Workers in the Era of the Great Migration.* Frederick, Md.: University Publications of America, 1985.

Grubbs, Donald H. *Cry from the Cotton: The Southern Tenant Farmers' Union and the New Deal.* Chapel Hill: University of North Carolina Press, 1971.

Guelzo. Allen C. *Reconstruction: A Concise History.* New York: Oxford University Press, 2018.

Guyatt, Nicholas. *Bind Us Apart: How Enlightened Americans Invented Racial Segregation.* New York: Basic Books, 2016.

Hahn, Steven. *A Nation Under Our Feet: Political Struggles in the Rural South from Slavery to the Great Migration.* Cambridge, Mass.: Harvard University Press, 2003.

Harvey, Paul. *Redeeming the South.* Chapel Hill: University of North Carolina Press, 1997.

Hawkins, Van. *Plowing New Ground: The Southern Tenant Farmers Union and its Place in Delta History*. Virginia Beach, Va.: Donning, 2007.

__________*A New Deal in Dyess: The Depression Era Agricultural Colony in Arkansas*. Jonesboro, Ark.: Writers Bloc, 2015.

Higgs, Robert. *Competition and Coercion: Blacks in the American Economy, 1865-1914*. Chicago: University of Chicago Press, 1980.

Hill, Ruth, ed. *Black Women Oral History Project*. Vol. II. Westport, Conn.: Meckler, 1991.

Hill, William N. *Story of the Arkansas Penitentiary*. Little Rock, Ark.: Democrat Printing & Lithographing Co., 1912.

Hine, Darlene Clark. *Hine Sight: Black Women and the Re-Construction of American History*. Brooklyn, N.Y.: Carlson Publishing, 1994.

Honigmann, E. A. J., ed. *Othello (Arden Shakespeare: Third Series)*. Walton-on-Thames Surrey, Great Britain: Thomas Nelson & Sons, 1997.

Huggins, Nathan I., Martin Kilson, and Daniel M. Fox, eds. *Key Issues in the Afro-American Experience*. Vol. II. New York: Harcourt Brace Jovanovich, 1971.

Hunter, Tera W. *To 'Joy My Freedom: Southern Black Women's Lives and Labors After the Civil War*. Cambridge, Mass.: Harvard University Press, 1997.

Jones, Jacqueline. *Labor of Love, Labor of Sorrow: Black Women, Work, and the Family from Slavery to the Present*. New York: Basic Books, 1985.

__________*The Dispossessed: America's Underclasses from the Civil War to the Present*. New York: Basic Books, 1992.

Kester, Howard. *Revolt Among the Sharecroppers*. New York: Arno Press,1969.

Key, V. O. *Southern Politics in State and Nation*. Knoxville: University of Tennessee Press, 1984.

Kirby, William Fosgate. *Supplement to the Digest of the Statutes of Arkansas*. Indianapolis, Ind.: Bobbs-Merrill Co., 1911.

Klarman, Michael J. *From Jim Crow to Civil Rights: The Supreme Court and the Struggle for Racial Equality*. New York: Oxford University Press, 2004.

Lancaster, Guy, ed. *Bullets and Fire: Lynching and Authority in Arkansas, 1840-1950*. Fayetteville: University of Arkansas Press, 2018.

__________ *The Elaine Massacre and Arkansas: A Century of Atrocity and Resistance, 1819-1919*. Little Rock, Ark.: Butler Center Books, 2018.

Lankford, George, ed. *Bearing Witness: Memories of Arkansas Slave Narratives from the 1930s WPA Collections*. Fayetteville: University of Arkansas Press, 1990.

Lanza, Michael. *Agrarianism and Reconstruction: The Southern Homestead Act*. Baton Rouge: Louisiana State University Press, 1990.

Lewis, David Levering. *W.E.B. Du Bois: The Fight for Equality and the American Century 1919-1963*. New York: Henry Holt and Company, 2000.

Litwack, Leon F. *Been in the Storm So Long: The Aftermath of Slavery*. New York: Vintage Books, 1979.

__________*Trouble in Mind: Black Southerners in the Age of Jim Crow*. New York: Alfred A. Knopf, 1998.

Lowitt, Richard and Maurine Beasley, eds. *One Third of a Nation: Lorena Hickok Reports on the Great Depression*. Urbana: University of Illinois Press, 1981.

Martin, Malachi. *Hostage to the Devil*. San Francisco, Calif.: Harper Collins, 1992.

Mays, Benjamin E. *Born to Rebel: An Autobiography*. Athens: University of Georgia Press, 1986.

Merton, Thomas. *Raids on the Unspeakable*. New York: New Directions, 1966.

Michaeli, Ethan. *The Defender: How the Legendary Black Newspaper Changed America*. New York: Houghton Mifflin Harcourt, 2016.

Mitchell, H. L. *Mean Things Happening in this Land: The Life and Times of H. L. Mitchell, Cofounder of the Southern Tenant Farmers' Union*. Montclair, N. J.: Allanheld, Osmun, 1979.

Moneyhon, Carl H. *The Impact of the Civil War and Reconstruction on Arkansas*. Fayetteville: University of Arkansas Press, 2002.

__________*Arkansas and the New South, 1874-1929*. Fayetteville: University of Arkansas Press, 1997.

Montejano, David. *Anglos and Mexicans in the Making of Texas, 1836-1986*. Austin: University of Texas Press, 1987.

Morrow, Lance. *Evil: An Investigation*. New York: Basic Books, 2003.

Nelson, Cary, ed. *Anthology of Modern American Poetry*. New York: Oxford University Press, 2000.

Nieman, Donald G., ed. *Black Southerners and the Law, 1865-1900*. New York: Garland Publishing, Inc., 1994.

__________ *To Set the Law in Motion: The Freedmen's Bureau and the Legal Rights of Blacks, 1865-1868*. Millwood, N. Y.: KTO Press, 1979.

Nixon, H. C. *Forty Acres and Steel Mules*. Chapel Hill: University of North Carolina Press, 1938.

Novak, Daniel A. *The Wheel of Servitude: Black Forced Labor after Slavery*. Lexington: University Press of Kentucky, 1978.

O'Connor, Thomas H. *Lords of the Loom*. New York: Scribners, 1968.

Packard, Jerrold M. *American Nightmare: the History of Jim Crow*. New York: St. Martin's Press, 2002.

Patterson, Orlando. *Slavery and Social Death: A Comparative Study*. Cambridge, Mass.: Harvard University Press, 1982.

Peck, Scott M. *People of the Lie: The Hope for Healing Human Evil.* New York: Simon & Schuster, 1983.

Percy, William Alexander. *Lanterns on the Levee: Recollections of a Planter's Son. New* York: Alfred A. Knopf, 1941.

Ransom, Roger L. and Richard Sutch. *One Kind of Freedom: Economic Consequences of Emancipation*. New York: Cambridge University Press, 2001.

Rasmussen, Randy. *Agriculture in the United States: A Documentary History*. New York: Random House, 1975.

Rawick, George P. *The American Slave. A Composite Autobiography*. Arkansas Narratives, Parts 5 and 6. Westport, Conn.: Greenwood Publishing Co., 1976.

Royce, Edward. *The Origins of Southern Sharecropping*. Philadelphia, Penn.: Temple University Press, 1993.

Royster, Jacqueline Jones, ed. *Southern Horrors and Other Writings: The Anti-Lynching Campaign of Ida B. Wells, 1892-1900*. Boston: St. Martin's, 1996.

Sadler, Genevieve Grant. *Muzzled Oxen: Reaping Cotton and Sowing Hope in 1920s Arkansas*. Little Rock, Ark.: Butler Center Books, 2014.

Salutos, Theodore. *Farmer Movements in the South, 1865-1933*. Berkeley: University of California Press, 1960.

Shannon, Fred A. *The Farmer's Last Frontier: Agriculture 1860-1897*. New York: Rinehart & Co., 1945.

Sinclair, Upton. *Letters to Judd: an American Workingman*. Pasadena, Calif., 1932.

Sinclair, William A. *The Aftermath of Slavery*. New York: Arno Press, 1969.

Sitkoff, Harvard. *A New Deal for Blacks: The Emergence of Civil Rights as a National Issue*. New York: Oxford University Press, 1978.

Snowden, Deanna, ed. *Mississippi County, Arkansas: Appreciating the Past and Anticipating the Future*. Little Rock, Ark.: August House, 1986.

Springle, Ray. *In the Land of Jim Crow*. New York: Simon and Schuster, 1949.

Stanley, Amy Dru. *From Bondage to Contract: Wage Labor, Marriage, and the Market in the Age of Slave Emancipation*. New York: Cambridge University Press, 1998.

Stanley, Henry Morton. *The Autobiography of Sir Henry Morton Stanley: The Making of a 19th Century Explorer*. Boston, Mass.: Houghton Mifflin, 1909.

Staples, Thomas. *Reconstruction in Arkansas, 1862-1874*. New York: Columbia University Press, 1923.

Stockley, Grif. *Blood in their Eyes: the Elaine Race Massacres of 1919*. Fayetteville: University of Arkansas Press, 2001.

__________*Ruled by Race: Black/White Relations from Slavery to the Present*. Fayetteville: University of Arkansas Press, 2009.

Street, James H. *New Revolution in the Cotton Economy*. Chapel Hill: University of North Carolina Press, 1957.

Taylor, Orville. *Negro Slavery in Arkansas*. Durham, N.C.: Duke University Press, 1958.

Terrell, Tom E. and Jerrold Hirsch, eds. *Such As Us: Southern Voices of the Thirties*. Chapel Hill: University of North Carolina Press, 1978.

Tindall, George Brown. *The Emergence of the New South, 1913-1945*. Baton Rouge: Louisiana State University Press, 1967.

Troeltsch, Ernst. *Social Teaching of the Christian Churches*. Louisville, Ky.: Westminster John Knox Press, 1992.

Vance, Rupert B. *All These People*. Chapel Hill: University of North Carolina Press, 1945.

Wallace, Henry A. *New Frontiers*. New York: Reynal & Hitchcock, 1934.

Watkins, T. H. *The Great Depression: America in the 1930s*. New York: Back Bay Books, 1993.

Wells-Barnett, Ida. *The Arkansas Race Riot*. Chicago, Ill.: Home Job, 1920.

Whayne, Jeannie M. and Willard B. Gatewood, eds. *The Arkansas Delta: Land of Paradox*. Fayetteville: University of Arkansas Press, 1993.

Whayne, Jeannie M., Thomas A. DeBlack, George Sabo III, and Morris S. Arnold. *Arkansas: A Concise History*. Fayetteville: University of Arkansas Press, 2019.

__________ *Arkansas: A Narrative History*. Fayetteville: University of Arkansas Press, 2002.

Whayne, Jeannie M. *A New Plantation South: Land, Labor, and Federal Favor in Twentieth-Century Arkansas*. Charlottesville: University Press of Virginia, 1996.

__________*Delta Empire: Lee Wilson and the Transformation of Agriculture in the New South*. Baton Rouge: Louisiana State University Press, 2011.

__________, ed. *Shadows Over Sunnyside: An Arkansas Plantation in Transition, 1830-1945*. Fayetteville: University of Arkansas Press, 1993.

Whitaker, Robert. *On the Laps of Gods. The Red Summer of 1919 and the Struggle for Justice that Remade a Nation*. New York: Crown Publishers, 2008.

Wilkerson, Isabel. *The Warmth of Other Suns: The Epic Story of America's Greatest Migration*. New York: Random House, 2010.

Williams, C. Fred, S., Charles Bolton, Carl H. Moneyhon, and LeRoy T. Williams, eds. *A Documentary History of Arkansas*. Fayetteville: University of Arkansas Press, 2005.

Wolters, Raymond. *Negroes and the Great Depression*. Westport, Conn.: Greenwood Publishing Co., 1970.

Woodruff, Nan Elizabeth. *American Congo*. Cambridge, Mass.: Harvard University Press, 2003.

Woods, Troy, ed. *A Delta Diary: Amanda Worthington's Civil War Diary*. Olive Woods Press, 2008.

Woodward, C. Vann. *Origins of the New South, 1877-1913*. Baton Rouge: Louisiana State University Press, 1951.

__________*The Strange Career of Jim Crow*. New York: Oxford University Press, 1955.

Wyatt-Brown, Bertram. *Southern Honor: Ethics and Behavior in the Old South*. New York: Oxford University Press, 2007.

Wright, Richard R. *Black Boy: A Record of Childhood and Youth*. New York: Perennial Library, 1966.

Dissertations and Theses

Craig, Shannon Klug. "Arkansas and Foreign Immigration: 1890-1915." M. A. Thesis. University of Arkansas, May 1979.

Lewis, Todd Everett. "Race Relations in Arkansas, 1910-1929." Pt. 2. Ph. D. Dissertation. University of Arkansas, May 1995.

Wagoner, William Delmer. "The Non-Free Worker in Post-Civil War American History." Ph. D. Dissertation. University of Texas, June 1961.

Journals and Periodicals:

Alexander, Charles C. "White Robed Reformers: the Ku Klux Klan Comes to Arkansas, 1921-1922." *Arkansas Historical Quarterly* 22:1 (Spring 1963): 7-23.

Anderson, William Cary. "Early Reaction in Arkansas to the Relocation of Japanese into the State." *Arkansas Historical Quarterly* 23:3 (Autumn 1964): 197-211.

Andrews, Sidney. "Three Months among the Reconstructionists." *Atlantic Monthly* 17 (February 1866): 238-245.

Aptheker, Herbert. "A Few Battles Against Racism." *The Black Scholar* 26:2 (Summer 1996): 3-8.

Arendt, Hannah. "Eichman in Jerusalem." *New Yorker* (February 1963-1967): 14 articles.

Baker, Ray Stannard. "A Pawn in the Struggle for Freedom." *American Magazine* 72 (September 1911): 608-610.

Barry, Richard. "Slavery in the South Today." *Cosmopolitan* 42 (March 1907): 481-491.

Bearss, Edwin C. "The Battle of Helena, July 4, 1863." *Arkansas Historical Quarterly* 20:3 (Autumn 1961): 256-297.

Biegert, M. Langley. "Legacy of Resistance: Uncovering the History of Collective Action by Black Agricultural Workers in Central East Arkansas from the 1860s to the 1930s." *Journal of Social History* (Fall 1993): 73-99.

Boehm, Randolph H. "Mary Grace Quackenbos and the Federal Campaign against Peonage: The Case of Sunnydale [sic] Plantation." *Arkansas Historical Quarterly* 50:1 (Spring 1991): 40-59.

Bond, Ulysses S. "Highlights in the Life of Scott Bond" *Arkansas Historical Quarterly*, 21:2 (Summer 1962): 146-152.

Brandfon, Robert L. "The End of Immigration to the Cotton Fields." *Mississippi Valley Historical Review* 50:4 (March 1964): 591-611.

Bull, Jacqueline P. "The General Merchant in the Economic History of the New South." *Journal of Southern History* 18 (February 1952): 37-59.

Castro, Justin. "Mexican Braceros and Arkansas Cotton: Agricultural Labor and Civil Rights in the Post-World War II South." *Arkansas Historical Quarterly* 75:1 (Spring 2016): 27-46.

Cathey, Clyde W. "Slavery in Arkansas." *Arkansas Historical Quarterly* 3:1 (Spring 1944): 66-90.

Cohen, William. "Negro Involuntary Servitude in the South, 1865-1940: A Preliminary Analysis." *Journal of Southern History* 42:1 (February 1976): 31-60.

"Cotton's Magical Rise Enriching the Nation," *Literary Digest* 53 (December 9, 1916): 156-184.

Crawford, Sidney. "Arkansas Suffrage Qualifications." *Arkansas Historical Quarterly* 2:4 (December 1943): 331-339.

Curry, Corliss. "Early Timber Operations in Southeastern Arkansas." *Arkansas Historical Quarterly* 19:2 (Summer 1960): 111-118.

__________"The Metamorphosis of Slavery, 1865-1900." *Journal of American History* 66:1 (June 1979): 88-99.

Desmarais, Ralph H., ed. "Military Reports in Arkansas Riots: 1919-1920." *Arkansas Historical Quarterly* 33:1 (Summer 1974): 175-191.

Dillard, Tom. "Madness with a Past: An Overview of Race Violence in Arkansas History." *Arkansas Review: A Journal of Delta Studies* 32:2 (August 2001): 93-101.

Finley, Randy. "Black Arkansans and World War One." *Arkansas Historical Quarterly* 49:3 (Autumn 1990): 249-277.

Frazier, Garrison. "Colloquy with Colored Ministers." *Journal of Negro History* 16:1 (January 1931): 91.

Freeman, Felton D. "Immigration to Arkansas." *Arkansas Historical Quarterly* 7:3 (Autumn 1948): 210-220.

Gatewood, Jr., Willard B. "Sunnyside: The Evolution of an Arkansas Plantation, 1848-1945." *Arkansas Historical Quarterly* 50:1 (Spring 1991): 5-29.

Gomez, Rocio. "Braceros in the Arkansas Delta, 1943-1964." *Ozark Historical Review* 39 (Spring 2010): 1-18.

Graves, William. "Negro Disfranchisement in Arkansas." *Arkansas Historical Quarterly* 26:3 (Autumn 1967): 199-225.

Grill, Johnpeter Horst and Robert L. Jenkins. "The Nazis and the American South in the 1930s: A Mirror Image?" *Journal of Southern History* 58:4 (November 1992): 667-694.

Hamilton, Don. "Jonesboro and Arkansas During the Flood of 1937." *Craighead County Historical Quarterly* 9:1 (Winter 1971): 2-11.

Holmes, William F. "The Arkansas Cotton Pickers Strike and the Demise of the Colored Farmers' Alliance." *Arkansas Historical Quarterly* 32:2 (Summer 1973): 107-119.

Holt, Dennis. "The Legend of Dead Man Camp." *Arkansas Historical Quarterly* 9:2 (Summer 1950): 116-119.

Kousser, J. Morgan. "A Black Protest in the 'Era of Accommodation': Documents." *Arkansas Historical Quarterly* 24:2 (Summer 1975): 149-178.

Lambert, Roger. "Hoover and the Red Cross in the Arkansas Drought of 1930." *Arkansas Historical Quarterly* (Spring 1970): 3-19.

Ledbetter, Calvin R. "The Long Struggle to End Convict Leasing in Arkansas." *Arkansas Historical Quarterly* 52:1 (Spring 1993): 1-27.

Lewis, Todd Everett. "Mob Justice in the 'American Congo': 'Judge Lynch' in Arkansas During the Decade After World War I." *Arkansas Historical Quarterly* 52:2 (Summer 1993), 156-184.

Lisenby, Foy. "A Survey of Arkansas's Image Problem." *Arkansas Historical Quarterly* 30:1 (Spring 1971): 60-82.

Lucas, Marietta Ann. "Bracero Labor in Northeast Arkansas." *Craighead County Historical Review* 6 (Summer 1968): 19-25.

Matkin-Rawn, Story. "'The Great Negro State of the Country': Arkansas's Reconstruction and the Other Great Migration." *Arkansas Historical Quarterly* 72:1 (Spring 2013), 1-41.

McDonald, Forrest and Grady McWhiney. "The South From Self-Sufficiency to Peonage: An Interpretation." *American Historical Review* 85:5 (December 1980): 1095-1118.

McKelvey, Blake. "Penal Slavery and Southern Reconstruction." *The Journal of Negro History* 20:2 (April 1935): 154.

Milani, Ernesto R. "Peonage at Sunnyside and the Reaction of the Italian Government." *Arkansas Historical Quarterly* 50:1 (Spring 1991): 34.

Mitchell, H. L. "The Founding and Early History of the Southern Tenant Farmers Union." *Arkansas Historical Quarterly* 32:4 (Winter 1973): 342-369.

Mitchell, John B. "An Analysis of Arkansas' Population by Race and Nativity, and Residence." *Arkansas Historical Quarterly* 2:8 (Summer 1949): 115-132.

Murray, Gail. "Forty Years Ago: The Great Depression Comes to Arkansas." *Arkansas Historical Quarterly* 29:4 (Winter 1970): 291-312.

Pickens, William. "American Congo: Burning of Henry Lowry." *Nation* 12 (March 1921): 426-428.

Pritchett, Merrill R. and William L. Shea. "The Afrika Corps in Arkansas, 1943-1946." *Arkansas Historical Quarterly* 37:1 (Spring 1978): 3-22.

Ransom, Roger L. and Richard Sutch. "Debt Peonage in the Cotton South after the Civil War." *Journal of Economic History* 32:3 (September 1972): 641-669.

Shea, William L., ed. "A German Prisoner of War in the South: The Memoir of Edwin Pelz." *Arkansas Historical Quarterly* 44:1 (Spring 1985): 42-55.

Shlomowitz, Ralph. "The Origins of Southern Sharecropping." *Agricultural History* 53:3 (July 1979): 557-575.

Shofner, Jerrell H. "Mary Grace Quackenbos, A Visitor Florida Did Not Want." *Florida Historical Quarterly* 58: 3 (January 1980): 273-290.

"Slavery: Seventy Years After." *Christian Century* 53 (December 9, 1936): 1645.

Smith, C. Calvin. "The Response of Arkansans to Prisoners of War and Japanese Americans in Arkansas, 1942-1945." *Arkansas Historical Quarterly* 53:3 (Autumn 1994): 340-366.

Smith, T. Lynn. "A Demographic Study of the American Negro." *Social Forces* 23:3 (1945): 379-387.

"Some Letters. From the South, May 8, 1911." *The Crisis: A Record of the Darker Races*, 2:4 (August 1911), 166-167.

A Southern Colored Woman. "The Race Problem-An Autobiography." *The Independent* 56 (March 17, 1904): 589.

Stockley, Grif. "The Legal Proceedings of the Arkansas Race Massacres of 1919 and the Evidence of the Plot to Kill Planters." *Arkansas Review: A Journal of Delta Studies* 32:2 (August 2001): 141-148.

Terrell, Mary Church. "Peonage in the United States: The Convict Lease System and the Chain Gangs." *Nineteenth Century* 68 (August 1907): 306-322.

Thrasher, Sue and Leah Wise. "The Southern Tenant Farmers' Union." *Southern Exposure* 1 (Winter 1974): 7, 19, 29.

Townsend, Belton O'Neall, "South Carolina Morals," *Atlantic Monthly* 39 (April 1877), 467-470.

Ward, Herbert D. "Peonage in America." *Cosmopolitan* 39 (August 1905): 423-30.

Ward, Jason Morgan. "Nazis Hoe Cotton: Planters, POWs, and the Future of Farm Labor in the Deep South." *Agricultural History* 81:4 (Fall 2007): 471-492.

Watkins, Beverly. "Efforts to Encourage Immigration to Arkansas, 1865-1874." *Arkansas Historical Quarterly* 38:1 (Spring 1979): 32-62.

Watson, Thomas E. "The Negro Question in the South." *Arena* 6 (October 1892): 540-550

Welch, Melanie. "Violence and the Decline of Black Politics in St. Francis County." *Arkansas Historical Quarterly* 60 (Winter 2001): 360-393.

Whayne, Jeannie. "Low Villains and Wickedness in High Places: Race and Class in the Elaine Riots." *Arkansas Review: A Journal of Delta Studies* 32:2 (August 2001): 102-118.

White, Walter. "The Negro and the Flood." *Nation* (June 22, 1927): 688-689.

Wilson, Lee, "Boss Lee's 1930 Message." *Delta Historical Review* (Spring 1998): 1-40.

Woodman, Harold D. "Post-Civil War Southern Agriculture and the Law." *Agricultural History* 53:1 (January 1979): 319-337.

___________"Sequel to Slavery: The New History Views the Postbellum South." *Journal of Southern History* 43: 4 (November 1977): 523-554.

Woodruff, Nan Elizabeth. "Pick or Fight: The Emergency Farm Labor Program in the Arkansas and Mississippi Deltas During World War II." *Agricultural History* 64:2 (Spring 1990): 74-85.

Worley, Ted. "Tenant and Labor Contracts, Calhoun County, 1869-1871." *Arkansas Historical Quarterly* 13:1 (Spring 1954): 102-106.

Wyatt-Brown, Bertram. "Leroy Percy and Sunnyside: Planter Mentality and Italian Peonage in the Mississippi Delta." *Arkansas Historical Quarterly* 50: 1 (Spring 1991): 60-84.

Zimmerman, Jane. "The Convict Lease System in Arkansas and the Fight for Abolition." *Arkansas Historical Quarterly* 8:3 (Autumn 1949): 171-188.

Legal Journals

Armstrong, Andrea C. "Slavery Revisited in Penal Plantation Labor." *Seattle University Law Review* (Spring 2012): 1-39.

Azmy, Baher. "Unshackling the Thirteenth Amendment: Modern Slavery and a Reconstructed Civil Rights Agenda." *Fordham Law Review* (December 2002):1-70.

Castle, John Thomas. "Embracing General Statutes." Supplement to *Kirby's Digest of the Statutes of Arkansas*. 2059.

Goluboff, Risa L. "Won't You Please Help Me Get My Son Home: Peonage, Patronage, and Protest in the World War II Urban South." *Law and Social Inquiry* 24 (Fall 1999): 777-806.

Huq, Aziz Z. "Peonage and Contractual Liberty." *Columbia Law Review* (March 2001): 1-40.

Kilpatrick, Judith. "(Extra) Ordinary Men: African-American Lawyers and Civil Rights in Arkansas Before 1950." *Arkansas Law Review* 53:299 (2000). 299-398.

Maddox, James G. "The Bankhead-Jones Farm Tenant Act." *Law and Contemporary Problems* 4 (October 1937): 434-455.

Perea, Juan F. "The Echoes of Slavery: Recognizing the Racist Origins of the Agricultural and Domestic Worker Exclusion from the National Labor Relations Act." *Ohio State Law Journal* (2011): 1-70.

Pope, James Gray. "Contract, Race, and Freedom of Labor in the Constitutional Law of 'Involuntary Servitude.'" *Yale Law Journal* (May 2010): 1-71.

Roback, Jennifer. "Southern Labor Law in the Jim Crow Era: Exploitative or Competitive?" *University of Chicago Law Review* 51 (Autumn 1984): 1161-1192.

Schmidt, Benno C. "Principle and Prejudice: The Supreme Court and Race in the Progressive Era, Part 1: The Heyday of Jim Crow." *Columbia Law Review* (April 1982): 1-69.

__________"Principle and Prejudice: The Supreme Court and Race in the Progressive Era, Part 2: The Peonage Cases." *Columbia Law Review* (May 1982): 1-65.

Public Documents

Anderson, A. W. S. "Proceedings of the Third Semi-Annual Session of the Alabama State Agricultural Society." Montgomery, Alabama, 1888, 93-95.

"Final Report and Physical Accomplishments of the Arkansas Works Projects Administration, March 1,1943." Background Section. National Archives, record group 69.6

Bayner plantation records and account book. February-December 1867. Field Office Records-Arkansas, Freedmen's Bureau, National Archives.

Biddle, Francis. Circular No. 3591. Attorney General Francis Biddle to all United States Attorneys. December, 12, 1941. Department of Justice, record group 60.

"Commissioner of Agriculture Report for the Year 1867." Department of Agriculture, Washington, D. C., 1868.

"Convict Labor. Report of the U. S. Commissioner of Labor, 1886." Washington, D. C., 1887.

"Dyess Project Book," Records Section, Rehabilitation Administration Management Division. National Archives, record group 96. Copy in Everett Henson Collection, Historic Dyess Colony, Arkansas State University, Record 2016-33-031.

"Farm Tenancy. Report of the President's Committee." Prepared under the auspices of the National Resources Committee. Washington, D. C.: U. S. Government Printing Office. February 1937.

"Federal Writers' Project: Slave Narratives, Vol. 2, Arkansas part 7." Vaden-Young, 1936. Manuscript/Mixed Material. Retrieved from the Library of Congress, https://www.loc.gov/item/mesn027/. Accessed April 16, 2017.

General Superintendent of Freedmen. Departments of Tennessee and Arkansas. December 31, 1864.

Glasshoff Report, November 15, 1867. Freedmen's Bureau, Field Office Records-Arkansas, National Archives.

Holt, John P. "An Analysis of Methods and Criteria Used in Selecting Families for Colonization Projects," Social Research Report No.1, 1937. Farm Security Administration and the Bureau of Agricultural Economics. National Archives, Record Group 96. Copy in Everett Henson Collection, Historic Dyess Colony, Record 2016-33-004.

McBride, Cornelius. "Testimony in U. S. Congress. Report of the Joint Select Committee, House of Representatives. Report 22, 42nd Congress, 2nd session." Washington, D. C.: Government Printing Office, 1872, II, 335.

Moton, Robert Russa, et al. "Final Report of the Colored Advisory Commission. Mississippi Valley Flood Disaster, 1927." Washington, D. C. : American Red Cross. May 21, 1929.

__________Memo for the Committee. No Date. Moton Family Papers: Library of Congress, Washington, D. C. General Correspondence 48.

Ord, E. O. C. "The Treatment of Freedmen in Arkansas." Report to the U. S. House of Representatives, 39th Congress, 2nd session. January 4, 1867. misc. doc. 14. University of Arkansas Special Collection.

Quackenbos, Mary Grace. "Report on Sunnyside Plantation. September 28, 1907." Department of Justice, 100937.

__________"Report on General Conditions at Delta Cotton Plantations. January 10, 1908." William Alexander Percy Memorial Library, Greenville, Miss.

Russell, Charles W. "Report Relative to Peonage Matters." U. S. Attorney General Annual Report. Washington, D. C., 1907.

__________Supplement to February 14, 1907, peonage report, 3-4. William Alexander Percy Memorial Library, Greenville, Miss.

U. S. Congress. *Congressional Record.* 39th Congress, Session II, 1867; 60th Congress, Session I, 1908; 75th Congress, Session II, 1937

Speeches, Oral Histories and Letters

Handcox, John L. Interviewed by Michael Honey and Joe Glazer. *Songs, Poems, and Stories of the Southern Tenant Farmers Union.* West Virginia University Press Sound Archive. December 13, 2000.

Johnson, Homer Joe. *The Delta Historical Review* 2:1. Mississippi County Genealogical Society. Summer 1990.

Kester, Howard. "The Struggle Against Peonage." Address delivered at the 26th Annual Conference of the National Association for the Advancement of Colored People. St. Louis, Missouri. June 26, 1935. STFU Papers, reel 59. Chapel Hill: University of North Carolina Press.

Redington, Edward. "Account of the Battle of Helena, Arkansas." "Transcribed letters, May 14, 1863-October 23, 1863; May 1867. *Wisconsin Goes to War: Our Civil War Experience*. State of Wisconsin Collection, University of Wisconsin System. http://digital.library.wisc.edu/1711.dl/WI.WIWarEdRed. Accessed July 1, 2019.

Rye, Johnny. Tyronza, Arkansas. Interview by author, May 22, 2003. Transcript. Southern Tenant Farmers Museum Collection, Arkansas State University.

Sullivan Hays. Burdette, Arkansas. Interview by author, March 24, 2002. Transcript. Southern Tenant Farmers Museum Collection, Arkansas State University.

Williams, Willie. Lake Village, Arkansas. Interview with Mike Bowman and Greg Hansen, September 20, 2003. Transcript, Lakeport Plantation Collection, Arkansas State University.

Index

www.ingramcontent.com/pod-product-compliance
Lightning Source LLC
Chambersburg PA
CBHW031937090426
42811CB00002B/216